Time, work and leisure

MANCHESTER
1824

er University Press

STUDIES IN POPULAR CULTURE

General editor: Professor Jeffrey Richards

Time, work and leisure

Life changes in England since 1700

HUGH CUNNINGHAM

Manchester University Press

The right of Hugh Cunningham to be identified as the author of this work has been asserted by him in accordance with the Copyright, Designs and Patents Act 1988.

Published by Manchester University Press
Altrincham Street, Manchester M1 7JA, UK
www.manchesteruniversitypress.co.uk

British Library Cataloguing-in-Publication Data is available

Library of Congress Cataloging-in-Publication Data is available

ISBN 978 1 7849 9355 9 *paperback*

First published by Manchester University Press in hardback 2014

This edition first published 2016

The publisher has no responsibility for the persistence or accuracy of URLs for any external or third-party internet websites referred to in this book, and does not guarantee that any content on such websites is, or will remain, accurate or appropriate.

Printed by Lightning Source

STUDIES IN
POPULAR
CULTURE

There has in recent years been an explosion of interest in culture and cultural studies. The impetus has come from two directions and out of two different traditions. On the one hand, cultural history has grown out of social history to become a distinct and identifiable school of historical investigation. On the other hand, cultural studies has grown out of English literature and has concerned itself to a large extent with contemporary issues. Nevertheless, there is a shared project, its aim, to elucidate the meanings and values implicit and explicit in the art, literature, learning, institutions and everyday behaviour within a given society. Both the cultural historian and the cultural studies scholar seek to explore the ways in which a culture is imagined, represented and received, how it interacts with social processes, how it contributes to individual and collective identities and world views, to stability and change, to social, political and economic activities and programmes. This series aims to provide an arena for the cross-fertilisation of the discipline, so that the work of the cultural historian can take advantage of the most useful and illuminating of the theoretical developments and the cultural studies scholars can extend the purely historical underpinnings of their investigations. The ultimate objective of the series is to provide a range of books which will explain in a readable and accessible way where we are now socially and culturally and how we got to where we are. This should enable people to be better informed, promote an interdisciplinary approach to cultural issues and encourage deeper thought about the issues, attitudes and institutions of popular culture.

Jeffrey Richards

Contents

General editor's introduction

It was in the 1970s that leisure became a major subject of investigation for social historians. One of the most important books to emerge from that interest was Hugh Cunningham's *Leisure in the Industrial Revolution c. 1780– c. 1880* (Croom Helm, 1980). Returning to the subject thirty years on, he set out to remedy what he now sees as deficiencies in the study of leisure as it was written in the 1970s and 1980s. He singles out in particular the neglect of women's experience of work and leisure, the over-concentration on the eighteenth and nineteenth centuries and the failure to address time-use generally rather than spare time in particular. He also seeks to address the now highly topical subject of work–life balance and the changes in the use and valuation of time over the past three centuries.

Beginning with changes in the perception of time in the eighteenth century – and taking in such diverse but related topics as oil lamps, sleep patterns, almanacs, clocks and watches, and the Christian calendar – he goes on to consider leisure and class, leisure and gender, leisure preference, and leisure and its critics. Under these broad headings and ever alert to changes in the relationship of work and leisure, he examines the conflict between rational and irrational recreation, the commercialisation of leisure and the emergence of the leisure industries, the attempts of central and local authorities to regulate leisure, the changing shape of the week, the redefinition and extension of childhood and the development of the concept of retirement.

Cunningham ends this elegantly written, cogently argued and consistently illuminating study with a soberly realistic conclusion. On the basis of three centuries of experience, he finds that the amount of people's time taken up by work – and therefore the amount of time available for leisure – has depended upon the strength or otherwise of the workers. When their organisation has been strong, working hours have been reduced. Where it is weak, as at present, the employers in a competitive capitalist system have always been reluctant to concede short working time.

Jeffrey Richards
March 2012

Acknowledgements

This book had its origin in five talks I gave for BBC Radio 3's The Essay programme in 2009. I am deeply indebted to Beaty Rubens who produced these talks, and helped enormously to shape both them and my own thinking; to Judy Fudge for her helpful comments on Chapter 8; and to the two anonymous readers for Manchester University Press for showing me the way to improve on my first draft.

Introduction

This book is about time past; but it is written out of a concern about time present and time future. The use of and attitude to time have changed radically since the 1970s. It was a commonplace of the 1960s and early 1970s that leisure time was going increasingly to eat into work time: robots would do the repetitive work, and most people would have much more free time at their disposal. An increase of leisure as against work can be traced back to the 1830s, and few people saw reason to doubt that the trend would continue and intensify. The concern about time in the 1970s lay in 'the problem of leisure', a worry that people wouldn't know what to do in their leisure time, or would misspend it. Now that worry seems somewhat fantastical; work has come to preoccupy us. Many people now work longer hours; some make themselves available for work 24/7, a term that would have made no sense in the 1970s. We increasingly talk about 'work–life balance' rather than 'work and leisure'.

I first became interested in time in the 1970s and 1980s. There was then a considerable scholarly output on the history of leisure.[1] Looking back on that body of publications, and leaving aside its considerable merits, three inadequacies now strike me. First, it was focused very largely on the experience of men to the neglect of that of women. Second, it concentrated on the eighteenth and nineteenth centuries, often petering out round about the time of the First World War or before. And third, it was about leisure, rather than time use more broadly, because of the assumption, so prominent then, that leisure time was on the increase. In returning to the topic after thirty years I have drawn extensively on that earlier work, including my own, but have brought to it a wider perspective. There is now a substantial literature addressing the three inadequacies, and that has informed this rethinking.

When I began to look at what has been written about work–life balance (and there is a lot of it, few topics in the social sciences being more generously funded), I was struck by five characteristics. First, its sense of the possibilities of time was extraordinarily narrow: time was either paid work, or it was life, which sounded good, but in the literature consisted of unpaid work raising a family. Second, it implicitly devalued 'work', reducing it to something that had to be done in order to fund 'life': who would not prefer 'life' to 'work'? Third, it was addressed, initially exclusively and still dominantly, to women. The 'work and leisure' discourse which 'work–life balance' replaced had been almost exclusively about men. Fourth, it was by no means comprehensive in its life course coverage. Its focus was on parents at the stage in their life course when they had young children. It took no account of the changes in the experience of time that have affected childhood, now prolonged beyond what anyone could have imagined in 1700, or of retirement which with increasing life expectancy occupies a much larger tranche of life than in previous generations. Fifth, no one writing about work–life balance seemed to have any sense of a past before about 1990. Scholars in the field were trapped into a way of thinking about time that assumed that both the present and to a large extent the future were determined and unalterable. The solutions offered to the problems people faced in trying to balance their work and their life focused on personal choice: be more organised, negotiate flexible hours at work and so on.

This book begins in 1700 in order to provide a longer perspective on current work–life balance discussions. In the late seventeenth and for most of the eighteenth centuries commentators were much concerned with what has come to be called the 'leisure preference' of workers. Men, it was complained, (the discourse was entirely about men) worked only as long as was needed to secure an adequate income – they might take three or four days off each week. There is much debate among historians as to the prevalence if not existence of leisure preference forms of behaviour (it was certainly not universal) but, whatever the conclusion, no one can doubt the volume of contemporary concern. Employers wanted a regular workforce. This was what they came near to securing in the harsher economic conditions of the later eighteenth and early nineteenth centuries when hours of work increased by a considerable margin. The fight-back against these long hours began with trade union agitation in the 1820s, and over the next one hundred and fifty years, largely owing to trade union pressure, the hours that were worked diminished by day, by week and by year.

Trade union action had been accompanied by wider public anxiety about the work that children were doing. Legislation in the form of factory acts and education acts, together with decisions by parents about the relative advantages of work or school, established a new pattern of life – children were, not entirely but to a considerable extent, taken out of the workforce. Childhood became a time for not working, or at least not working for wages – children now did schoolwork. At the other end of the life course, in the late nineteenth century people began to campaign for a period of 'retirement'. State-funded old age pensions were introduced in 1908, but were set at such an inadequate level that in themselves they didn't stop people working. Only after the Second World War did retirement become a reality for most workers.

By the 1970s the invention of a non-working childhood at one end of life and of retirement at the other had reshaped the life course. Work was now concentrated in the years between childhood and retirement, and the hours spent at work had diminished and seemed likely to continue to do so. This situation had been achieved by a combination of trade union activity, more widespread public pressure and legislation. Capitalism had been brought under control. In the 1980s and subsequently those controls were lifted.

From the 1950s married women increasingly entered the labour market. Women had been remarkably absent from discussions about work and leisure in the nineteenth and first half of the twentieth centuries. In the upper classes the ability of a husband to earn enough to keep his wife at home, outside the paid workforce, was a mark of status. The majority of women, by contrast, sought waged work wherever they could find it and laboured endlessly, unpaid, to maintain households – if asked, they often found it difficult to think of any leisure that they had. In the second half of the twentieth century as household tasks become less arduous they increasingly sought paid work, usually part-time and badly paid. In the nineteenth century there were strong pressures to prevent women from taking paid work so that they could con-centrate on their central home-keeping tasks; in the twenty-first century the opposite happens: women, including mothers of young children, are pressured into the labour market.

The combination of the lifting of controls on capitalism and the entry of more women into the labour market has produced the current situation where time pressures are acute – at least for those who are in work. For it is a feature of the period since the 1970s that long hours of work for some have sat alongside unemployment, underemployment or retirement for others. For some time is scarce, for others plentiful.

Work not only takes up time. It also gives many people their sense of identity. If we ask someone 'What do you do?' we expect the answer to be

'I'm an engineer', 'I'm a gardener', 'I'm a housewife' and so on. Work also often influences time spent not working, especially leisure, that residue of time left over after work, sleep and other obligations have been met. But leisure can equally be free of work associations. Historically leisure has been closely linked to class. The word first began to be used by the upper classes in the early modern period to describe the time they spent amusing themselves and the activities they engaged in.[2] In the eighteenth century the middling sorts began to develop a calendar of leisure and specific places, such as spas, in which to spend it. By the mid-nineteenth century people began to write about 'the leisured class', people of wealth who had no need to work though they often felt a sense of obligation to carry out public duties. In a society that placed huge value on work, those at the top of the status ladder proclaimed their leisure. The incentive to work for the wealthy seemed to be the hope of achieving the status of not needing to work.

There was much debate in the eighteenth and early nineteenth centuries as to whether the common people should have any leisure. Leisure for the upper classes was idleness for the lower. There were innumerable attempts to control the ways in which non-work time was spent which sparked a counter movement to provide time and space and facilities for working-class leisure. But leisure was often presented as a 'problem', entrepreneurs offering attractions that many commentators found anything but life-enhancing.

The book opens by examining the variety of ways in which time was imagined and experienced in the eighteenth century and the changes that happened within that century. Chapter 2 analyses the prevalence and attractions of leisure preference and the increasing difficulties of exercising it in the late eighteenth and early nineteenth centuries as hours of work rose. Chapter 3 focuses on the attempts to control and shape working-class leisure in the face of entrepreneurs who began to sense a mass market for popular leisure. Chapter 4 traces the long decline in the amount of life devoted to work between 1830 and 1970. Chapter 5 looks at how working-class men experienced work and leisure and the weight each had in shaping their sense of their own identity. Chapter 6 analyses the leisure class, its members from the late nineteenth century all too likely to be described as the 'idle rich'. Co-existing with this, a much-feared speeding up of life for the middle classes led to calls for 'a gospel of recreation': time for leisure was in competition with the demands of work. Chapter 7 looks at the emergence of work–life balance discourse against the background of married women's entry into the labour force and the end of the long decline in working hours.

Time – how it has been imagined and how it has been spent – is the unifying theme of the book. Few words have gathered around themselves so many associations as time. We pass it, we spend it; we find it and lose it; it flies, or hangs heavy, or we while it away. Time, we know, is money, and many of the words used to describe it would do for money as well. Time is divided up into seconds, minutes, hours, days, weeks, months, years, decades (a recent innovation), lifetimes, centuries, 'time immemorial'. Everyone is at some level aware, as Isaac Watts put it in 1719 reflecting on Psalm 90, that 'Time, like an over-rolling stream, bears all its sons away', that death at some time awaits us. But time can be not only linear, pointing forwards, but also cyclical: it repeats itself, in days and nights, in the seasons of the year, in menstruation.[3]

Time cannot be understood on its own. Its closest relationship is to space, for time is necessarily passed somewhere, in bed, at work, at home, in the pub and so on. The politics of time, particularly time for leisure, intermesh with those of space, for somewhere to spend it. Time is also bound up with class and the power relationships that go with it for the legitimacy of ways of spending time has never been free of legal, governmental and cultural constraints. Christianity, starting from the premise that time is a gift from God, has historically had a huge impact on how it has been spent and imagined. Perhaps most obviously, time and economic life are closely related. Economists picture individuals and families making decisions about time, trading leisure, income and consumption.[4]

Thinking about time in these ways and in historical perspective carries one basic message: times change. The future is unlikely to be as we imagine it, and the present need not be as we experience it.

Notes

1 Major works were R. W. Malcolmson, *Popular Recreations in English Society 1700–1850* (Cambridge: Cambridge University Press, 1973); J. H. Plumb, *The Commercialisation of Leisure in Eighteenth-Century England* (Reading: Reading University, 1973); J. Lowerson and J. Myerscough, *Time to Spare in Victorian England* (Brighton: Harvester Press, 1977); P. Bailey, *Leisure and Class in Victorian Britain: Rational Recreation and the Contest for Control, 1830–1885* (London: Routledge and Kegan Paul, 1978); J. Walvin, *Leisure and Society, 1830–1950* (London: Longman, 1978); H. Cunningham, *Leisure in the Industrial Revolution c. 1780–c. 1880* (London: Croom Helm, 1980); E. and S. Yeo (eds), *Popular Culture and Class Conflict, 1590–1914: Explorations in the History of Labour and Leisure*

(Brighton: Harvester Press, 1981); R. Storch (ed.), *Popular Culture and Custom in Nineteenth-Century Britain* (London: Croom Helm, 1982); J. K. Walton and J. Walvin (eds), *Leisure in Britain 1780–1939* (Manchester: Manchester University Press, 1983); J. M. Golby and A. W. Purdue, *The Civilisation of the Crowd: Popular Culture in England, 1750–1900* (London: Batsford, 1984).

2 P. Burke, 'The invention of leisure in early modern Europe', *Past & Present*, 146 (1995), 136–50.

3 P. Borsay, *A History of Leisure: The British Experience since 1500* (Basingstoke: Palgrave Macmillan, 2006), pp. 200–7.

4 G. Becker, 'A theory of the allocation of time', *Economic Journal*, 75 (1965), 493–517.

Time and society in the eighteenth century

People's perception of time, of how it might be measured or divided up, and how it ought to be spent, depended very much on whether they lived in town or country, and where they stood in the social hierarchy. England in 1700 was a dominantly rural society. Just under a quarter of the population inhabited towns with a population over 2,500, nearly half of these urban dwellers living in London.[1] If the minimum population of a town is raised to 5,000, then 83 per cent of the population were rural dwellers in 1700, a proportion down to 72 per cent by 1800.[2] Living in the countryside did not necessarily mean working in agriculture, or not full-time in agriculture. Agriculture was by a long way the biggest single occupation, but the countryside was also the location for much industry.

The English in the eighteenth century thought of their society as made up of distinct ranks, with the aristocracy at the top, and labourers and the poor at the bottom. One of the distinctive features of the century was the growth in numbers and influence of 'the middling sort'. This middle rank in the course of the century developed ways of living and of spending time that began to mark it out from the bulk of the population. This chapter will explore these different and changing ways of thinking about and experiencing time, on a daily, weekly, monthly, annual and life course level.

Light and darkness

In 1680 John Butler, an astrologer, wrote: 'pretty it is to observe, how a Child, as soon as it draws breath, becomes Time-smitten by the Face of Heaven; and receives an impression from all parts of Heaven, and the Stars therein'.[3] In a largely agricultural society, without much light pollution even in cities, the sky was the most obvious resource for learning about time. The child,

Butler went on, would find by looking at the sky that 'different times seem to fly out'. Days were measured from sunrise to sunset, years by the change from shortest day to longest and back again to shortest. The moon marked out a shorter cycle, its different phases always detailed in the most popular literature of the day, the almanac. Knowledge of the phases of the moon was essential for farmers. Pigs were not to be killed when the moon was waning, sheep were to be shorn during the moon's increase, and the times for sowing, planting and grafting were all determined by the moon. For everyone, the time for taking pills, having a purge, cutting one's hair, and, if hoping for a child, the best times of the month for getting the desired gender, were all suggested by the phase of the moon.[4]

People's sense of time was dominated by the availability of light. Darkness, night-time, was feared. Dame Sarah Cowper wrote in her diary in 1709, 'At night I pray Almighty God to keep me from ye power of evil spirits, and of evil men; from fearfull dreams and terrifying imaginations; from fire, and all sad accidents'. Satan, the Prince of Darkness, was abroad in the night, as were the 'evil spirits' that Sarah Cowper feared. Evil men equally abounded. 'In the night', wrote Isaac Watts, 'we are exposed here on earth to the violence and plunder of wicked men, whether we are abroad or at home.' Samuel Johnson wrote of London in 1739: 'Prepare for death, if here at night you roam, and sign your will before you sup from home'. It was a sentiment put at greater length by the City Marshal in 1718: 'It is the general complaint of the taverns, the coffee-houses, the shopkeepers and others, that their customers are afraid when it is dark to come to their houses and shops for fear that their hats and wigs should be snitched from their head or their swords taken from their sides, or that they may be blinded, knocked down, cut or stabbed'. In town and country crime was most common at night; in rural Somerset in the eighteenth century three-quarters of thefts were committed after dark.[5]

The moon was the main source of light at night. Without it, people stayed at home. Fanny Boscawen in 1756 wrote to her husband, an admiral, 'I have made such profession of my aversion to *groping* that at length I seem to have obtained a dispensation never to visit in the dark'. To grope, to feel your way, was the only safe way to proceed on dark nights. Social life was constricted. Nancy Woodforde in 1792 wrote of a Norfolk neighbour that 'He would not dine with us on account of there being no moon'. Full moon was the time for gatherings at night-time, most famously in the eighteenth century for the intellectuals of Birmingham's Lunar Society, who met once a month at full moon.[6]

The restrictions imposed by darkness, especially in towns, sharply diminished in the course of the eighteenth century. Change began in the 1680s. Until then the lighting regulations, which most towns had, covered only the nights from All Hallows' Eve (31 October) to Candlemas (2 February), from dusk to curfew, normally set at nine o'clock, and even then only 'when the moon is dark', from the second night after a full moon until the seventh after a new moon. Thus in London for much of the seventeenth century there was lighting annually for only 63 nights and for a total of 189 hours. The nights to be lit were extended in London in 1662 to cover the period from Michaelmas to Lady Day, but it was not until the 1680s that three developments signalled significant change. First, oil-burning street lamps began to replace those lit by candle. Second, the responsibility for street lighting passed from the individual householder to lighting contractors. And third, local authorities rather than individuals began to bear the costs. Oil-burning lamps were soon installed in a range of provincial towns and in 1700 England's two biggest provincial cities, Bristol and Norwich, both secured Acts of Parliament for improved lighting. In 1736 London's Act for 'better enlightening the streets' allowed a rate to be raised, and extended the lighting season through the whole year. Many towns established Improvement Commissioners and better lighting was a crucial task allocated to them. In York, for example, under the Act of 1763, commissioners set up four hundred lamps for six months in the year on dark nights from sunset until morning twilight.[7] Oil lamps were improved in the 1780s with the introduction of Argand lights, but it was the invention of the coal gas light, first on display in Pall Mall in 1807, and with a strength ten or twelve times that of a candle or oil lamp, which truly revolutionised street lighting.[8]

It was not only the main streets and public places that were becoming better lit; so also were shops and places of entertainment. Tobias Smollett in 1771 described Ranelagh Gardens in London as 'enlightened with a thousand golden lamps'. In London it was reported in 1789 that 'All the shops are open till ten o'clock at night, and exceedingly well lighted'. Forty years later, in 1829, a visitor marvelled at how 'Thousands of lamps, in long chains of fire, stretch away to enormous distances. The display of the shops, lighted up with peculiar brilliancy . . . is most striking in effect.'[9]

Improved lighting had a marked impact on social life. The night began to be colonised. Richard Steele in 1710 wondered 'at this perverted relish of those who are reckoned the most polite part of mankind, that prefer sea-coals and candles to the sun, and exchange so many cheerful morning hours for the pleasures of midnight revels and debauches'. Social occasions for the wealthy began later in the day than previously. In the course of the eighteenth century the hour of dining shifted from about one or two o'clock to five or six o'clock, and in tune with this evening entertainments began later – and extended further into the night. Those 'which used to begin at six in the evening', it was said in 1779, 'are now begun at eight or nine'.[10]

Better lighting also began to change sleep patterns. The common experience was to have two roughly equal periods of sleep. The 'first sleep' lasted till about midnight, and was followed by an hour or so of wakefulness, during which people might get up for a drink or smoke or to relieve themselves, or reflect on their dreams. A second or morning sleep then followed. Tallow candles or rushlights, the common form of domestic lighting, one hundred times weaker than a single electric light bulb, didn't encourage late nights. The upper classes, however, were by the late seventeenth century moving towards a single period of sleep, and gradually this became the common pattern. But segmented sleep was still experienced in the nineteenth and even early twentieth centuries. In 1869 Thomas Wright described how labourers who had to turn out early were 'already in their first sleep' while the streets were 'still in a state of comparative bustle'. And in 1912 Richard Sturt in rural Surrey could still write of his 'first sleep'.[11]

Almanacs and calendars

If the sun and the moon provided the easiest guide to time, they were not alone in providing one from observation of the sky. Astrologists' influence among the educated was distinctly on the wane as the eighteenth century dawned, but at a popular level their prognostications from the movements of planets and stars still held sway, purveyed annually in the almanacs. Towards the end of the seventeenth century sales reached about four hundred thousand a year, roughly one almanac for every three families. Moore's Almanac, starting in 1699, became dominant in the eighteenth century and beyond, its nineteenth-century sales reaching a peak of 560,000 in 1839.[12] John Clare in the early nineteenth century described its impact:

> Old Moore's annual prophecies
> Of flooded fields and clouded skies;
> Whose Almanac's thum'd pages swarm
> With frost and snow, and many a storm,
> And wisdom, gossip'd from the stars,

> Of politics and bloody wars.
> He shakes his head, and still proceeds,
> Nor doubts the truth of what he reads.[13]

Of the same period Charles Knight wrote how 'There was scarcely a house in Southern England in which this two shillings worth of imposture [Moore's Almanac] was not to be found. There was scarcely a farmer who would cut his grass if the Almanack predicted rain. No cattle-doctor would give drench to a cow unless he consulted the table in the Almanack showing what sign the Moon is, and what part of the body it governs.'[14]

The almanacs' contribution to the sense of time stretched beyond astro-logical predictions and advice. Coastal dwellers could learn from almanacs about the tides. For everyone, almanacs gave dates in the history of the world since its creation, the time-lines of their day. They also provided a recent history of England, stressing different events and dates according to their political persuasion. Above all, almanacs gave a calendar for the year, or rather a number of overlapping calendars. As Samuel Johnson put it in 1773, 'We compute from calendars differing from one another; the compute of one differing from that of another'.[15]

There was, first, the ecclesiastical calendar. Before the Reformation, there were each year, besides Sundays, some forty or fifty saints' days that were taken as holidays. These days were reduced in number but not done away with in their entirety in the Reformation and thereafter. The 1552 Act 'for the keeping of holy days and fasting days' gave approval to all Sundays, Monday and Tuesday in Easter and Whitsun weeks, and a further twenty-three Christian feasts, including five days in Christmas week.[16] These were the red letter saints' days first published in the 1559 prayer book, and sub-sequently included in popular almanacs. If their existence and number seem surprising in a post-Reformation and Protestant world, it is explicable in large part because they often coincided with the dates of fairs or wakes, for paying rent, or hiring labour. Lady Day, for example, the day marking the Annunciation of the Blessed Virgin Mary, was on 25 March. It was still in England until 1752 the official date for the beginning of the year, and it was a quarter day, and therefore a day for contracts to be signed and dues to be paid. It was a day that needed to be remembered, as were the other quarter days, at mid-summer, Michaelmas and Christmas (25 June, 29 September, 25 December), and the mid-quarter days on Candlemas (the Purification of the Blessed Virgin May on 2 February), May Day (the Nativity of St John the Baptist), Lammas Day (1 August, traditionally the day for the first gathering of harvest) and

Martinmas (11 November).[17] Ninety per cent of labour hirings in the eighteenth century ran from either Michaelmas or Martinmas, common in arable
districts, or Lady Day or May Day in pastoral. Marriages were often celebrated
immediately after these hiring days, the days taking on a double importance.[18]

Add all the Sundays, the Mondays and Tuesdays at Easter and Whitsun, and
the saints' days, and it amounted to seventy-nine days in the year when 'lawful
bodily labour' could be set aside for prayer and worship.[19] On top of this there
were other church-organised events and days, for example Rogation Day,
dating back to 747, when the parish boundaries were patrolled and reaffirmed.
It survived through the Interregnum, and then enjoyed something of a revival,
not least (for rural customs could be transposed to towns) in London parishes.
Elsewhere, at Whiston in South Yorkshire, for example, the parish provided
bread, beer, tobacco, pipes and a bonfire at the end of the walk.[20]

The national Christian calendar co-existed and overlapped with a multiplicity of more obviously secular annual events. In arable communities, Plough
Monday, celebrated in January on the first Monday after Twelfth Day, marked
the beginning of the agricultural year. There might be morris dancing, and
processions to collect money for a feast in the evening. Shrove Tuesday was
another holiday, particularly for apprentices, and an occasion for football. At
Newcastle-upon-Tyne, it was reported, the church bell was rung at twelve
o'clock and 'Shops are immediately shut up, Offices closed, and all Kind of
Business ceases; a Sort of little Carnival ensuing for the remaining Part of the
Day'.[21] At Easter, it was said, 'it is customary for Work to cease, and Servants
to be at Liberty'.[22] May poles had been widely revived at the Restoration in
1660, and they formed the centre of attraction for May Day celebrations,
young people having gone out early to collect shrubs and flowers with which
to decorate them. Nearly every community had an annual feast, wake or fair,
and, if the latter had an economic rationale, the former two originated in
annual celebration of the parish church's name and in fund-raising for it. By
the second half of the seventeenth century the fund-raising aspect of wakes
and feasts had gone, and there were some reports that the wakes themselves
had, as one reporter said in 1695, fallen into disuse in much of southern
England because of 'popular prejudice', though the nature of that prejudice
was not elaborated.[23] But, by and large, the occasions themselves remained,
and, if some parts of southern England had indeed lost them, their place
tended to have been taken by fairs. Many of the feasts, wakes and fairs occurred
either around Whitsun or in the period after harvest. Whit Monday, it was
said, 'is a universal festival in the humble ranks of life throughout the

kingdom'.[24] In September 1738 a contributor to the *Gentleman's Magazine* described how 'I am now in the Country, and at that Season of the Year in which Parish Feasts abound'.[25]

Every parish or manor had its own calendar within a common framework. The Rev. William Cole of Bletchley, for example, noted in his diary for 1766–7 a Rogation Week Parish Perambulation, children 'hallooing under my chamber window before I was up' on Valentine's Day, Shrove Tuesday football on the village green, morris dancing on Whit Monday, a Whitsuntide Fair at nearby Buckingham the following Thursday, a hay harvest dance and supper, a harvest home, the local parish feast on 14 September, and bonfires on the green on 5 November.[26] As the visit to the Buckingham fair indicates, people were not confined to their parishes. Any entertainment within a distance of about ten miles might attract them. John Hobson in Yorkshire in 1726 recounts visiting Holmfirth feast on 22 May, Dodsworth feast on 12 June, Birchouse feast on 17 July, Skilston feast on 1 August and Woosboroug feast on 14 August, a summer of feasts spread out between May and August.[27]

This annual calendar had never been without its opponents. There were always those who argued that the interruption to work that holidays entailed could be ill-afforded. It was concern about idleness, for example, that prompted Norwich in the early seventeenth century to prohibit plays 'by reason that the maintenance of the inhabitants here doth consist of work and making of manufactures'.[28] A concern for the priority of work was one factor in the movement against popular festivals and entertainment. Another was the Puritan distaste for any recreation: in the 1670s, for example, Richard Baxter was fulminating against any Sunday games and condemning 'voluptuous youths that run after wakes, and May games, and dancings and revellings, and are carried by the love of sports and pleasure . . . into idleness, riotousness and disobedience to their superiors'.[29] But such statements may well be read as coming from those who are aware that they are fighting a losing battle. The campaign against popular festivals 'was almost invariably divisive', and not always wholly successful. Take Rangeworthy, a few miles north of Bristol, where an attempt to curtail the Whitsun revel was resisted by people claiming that its purpose was 'the refreshing of the minds and spirits of the country people, being inured and tired with husbandry and continual labour'.[30]

Keith Wrightson argued that already by 1600 the communal sociability of the parish festival had been replaced by the 'fragmented sociability of the alehouse'.[31] Elite patronage of and participation in such occasions, he implied, had gone. But that is not the whole story. On top of underlying economic and social forces that were dividing communities were political and religious ones that could work either way. Puritans were certainly against wakes, revels and anything like them (though sometimes supportive of the anti-Catholic 5 November celebrations). But correspondingly royalists often supported them, even sometimes initiating new ones, like the Dover Games in the Cotswolds. Sports, it was thought, could contribute to social and political harmony. The marquis of Newcastle urged the newly restored Charles II to revive

> May-games, morris dancers, the Lords of the May and the Lady of the May, the fool – and the hobby-horse must not be forgotten. Also the Whitsun Lord and Lady, thrashing of hens at Shrovetide, carols and wassails at Christmas, with good plum porridge and pies which are now forbidden as profane ungodly things . . . and after evening prayer every Sunday and holy day – the country people with their fresher lasses to trip on the town green about the May-pole to the louder bagpipe there to be refreshed with their ales and cakes.[32]

It was to many people an attractive prospect. Through the later seventeenth century, right through the eighteenth and deep into the nineteenth, the argument between suppression and patronage of popular recreation continued, and neither side could ever be confident of victory.

There were other calendars besides these notionally ecclesiastical but by the eighteenth century more obviously rural economic ones. Some were distinctively urban, such as the annual pattern of civic life. Alderman Samuel Newton's year in Cambridge, for example, was structured by 'civic observances, mayoral dinners, scarlet robings, leet courts, quarter sessions, anniversary sermons, audit dinners and fairs'.[33] Legal life was patterned by the three Law Terms, their dates requiring elaborate calculation.

In the sixteenth and seventeenth centuries new days with a royal and political meaning had provided further markers to the calendar. Queen Elizabeth was the first monarch to introduce the celebration of her birthday, and accession days and other notable days in the history of the Stuarts were added to it. 'The English', wrote David Cressy, 'developed a relationship to time – current time within the cycle of the year, and historical time with reference to the past – that set them aside from the rest of early modern Europe . . . It was based on, and gave expression to, a mythic and patriotic sense of national identity.'[34] There was 30 January to remember the execution of Charles I, 29 May, Royal Oak Day, to celebrate Charles II's escape by hiding in an oak tree near Worcester, and also the day of his formal entry into London on the Restoration in 1660 and, more important, his birthday. Charles II and James II both had their coronations on St George's Day,

23 April.[35] On top of this there was, from the early seventeenth century, Guy Fawkes Day on 5 November, coincidentally also the day when William III landed in England.

In 1752 the established annual cycle was thrown into confusion by the adoption in England of the Gregorian calendar, thus bringing it into line with Scotland and continental Europe. This meant that eleven days had to be omitted, Wednesday 2 September being followed by Thursday 14 September. But the calendar was only 'half-reformed'; in economic life the change was ignored. The dates for payment of rents and similar transactions and for holding fairs were after 1752 eleven days behind those of the 'new-style' calendar.[36] The consequences were considerable. In the south and east of the country the new-style ecclesiastical calendar became separated from the old-style wakes and fairs, the latter now cut off from links with the church. It marked, writes Robert Poole, 'the point at which elite and popular culture drew decisively apart at parish level'. In the north-west, by contrast, most fairs and wakes decided to go new-style; the church link was maintained, and survival prospects considerably enhanced.[37]

Clocks and watches

On a daily basis time was increasingly measured by clocks and watches. In the late seventeenth century the invention of the pendulum clock, providing more accurate timing, has suggested to some historians a step forward to modernity in time-consciousness. Such a narrative underestimates the clock-time awareness of previous generations. Already by the late sixteenth century there were a large number of public clocks, and they signalled the time of the working day, the opening of markets, public meetings, church services, guild, fraternity or vestry meetings, and so on.[38] They could be seen and heard not only on churches but on the frontages of hospitals, assembly rooms and exchanges, and in the interior of pubs. Schools played a major role in inculcating a sense of clock-time. In the sixteenth and seventeenth centuries they operated strict hours, 6.00 a.m. to 5.00 p.m. in summer, 7.00 a.m. to 5.00 p.m. in autumn and spring, and 8.00 a.m. to 4.30 p.m. in winter. Not only were these hours rigidly adhered to, but the evidence of attempts by schools to inculcate a sense of time suggests that it was assumed that children had acquired a knowledge of and ability to use clock-time before they started school.[39] Of course not every child attended school, but all would have acquired an aural sense of clock-time from listening to the different clock bells. They would have known that some bells simply measured the passing of time, the hours, half-hours and quarter-hours; that others told the time for prayer, time to start or stop work, time for curfew; and that yet others might mark out anniversaries, such as the beginnings of wakes week or the date of a sovereign's birthday.

Telling or reading the time from a complicated clock-face, a visual way of knowing the time, was a more difficult skill to acquire than an aural one, and probably came with the spread of private clock ownership. Unusual before the late seventeenth century, it soon spread widely. Only nine per cent of probate inventories reveal clock ownership in the 1670s, compared with 34 per cent in the 1720s. It's true that inventories were skewed towards the better-off, but there were clocks to be found even amongst the poor. In Bristol in the 1740s clock ownership was evident in upwards of 40 per cent of inventories, including amongst those of 'very modest worth'. In nine eighteenth-century rural parishes in north Essex about one in five inventories of paupers had clocks or watches.[40] The rise of clock ownership was paralleled by a rise in opportunities for clock-makers – in the second half of the eighteenth century Bristol had at least 372 clock-makers.[41] Watch ownership has left less trace than clock ownership, but the trade in making them was booming in the late eighteenth century, perhaps about fifty thousand a year for home consumption until there was a misguided attempt to tax them in 1797–8. Imports thereafter increased, but for most people a watch could be afforded only after careful saving or a windfall.[42]

Clocks and watches were status symbols, but they were primarily for use. Inventories show that clocks were most commonly to be found, not in hall-ways or public rooms, but in kitchens, suggesting use largely by women, perhaps to time meal preparation.[43] Diaries and court records reveal that people noted the times of events, and could remember them accurately. Besides clocks, watches and bells, there were constant prompts to what time it was. In Bristol, for example, in the late eighteenth century postal workers set out on their rounds promptly each day at 8.30, 12 and 5.30, just as coaches departed at set and regular hours. Seeing the postman or the coach would tell people what time it was. By the eighteenth century a sense of clock time was universal in settlements of any size.

God's time

There was another kind of time, less universal, but hard to escape in its entirety – the idea that all time was God's time, and that people would be accountable for how they had spent it. This idea had been strongly voiced by Puritans in the sixteenth and seventeenth centuries, and was endlessly repeated in the eighteenth and nineteenth centuries. Richard Baxter put the matter both simply and forcibly in his *Christian Directory* (1673): 'O where are the brains of those men, and of what metal are their hardened hearts made, that can idle and play away that Time, that little Time, that only Time, which is given them for the everlasting saving of their souls?' Time was not to be idled with or played with, but 'used'. 'Use every minute of it', Baxter urged, 'as a most precious thing, and spend it wholly in the way of duty'.[44]

Duty encompassed work. Protestant sermons, catechisms and advice literature were at one in stressing the importance of work carried out diligently. God intended us to work, just as he worked in creating the world. Biblical precepts and Pauline injunctions rammed home the basic message: if you didn't work, you deserved to starve. No one was exempt from this. Beyond this basic requirement to work, Protestants developed the idea of a 'calling', the employment that God intended for each individual. It could be – for most people it necessarily was – a humble employment, but done in the right spirit it met with God's approval. 'Drudgerie', as George Herbert famously wrote in 1633, could be 'divine': 'Who sweeps a room, as for thy laws, / Makes that and th'action fine'.[45] Others might be called to higher occupations, but God required of them a diligence equal to that of the servant sweeping the room. After the Fall, work was part of God's plan for us.

The title of Max Weber's essay on *The Protestant Ethic and the Spirit of Capitalism* (1904–5) suggests the potentially enormous importance of the Protestant emphasis on work. Weber posited a link, what he called an 'elective affinity', between 'ascetic Protestantism' and the profit-making that was intrinsic to capitalism. He and others noted how prominent Protestants were as entrepreneurs in the years leading up to and including the industrial revolution – Quakers, for example, the most ascetic of the Protestant sects, were among the early industrialists. Weber turned to the Protestants themselves for an explanation for this. For all Protestants, faith, not what you did, was the route to heaven, but people understandably looked for reassurance that their faith was sufficient. They had a nagging anxiety as to whether they were saved. It was most acute for Calvinists who believed in predestination, that people's destinies lay not in anything they might do but in God's unknowable decision. Misuse of time, they knew, must be displeasing to God. If God had reserved for each person a calling, then it was incumbent on them to spend their time diligently in that calling. Psychologically, success in the calling was likely to be experienced as a sign of God's approval. There was an analogy between how people spent time in their calling and how they spent it in God's service. 'Remember', Baxter wrote, 'how gainful the Redeeming of Time is . . . in Merchandize, or any trading; in husbandry or any gaining course, we use to say of a man that hath grown rich by it, that he hath made use of his Time'.[46] The same should be true of all time. The material benefits of the proper use of time were potentially far outweighed by its spiritual ones. Or rather, as it was usually put negatively, the loss of time, the waste of time, would lead to everlasting hell. 'Sleep now', warned the Rev. Oliver Heywood, 'and awake in hell, whence there is no redemption'.[47]

John Wesley took up this theme in the eighteenth century. 'Leisure and I have now taken leave of each other', he wrote to a correspondent in 1727, 'I propose to be busy as long as I live'. He certainly was, cutting down on sleep, preaching at 4 a.m., even urging his followers to sing their hymns more quickly so as not to waste time.[48] He stressed to Methodists the importance of 'saving all the time you can for the best purposes; buying up every fleeting moment out of the hands of sin and Satan, out of the hands of sloth, ease, pleasure, worldly business'.[49] The interesting point here is the inclusion of 'worldly business' alongside 'sloth, ease, pleasure'. Weber was inclined to oppose 'worldly business' and faith on the one hand against leisure on the other, but for the Protestant preachers time for God was the absolute priority, and work should take second place to it: the spiritual ethic trumped the work ethic. Wesley himself prayed to be delivered 'from too intense an application even to necessary business'. George Whitefield, in a sermon entitled 'Worldly Business No Plea for the Neglect of Religion', preached that 'though business may assume an air of importance when compared with other trifling amusements, yet when put in the balance with the loss of our most precious souls, it is equally frivolous . . . The most lawful callings cannot justify our neglect with the grand concern of religion.'[50]

Methodism made heavy demands on the time of its adherents, and was much criticised for so doing. As one writer put it, for Methodists, Sunday, far from being a day of rest, was a day of constant services and 'imposes on the little mechanic, servant and labourer . . . the hardest day's work he performs in the whole week'. More alarming to many was the way in which on weekdays popular preachers could attract huge crowds, could 'detain 5 or 6,000 of the vulgar from their daily labour', many of 'the vulgar' being colliers whose absence from work would lead to 'a prodigious rise in the cost of coals' as well as bringing ruination on their families. Far from being seen as reliable hard workers, Methodists to their critics seemed sometimes to have an aversion to work comparable to those who regularly drank away Monday and sometimes Tuesday. Lengthy revivalist meetings, over-long prayer meetings, a service which in 1791 reputedly lasted sixteen hours, all these kept Methodists from regular work. Many of the better-off withdrew from work as soon as they felt that they could so that they could spend more time on religion.[51]

Quakers, too, put spiritual concerns uppermost. The London Yearly Meeting issued a stream of condemnations both of the old leisure centred on the alehouse and of the new leisure with its 'sports, plays, and all such diversions', its 'pernicious works of stage-authors, and romances'. In 1778 Quakers were warned 'against spending their time, and the substance of their hands, unprofitably, by resorting to places of vain, irreligious, and dissipating entertainment'. As to work, Quakers accepted it as 'not only praiseworthy, but indispensable', but hardly waxed lyrical about it. They had, writes Michael A. Mullett, 'a suspicion of labour insofar as it made incursions on spirituality'.[52]

Protestants were certainly anxious about the way that time was spent, but they did not give priority to time spent working. God's work came first. Moreover, taking a broader view, there doesn't seem to be very much that is distinctly Protestant about such attitudes. In 1740 Richard Challoner, the Vicar Apostolic, described as 'the supreme mentor of English Catholicism between the mid-eighteenth and mid-twentieth centuries', in his *Garden of the Soul* reminded readers that 'In the sweat of thy brow thou shalt eat they bread', urged them to 'submit yourselves to the labours of your calling', and to 'fly idleness as the mother of all mischief', and concluded as any good Protestant might: 'Perform all your works with due care to do them well, not as pleasing in the eyes of men, but the eyes of God; in whose presence, and for whom you ought to do all that you do'. Catholic holidays, too, were by the later eighteenth century in line with Protestant ones, the feast days reduced by papal decree to twelve, or ten if permission was given to work on two summer harvest days.[53]

The proper use of time was the more urgent because of the ever-present danger of sudden death, not least to children. Lessons in the proper use of God's time had to be inculcated from birth. As Isaac Watts put it:

> There is an hour when I must die,
> Nor do I know how soon 'twill come.
> A thousand children, young as I,
> Are call'd by death to hear their doom.[54]

It is impossible to measure in any accurate way how far in the eighteenth or nineteenth centuries people internalised this sense that they were accountable to God for the use of every minute of their time. What impact did it have, for example, on the sixteen-year-old daughter of an Essex nonconformist wool merchant-farmer who in 1821 was given a commonplace book inscribed on the title page: 'The improvement of our time is the first consideration in human life, for on time depends eternity . . . let no hour or minute be without its use'?[55] Diary writing, extensively encouraged, especially for girls, was a reminder of the need constantly to account for time spent.

There was another way in which God's time impacted on people's sense of time. Many believed that the second coming was imminent, that the day of judgement was at hand, that there were signs in the heavens and on earth that time as humankind had known it was coming to an end. Millenarian beliefs were widespread, to be found amongst leading Anglicans and scientists, as well as being promulgated through the almanacs. The pope or the Turks or both were seen as the anti-Christ. Their fall, it was increasingly believed in the eighteenth century, would be followed by an era of peace and prosperity. Time, therefore, did not stretch unchangingly ahead. Any significant event – the Glorious Revolution of 1688–9 or the Lisbon earthquake of 1755 – was interpreted as signalling some new era for humankind. Moore's almanac for 1761 discussed the key prophetic texts, and two years later returned to the theme in response to reader demand.[56]

The upper and middling sort

The idea that time was a gift from God to be used in his service was by no means universally held. There was emerging by 1700 and growing significantly through the eighteenth century an attitude to and structuring of time that distinguished itself sharply both from God's time and from the older calendar customs. The upper and middling ranks were creating their own calendars of social life centred on cities and towns. They were able to do this, perhaps needed to do it, because they had time to spare – and the money to go with it. The contrast between the time of the rich and the time of the poor was constantly drawn. 'The Time of People of Fashion may be indeed of very little Value', admitted a writer in the *Gentleman's Magazine* in 1743, 'but in a trading Country, the Time of the meanest Man ought to be of some Worth to himself, and to the Community'.[57] As Henry Fielding, himself a busy man, put it in 1751, 'to the upper part of mankind, time is an enemy . . . Their chief labor is to kill it.' If there was any truth in that negative assessment, then it must also be admitted that the means adopted to kill time were far-reaching, ingenious, and had the effect of transforming social life. 'Diversions', it was admitted in 1757, 'may be necessary to fill up those dismal Chasms of burdensome Time among People of Fortune'.[58] And diversions there were.

Many of these diversions were in people's homes which were the chief locales for sociability.[59] But it was the more public socialising which caught the attention of contemporaries and historians. London was at the heart of this. In 1700 it had perhaps as many as two thousand coffee-houses, centres of sociability, often with newspapers, sometimes libraries, and host to the growing numbers of clubs and societies.[60] In the later seventeenth century the London Season for the aristocracy began to be paralleled by seasons of sociability in provincial towns. There was often a resident population of 'urban gentry', families without land but with money and, typically coinciding with the meeting of the Quarter Sessions or some other civic occasion, families from the countryside would move to the town, there to enjoy assemblies, horse racing, theatre, promenades, music and libraries – and also to have the opportunity to find marriage partners for their children. The oldest provincial towns, Norwich, Exeter, York or Preston, had the earliest and most elaborate provision, but even a small town like Loughborough could in the reign of George III mount an impressive round of balls, assemblies, concerts, lectures and card parties with a population of only three thousand.[61]

The annual race meeting might well be the high spot of a town's round of pleasure, but probably what were more important for urban dwellers were the permanent, year-round ways of passing time. Clubs and societies mushroomed in eighteenth-century towns; historians have counted about twelve thousand of them with over one hundred different types. Bristol and Norwich could each boast two to three hundred clubs and societies. Even in small towns, by the late eighteenth century there were, concentrated in the Midlands, at least sixty book clubs and literary societies. Much of this middling-sort associational life was exclusively male.[62] As Shani D'Cruze has put it with reference to Colchester, 'Males of the eighteenth-century middling sort could organise their lives to have time free'; wives, children, apprentices and servants could be called on to mind the business while the men went off to their clubs.[63] Much of the time there, as Sir Charles Hanbury-Williams complained in a letter of 1751, was spent '*lounging*, which is a painful manner of letting time slip though one's hands . . . I have often wished that it were possible for me to buy at a good price that time that sits so heavily upon them, and to purchase the hours which they so lavishly squander.'[64]

Women certainly participated in the assemblies and nearly every town by the reign of George III had an assembly, normally weekly.[65] But such meetings may not have been such fun as they are sometimes assumed to be. For many well-to-do women, as James Thomson lamented in 1748:

> Their only Labour was to kill the Time;
> And Labour dire it is, and weary Woe.[66]

As Fanny Burney wrote of social life in country towns, 'all the conversation is scandal, all the attention, dress, and almost all the heart, folly, envy and censoriousness'.[67]

From the sixteenth century, but growing rapidly in the later seventeenth century, a new type of town, the spa, catered for the wealthy with time on their hands. They were located primarily in southern England. Epsom, near London, a town according to Defoe 'adapted wholly to pleasure',[68] and Tunbridge Wells grew rapidly. Further afield from the pull of London, Scarborough was fashionable from the 1720s and Bath, already with a substantial range of visitor facilities in the late seventeenth century, was about to embark on heady expansion to become the premier inland spa of the eighteenth century. From the 1720s another new type of leisure town, the seaside resort, began to make its mark, again mainly in the south of England (Margate, Brighton and Weymouth), but Scarborough in the north was able to take on a double role as spa and seaside resort.[69]

The experience of time in these developments, whether in new towns or old, differed substantially from that in the villages and rural areas where most of the population lived. The old feasts, wakes and revels were of no relevance. The 'new timetable based on polite recreations' writes Peter Borsay, '. . . cut right across that of the customary year'.[70] Provincial capitals and shire towns tended to have a winter season, spas a summer one. Bath went its own way with a spring and autumn season to distinguish itself from the more common spa or resort summer season. Within its season a town might, like Bath or Tunbridge Wells, have a master of ceremonies, part of whose job was to create a daily and weekly timetable that ensured that all visitors were doing the same thing at the same time. In Bath in the 1740s 'the Balls begin at six o'Clock, and end at Eleven; nor will the King of Bath [Beau Nash, the Master of Ceremonies] suffer them to continue a Moment longer'.[71] The aim was to create an enclosed world where people of similar status could meet and socialise.

As the promoter of a new mid-eighteenth-century theatre in Bath expressed it, 'nothing can be more disagreeable, than for Persons of the first Quality, and those of the lowest Rank, to be seated in the same Bench together'. The new theatre, it was claimed, would prevent that.[72]

This class separation in leisure was not confined to towns – it was also becoming increasingly apparent in rural areas. The rich began to cordon off areas of activity for themselves. An Act of 1671 had disqualified all except the landed classes from game hunting, and a further 1692 Act stipulated that 'inferior Tradesmen, Apprentices, and other dissolute Persons neglecting their Trades and Employments' should not 'presume to hunt, hawk, fish or fowl'. When, a century later, there was an attempt to remove the qualifications, the prime minister, William Pitt, defended exclusive amusements for 'the higher orders of the state', though prepared to admit that 'the second class, to whom a participation of this right might properly be given, were the occupiers of land, but in a more limited degree, and only on their own grounds; lest by too liberal an indulgence in this amusement, they might be diverted from more serious and useful occupations'. There were also attempts to make horse racing more exclusive, with an Act of 1740 'to restrain and prevent the excessive Increase of Horse Races', passed in part because 'the great Number of Horse Races for small Plates, Prizes, or Sums of Money, have contributed very much to the Encouragement of Idleness, to the Impoverishment of many of the meaner Sort of the Subjects of this Kingdom'.[73] The Act had a considerable effect, reducing the number of courses and races by two-thirds, the recovery from mid-century being concentrated on the bigger courses. In addition the gentry and their womenfolk by the 1770s were gaining some seclusion from 'the meaner Sort' in stands which provided better viewing and exclusivity.[74]

An annual calendar for the aristocracy and very rich emerged in the eighteenth century. The year was marked by living in London during the Season, retreating to their country estates in the summer, the men then participating in game shooting and fox-hunting in the autumn and early winter. On occasions they might fraternise with their principal tenants, at a harvest or Christmas dinner, or provide more extensive largesse to celebrate a military victory or royal accession, but the calendar they lived by bore little relation to that of the bulk of the population. Below the aristocracy, the 'middling sort' were creating their own calendar, centred more on local urban centre or nearby spa or seaside resort but, like that of the aristocracy, socially exclusive. A service industry of luxury shops, entertainment, accommodation, transport, gamekeepers and grooms grew up to support these calendars. Many people below the rich and 'middling sort' thus had their lives shaped by and dependent on them.

The life course

There were, then, many different ways of experiencing time in the eighteenth century. One thing, however, common to all people, was a sense of the life course. From the Middle Ages came a depiction of it, common on church walls, reiterated in words, most famously by Jaques in Shakespeare's *As You Like It*, of life as an ascent by stages from birth to mature adulthood followed by a descent into old age, infirmity and death. Infancy, childhood, youth, adulthood and old age were the markers. Of course, they were experienced differently in different social classes, but in none were they absent. There is evidence, too, that in the eighteenth century birthdays were increasingly recognised and celebrated as signs of progress through the life course.[75] For the majority of the population the age of leaving home, commonly at fourteen to enter service, was the end of a childhood which would itself have entailed contributions to the family economy. Adulthood would come with marriage, roughly in the mid-twenties. The age of sixty was seen as the beginning of old age, about ten per cent of the population in the early eighteenth century falling into that category. Retirement as such was unknown – the expectation was that people would work until no longer able to. But it was recognised that many people would need support in old age. The Poor Law was one resource, but rarely met more than enough for a bare survival diet – and only a minority of the old applied for help. They were expected, and expected, to access other sources of income, from family or from odd jobs.[76] For some there was help from the growing number of friendly and benefit societies in the later eighteenth century; they nearly all included pension schemes for members. Almshouses, too, were a visible sign in nearly every community that care needed to be, and was, provided for the old. There was never enough, however, and conditions for the elderly poor deteriorated in the later eighteenth century, leading, perhaps for the first time, to a sense of the elderly being a burden on society. 'It is impossible', writes Susannah Ottaway, 'to exaggerate the desperate misery of the aged poor of both sexes' in the later eighteenth century.[77]

Charles Lamb in 1825 provided a more positive view of retirement and of time in the life course. In 'The Superannuated Man', he imagines a clerk being unexpectedly offered a pension for life of two-thirds of his salary. For the clerk, 'It was like passing out of Time into Eternity – for it is a sort of Eternity for a man to have his Time all to himself. It seemed to me that I had more time on my hands than I could ever manage. From a poor man, poor in Time, I was suddenly lifted up into a vast revenue.' The clerk proceeded to calculate that he was in fact quite young since he couldn't include time working as contributing to his age. 'For *that* is the only true Time, which a man can properly call his own, that which he has all to himself; the rest, though in some sense he may be said to live it, is other people's time, not his'.[78] It was a view of time that many shared in the eighteenth and nineteenth centuries.

Conclusion

Fear of darkness and the night, the prognostications of the almanacs, the calendars and customs of the community in which people lived, clocks and watches, the sense that all time belonged to God, the demands of the social round for the well-to-do, these were the variety of ways in which time was experienced in the eighteenth century.

It is tempting to think that some of these ways of experiencing time such as faith in the almanacs simply faded away with the advance of clock time. In fact they had a capacity to endure and indeed flourish in new formats into the nineteenth and twentieth centuries, often resistant to campaigns to do away with them.

The history of almanacs is indicative. In 1828 the utilitarian Society for Diffusing Useful Knowledge (SDUK) launched the *British Almanac*, hoping that it would eliminate the 'superstitions' of the existing almanacs – it excluded lunar time, and included much of the new science of statistics. Statistics dominated many later nineteenth-century almanacs; Whitaker's, the most famous, starting in 1869, carried 368 pages of data. But the old almanacs lived on, reinvigorated by the removal of stamp duty in 1834.[79] There was another attempt to clean up time and rewrite history with the repeal in 1859 of the Acts for the observance of 30 January, 29 May and 5 November – but 5 November at least seemed to be unaffected. As to the calendar, in 1879 Richard Jefferies reported how 'An old man will . . . tell you the dates of every fair and feast in all the villages and little towns ten or fifteen miles round about. He quite ignores the modern system of reckoning time, going by the ancient ecclesiastical calendar and the moon.'[80] The old man had lived through a period when there had been concerted efforts to extinguish his ways of reckoning time, but he and many others had brushed them off.

Other attitudes to time that critics labelled 'superstitious' proved to have powers of survival. Fortune-telling had been made illegal in the 1736 Witchcraft Act, but that did not stop the practice. The Society for the Suppression of Vice, founded in 1802, brought fortune-tellers to court, the Vagrancy Act of 1824 reinforced the illegality of fortune-telling, the new police forces of mid-century brought prosecutions, but in 1912 *The Times* estimated that the number of fortune-tellers in London had increased and now numbered six to seven hundred. The middle classes formed a substantial part of the clientele.[81] Dreams and the interpretation of them, another superstition, until Freud seen as a guide to the future not the past, were linked by the dominant culture to mental and physical illness, particularly female, but the barrage of criticism again did little to stop the practice.[82]

Time was central to these attempts at reform of superstition. The predictions of the future that the almanacs made were essentially pessimistic, an abrogation of any idea that humans might be able to control their own destiny.[83] Advocates of the new, progressive and linear sense of time wanted to do away with all that. 'At the heart of the attack on superstitious modes of thinking and behaving', writes David Vincent, 'was the desire to generate a far more precise and disciplined attitude towards time.' Schools were in the frontline of this attack and placed a premium on instilling a sense of time. Joseph Lancaster, one of the early nineteenth-century pioneers, was adamant that 'In education nothing can be more important than economy of time'.[84]

If continuity beyond the eighteenth century is one theme in the history of the experience of time, another is the extent of change. It was most obvious in the eighteenth century amongst the aristocracy and middling sorts who developed their own calendars of time, both annually and on a daily basis – the latter much aided by the improvements in lighting. They learned how to 'kill time'. For the majority of the population, however, the critical issue in the spending of time in the eighteenth century and into the early nineteenth century was the separation of time between work and leisure, and here too there was both change and continuity.

Notes

1 P. Borsay, *The English Urban Renaissance: Culture and Society in the Provincial Town 1660–1770* (Oxford: Clarendon Press, 1989), p. 20.

2 E. A. Wrigley, *People, Cities and Wealth: The Transformation of Traditional Society* (Oxford: Blackwell, 1987), p. 170.

3 Quoted in P. Curry, *Prophecy and Power: Astrology in Early Modern England* (Cambridge: Polity Press, 1989), p. 10.

4 Ibid., pp. 97–8.

5 A. R. Ekirch, *At Day's Close: A History of Nighttime* (London: Weidenfeld and Nicolson, 2005), pp. 9, 33, 44, 34.

6 Ibid., pp. 134, 129.

7 M. Falkus, 'Lighting in the dark ages of English economic history: town streets before the industrial revolution', in D. C. Coleman and A. H. John (eds), *Trade, Government and Economy in Pre-Industrial England* (London: Weidenfeld and Nicolson, 1976), pp. 248–73.

8 Ekirch, *At Day's Close*, p. 331.

9 Ibid., pp. 212, 326, 333.

10 Ibid., pp. 304, 328; P. Clark and R. A. Houston, 'Culture and leisure 1700–1840', in P. Clark (ed.), *The Cambridge Urban History of Britain, vol. 2, 1540–1840* (Cambridge: Cambridge University Press, 2000), pp. 589–90.

11 Ekirch, *At Day's Close*, pp. 300–1, 104–10, 334, 337.

12 B. Capp, *Astrology and the Popular Press: English Almanacs 1500–1800* (London: Faber & Faber, 1979), pp. 23, 43, 263.

13 Quoted in Curry, *Prophecy and Power*, p. 102.

14 Quoted in ibid., p. 102; see also S. Yeo, *Religion and Voluntary Organisations in Crisis* (London: Croom Helm, 1976), p. 299.

15 Quoted in R. Poole, *Time's Alteration: Calendar Reform in Early Modern England* (London: UCL Press, 1998), p. 121.

16 D. Cressy, *Bonfires and Bells: National Memory and the Protestant Calendar in Elizabethan and Stuart England* (London: Weidenfeld and Nicolson, 1989), p. 7.

17 R. Hutton, *The Stations of the Sun: A History of the Ritual Year in Britain* (Oxford: Oxford University Press, 1996), pp. 139–45, 327–31.

18 Poole, *Time's Alteration*, p. 138.

19 Ibid., pp. 6–7, 20, 29.

20 R. Hutton, *The Rise and Fall of Merry England: The Ritual Year 1400–1700* (Oxford: Oxford University Press, 1994), pp. 52, 247.

21 John Brand, quoted in R. W. Malcolmson, *Popular Recreations in English Society 1700–1850* (Cambridge: Cambridge University Press, 1973), p. 28.

22 Henry Bourne, quoted in ibid., p. 29.

23 Hutton, *Rise and Fall of Merry England*, pp. 229, 237.

24 Malcolmson, *Popular Recreations*, p. 31.

25 Ibid., p. 16.

26 B. Bushaway, *By Rite: Custom, Ceremony and Community in England 1700–1880* (London: Junction Books, 1982), pp. 36–8.

27 E. Griffin, *England's Revelry: A History of Popular Sports and Pastimes 1660–1830* (Oxford: Oxford University Press, 2005), pp. 33, 52–4.

28 D. Underdown, *Revel, Riot, and Rebellion: Popular Politics and Culture in England 1603–1660* (Oxford: Clarendon Press, 1985), pp. 49–50.

29 Hutton, *Rise and Fall of Merry England*, p. 231.

30 Underdown, *Revel, Riot, and Rebellion*, pp. 53–62.

31 Quoted in ibid., p. 50.

32 Hutton, *Rise and Fall of Merry England*, p. 233; E. R. Vyvyan (ed.), *Cotswold Games: Annalia Dubrensia* (London: The Tabard Press, 1970).

33 Cressy, *Bonfires and Bells*, pp. 14–15.

34 Ibid., p. xi.

35 Hutton, *Rise and Fall of Merry England*, pp. 251, 253.

36 Poole, *Time's Alteration*, passim, quoting p. 122.

37 Ibid., pp. 141–52.

38 P. Glennie and N. Thrift, *Shaping the Day: A History of Timekeeping in England and Wales 1300–1800* (Oxford: Oxford University Press, 2009), pp. 144, 408.

39 Ibid., pp. 124, 225–31.

40 Ibid., pp. 109, 163–8.

41 Ibid., p. 115.

42 E. P. Thompson, 'Time, work-discipline and industrial capitalism', *Past & Present*, 38 (1967), reprinted in M. W. Flinn and T. C. Smout (eds), *Essays in Social History* (Oxford: Clarendon Press, 1974), pp. 46–9.

43 Glennie and Thrift, *Shaping the Day*, pp. 174–5.

44 Quoted in Thompson, 'Time, work-discipline and industrial capitalism', pp. 61–2.

45 Quoted in K. Thomas (ed.), *The Oxford Book of Work* (Oxford: Oxford University Press, 1999), p. 111.

46 Quoted in Thompson, 'Time, work-discipline and industrial capitalism', p. 61.

47 Quoted in ibid., p. 62.

48 J. Walsh, '"The bane of industry"? Popular evangelicalism and work in the eighteenth century', in R. N. Swanson (ed.), *The Use and Abuse of Time in Christian History* (Woodbridge: The Boydell Press, 2002), pp. 223–4.

49 Quoted in Thompson, 'Time, work-discipline and industrial capitalism', p. 62.

50 Walsh, '"The bane of industry"', pp. 232–3.

51 Ibid., pp. 235–7.

52 Michael A. Mullett, 'Catholic and Quaker attitudes to work, rest, and play in seventeenth- and eighteenth-century England', in R. N. Swanson (ed.), *The Use and Abuse of Time in Christian History* (Woodbridge: The Boydell Press, 2002), pp. 198–209.

53 Ibid., pp. 190–8.

54 I. Watts, *Divine Songs Attempted in Easy Language for the Use of Children* (London, 1715).

55 Quoted in L. Davidoff and C. Hall, *Family Fortunes: Men and Women of the English Middle Class 1780–1850* (London: Hutchinson, 1987), p. 359.

56 Capp, *Astrology and the Popular Press*, pp. 164–79, 251–3.

57 Quoted in Malcolmson, *Popular Recreations*, p. 92.

58 Quoted in ibid., p. 98.

59 B. Heller, 'Leisure and the use of domestic space in Georgian London', *Historical Journal*, 53 (2010), pp. 623–45.

60 Clark and Houston, 'Culture and leisure', p. 579.

61 Borsay, *English Urban Renaissance*; A. Everitt, 'The English urban inn 1560–1760', in A. Everitt (ed.), *Perspectives in English Urban History* (London: Macmillan, 1973), pp. 91–137.

62 Clark and Houston, 'Culture and leisure', pp. 587–8.

63 S. D'Cruze, 'The middling sort in eighteenth-century Colchester: independence, social relations and the community broker', in J. Barry and C. Brooks (eds), *The Middling Sort of People: Culture, Society and Politics in England, 1550–1800* (Basingstoke: Macmillan, 1994), p. 196.

64 Quoted in Thomas, *Oxford Book of Work*, p. 43.

65 Clark and Houston, 'Culture and leisure', p. 582; Borsay, *English Urban Renaissance*, p. 153.

66 Quoted in Thomas, *Oxford Book of Work*, p. 42.

67 Quoted in P. Clark, 'Small towns 1700–1840', in Clark (ed.), *Cambridge Urban History, vol. 2*, p. 767.

68 Quoted in D. Underdown, *Start of Play: Cricket and Culture in Eighteenth-Century England* (London: Allen Lane, 2000), p. 8.

69 P. Borsay, 'Health and leisure resorts 1700–1840' in Clark (ed.), *Cambridge Urban History, vol. 2*, pp. 776–7.

70 Borsay, *English Urban Renaissance*, p. 289.

71 Quoted in P. Borsay, *A History of Leisure: The British Experience since 1500* (Basingstoke: Palgrave Macmillan, 2006), pp. 197–8.

72 Quoted in H. Cunningham, *Leisure in the Industrial Revolution, c. 1780–c. 1880* (London: Croom Helm, 1980), p. 16.

73 Ibid., pp. 17, 19.

74 Borsay, *English Urban Renaissance*, pp. 180–96; J. H. Plumb, *The Commercialisation of Leisure in Eighteenth-century England* (Reading: Reading University, 1973), p. 18.

75 S. R. Ottaway, *The Decline of Life: Old Age in Eighteenth-Century England* (Cambridge: Cambridge University Press, 2004), pp. 46–9.

76 P. Thane, *Old Age in English History: Past Experiences, Present Issues* (Oxford: Oxford University Press, 2000), pp. 114–59.

77 Ottaway, *Decline of Life*, pp. 7–14, 22.

78 Quoted in Thomas, *Oxford Book of Work*, pp. 598–9.

79 M. Perkins, *Visions of the Future: Almanacs, Time , and Cultural Change 1775–1870* (Oxford: Clarendon Press, 1996), pp. 53–63, 77–8, 81.

80 Quoted in Bushaway, *By Rite*, p. 48.

81 O. Davies, *Witchcraft, Magic and Culture 1736–1951* (Manchester: Manchester University Press, 1999), pp. 2, 54–71.

82 M. Perkins, *The Reform of Time: Magic and Modernity* (London: Pluto Press, 2001), pp. 59–83.

83 Ibid., pp. 2–6.

84 D. Vincent, *Literacy and Popular Culture in England 1750–1914* (Cambridge: Cambridge University Press, 1989), pp. 181, 188, 315. See also B. Adam, *Timewatch: The Social Analysis of Time* (Cambridge: Polity Press, 1995), pp. 59–83.

3

Leisure preference and its critics, 1700–1850

Commentary on the relationship between work and leisure, both at the time and amongst historians, tends to be based on a fundamental and misleading assumption: it is that workers were adult males who had one occupation for which they were paid in wages. In the eighteenth century the assumption was correct for some workers but by no means for all. It failed to cover children, women, servants, apprentices, multi-occupation men, the unemployed and the underemployed, and those who survived by getting by in an economy of makeshifts. In short, it applied to only a minority of those who worked. Nevertheless, the dominant discourse about work and leisure has been framed by this assumption.

Eighteenth-century commentators inherited a belief, strongly voiced in the later seventeenth century, that the lower orders would work long hours only if wages were low and prices high; if wages were high and prices low, they would simply stop work. Sociologists call this 'leisure preference', a preference for leisure over higher wages. Economists describe it as a 'backward-sloping supply curve' for labour, a situation where workers do not respond to the possibility of maximising income and consumption by working harder; rather, they simply withdraw their labour. Eighteenth-century commentators were blunter; for them the workers had an addiction to idleness.

This chapter starts by looking at the reality of working lives before turning to the debates about leisure preference amongst both contemporaries and historians. It broadens out to engage with central issues in eighteenth-century social and economic history, the ideas that there was an 'industrious revolution' and a 'consumer revolution', neither of which allows much space for leisure preference. It concludes by examining employer strategies, their success or failure, and the possibility that workers themselves, largely through Methodism, had internalised a new sense of time that was consonant with the demands of an industrial age.

Working lives

Concern about leisure preference long predated the eighteenth century. Most adult male workers were paid by the day, and there had been attempts by statute, dating back to 1495, to set its length. The concern was not that the working day might be too long but that many artificers and labourers 'waste much part of the day and deserve not their wages, some time in late coming unto their work, early departing therefrom, long sitting at their breakfast, at their dinner and noon meat, and long time of sleeping at afternoon'. Between mid-March and mid-September, it was laid down, workers were to start at 5 a.m., have breaks of no more than two and a half hours, and remain at work until 7 or 8 p.m. During the winter they were to be 'at their work in the springing of the day and depart not til the night of the same day'. These times were repeated in subsequent acts including the Statute of Artificers of 1563. Twelve hours of actual work were, then, the desired norm. Sunday was a day without work, but the assumption was of a full day's work on the other six days.[1]

Statute law represented an ideal, reality was often different. This was not so much because workers or employers did not accept the assumptions of the law but because circumstances made it impossible to uphold them. The most obvious reason was the weather. Building workers might lose as much as three months' work – and wages – in a bad winter. As Adam Smith put it, the bricklayer and the mason 'could work neither in frost nor in foul weather'. Other trades, too, were affected by the cold: 'Calico printers could not wash their fabric, weavers could not size their cloth, shoemakers could not use frozen waxed-threads'.[2] In textile work dependent on mills driven by water, floods could stop work for a week at a time and drought 'part of every day for many weeks'.[3] Similarly for papermakers, dependent on a steady flow of water, summer was often a slack time. The lack of light in winter, as the 1495 statute recognised, was another reason for shorter hours. It affected many trades. Exeter woolsorters, for example, worked 'from the time of being able to discern the quality of wool until the evening', amounting to about eight and a half hours in winter and twelve in summer.[4] A quite different reason for not working regularly the full twelve hours was fluctuating demand from consumers, particularly in the fashionable clothing trades. Journeyman tailors in London had their hours fixed by statute in 1721, requiring them to work from 6 a.m. to 8 p.m. with an hour for dinner, but they complained that in fact they were out of employment for half the year, particularly in summer when the quality retreated to their country estates, 'cucumber time' as it was known in the trade, for they could afford to eat little else.[5]

The middle of the eighteenth century provides some firmer data on the pattern of the working day and the working week, at least for London. First, Richard Campbell's 1747 compilation *The London Tradesman* suggests a norm of a fourteen-hour day (perhaps twelve hours of work) for many trades. The average work starting time in 182 occupations was just after 6 a.m. – and there is evidence that this might also be the case outside London.[6] Second, some ingenious research by Hans-Joachim Voth gives clues to the pattern of Londoners' days. Voth examined witness statements in Old Bailey cases, where people might have seen a crime just after they had got up in the morning, or on their way to work, or as they were going to bed, and so on. For the period 1749 to 1763, Voth found that on average people got up just before 6 a.m. and were at work from shortly before 7 a.m. until about 7 p.m., two hours in total less than Campbell's evidence indicated. They were in bed by 11 p.m. This pattern had hardly changed by the end of the century, though working hours were about half an hour longer.[7] The same pattern, extending for a further half century, has been argued for towns in general, with particular reference to Bristol: '[B]etween 1750 and 1850', writes Mark Harrison, 'almost all employed people, particularly in the towns, were to be found at work between the hours of 6 a.m. and 6 p.m.', probably taking off two hours between noon and 2 p.m. '[T]he working week in Bristol', he finds, 'was ordered, predictable and long'.[8]

The big exception to this was Monday. Monday in Bristol was effectively a holiday, the most popular day for 'crowd events' as Harrison calls them, most of them inside working hours. The same was true in London in mid-century, though not, according to Voth, by its end.[9] If this is true, then London was rather exceptional, for the nationwide evidence suggests that Monday was widely taken as a holiday deep into the nineteenth century. It was in many places, particularly in rural industrial parishes, the favoured day on which to get married, with nationally 30 per cent of marriages in 1780. In Birmingham nearly 40 per cent of weddings between 1791 and 1850 were on Monday.[10]

Saturday, by contrast, was a working day, though often shorter than other working days. In the fourteenth century work had been prohibited on

Saturdays, but the Saturday holiday was thereafter eroded to the point where it 'had become a rarity' in the eighteenth century.[11] Where home was the workplace, it was a day to hand in to the master manufacturer the completed work, perhaps after long hours of work through Friday night and into Saturday morning. In 1777 John Brand, commenting on Henry Bourne's claim of fifty years earlier on 'the present Custom of spending a Part of Saturday afternoon, without servile Labour', thought that 'An Inference might easily be deduced from it in favour of Idleness. Perhaps Men who live by manual Labour, or have Families to support by it, cannot better spend their Saturday afternoons than in following the several Callings in which they have employed themselves on the preceding Days of the Week – Industry will be no bad Preparation for the Sabbath.'[12] This suggests that leaving work early on Saturday was by no means unknown, and there are scattered examples of the habit in the eighteenth and first half of the nineteenth centuries. But it was by no means universal. At the Quarry Bank Mill in Cheshire in 1790 hours worked on Saturdays were greater than on any other day of the week.[13]

The Puritans in the sixteenth and seventeenth centuries made strenuous attempts to restrict work and recreation on Sundays. The *Book of Sports*, by contrast, issued by James I in 1618, and reissued by Charles I in 1633, encouraged sport and recreation on Sundays after divine service. Charles II was on the side of Sunday sport and recreation, but his reign was punctuated by attempts, mostly unsuccessful, to pass sabbatarian legislation. Eventually in 1677 an Act, originating in the Lords, and probably promoted by bishops, was passed very rapidly, but only after the inclusion of a clause banning 'all sports and pastimes' had been dropped. The Act itself focused on banning work and trade.[14] Its immediate impact is not clear, but after the Societies for the Reformation of Manners had been founded from 1690 onwards – there were at least twenty in London and a minimum of forty-two in the provinces at the turn of the seventeenth and eighteenth centuries – prosecutions for Sabbath breaking were high on their agenda.[15] A 1738 Account recorded over a hundred thousand prosecutions for Sabbath breaking in or near London in the previous forty-four years – mostly against people continuing to work on Sundays.[16]

Mark Harrison suggests for Bristol 'a working Saturday, domestic Sunday and recreational Monday', with regular long days of work filling up Tuesday to Friday.[17] This neat picture of order fails to allow for a number of uncertainties. The first is unemployment and underemployment, some of it seasonally based, but much of it due to a quantity of available labour surplus to demand. 'Among the adult population as a whole', concludes Keith Wrightson, 'continuity in employment was not to be expected save among a minority of exceptionally skilled and valued employees ... The bulk of the labouring population, both male and female ... constituted a large pool of partially employed labour, which was drawn upon selectively as need arose.'[18] The number of days worked per year is difficult to gauge, though some heroic estimates have been made. Gregory Clark and Ysbrand Van der Werf have argued that 'There is ... no evidence of any increase in days worked per year between the Middle Ages and the nineteenth century'; they think that the number of days worked in the Middle Ages was high: assuming Sundays were a non-work day, near the maximum of about three hundred. Many medievalists think this three hundred days a year baseline a considerable inflation of reality. Ian Blanchard, for example, stressing the seasonality of work in agriculture, estimates somewhere between two hundred and 264 days of work. Clark, by contrast, sees little variation by period or season, male agricultural workers, he argues, being typically employed for three hundred or so days each year throughout the period 1670–1869, threshing work keeping up the work level in winter.[19] Craig Muldrew pushes the work level in agriculture even higher, assuming 312 days, though he admits, as his evidence very clearly shows, that 'many day labourers', actually a considerable majority, worked less than this.[20] The reality seems to have been that big estates might employ core workers for three hundred or more days, but that alongside them was a much larger group of casual workers employed in some places for as little as three weeks or two months a year.[21]

The same picture emerges from a study of the building trades in northern England. Very few workers in the building trades had guaranteed work throughout the year – they typically moved from one contract to another, a master with his journeymen and apprentices forming a mobile team, travelling to wherever there was work. Such people might with luck find work on a regular and consistent basis. We know of a Hull carpenter, William Newlove, who in the 1670s worked an average of 270 days a year for the council, exceeding 250 days in five years in that decade. But even he was doubtless affected by the seasonality of employment: 37 per cent of man days worked in Hull building trades were concentrated in the three summer months as against only 12 per cent in the three winter months.[22] Rather than a norm of three hundred days a year, we might instead conclude with Keith Wrightson that 220 days is 'a generous estimate' of what might be expected.[23]

Second, many people in the eighteenth century worked at more than one job, juggling their activities as best they could, but certainly not assuming that they would be working regular hours from Monday or Tuesday to Saturday, nor imagining that the sole recompense for their work would be money wages. Family incomes were typically made up of a combination of cash wages, grazing rights, perquisites such as fuel, the produce of vegetable gardens, charity, poor relief and credit. Until the early nineteenth century there was a serious shortage of small-denomination coins which meant that 'much of the wage was necessarily paid in credit or in kind'.[24] Agriculture was by a long way the biggest single occupation and most people lived in the countryside. Some combined small-scale farming with domestic textile working. Others had rights to common land, and could combine grazing their livestock there with work as an (occasional) day labourer. Women, certainly in the south and east, losing out on opportunities in agriculture as the century progressed, in part as the scythe (a male tool) replaced the sickle (a female one), found opportunities to bring in non-monetary resources to the family economy through gleaning after harvest, perhaps in that way adding ten per cent to household incomes.[25] For such people there was no resonance at all in the notion of regular working days and weeks. They took opportunities as they arose to add to their scanty budgets. Their time was marked out by the presence or lack of such opportunities.

Third, servants and apprentices worked in situations where they had no control over their hours. A 1743 diatribe against cricket for drawing 'numbers of people from their employments', noted also that 'It brings together crowds of apprentices and servants, whose time is not their own' – it belonged to their employers, though in this case the apprentices and servants seemed to have exercised some control over it.[26] Both service and apprenticeship were periods in the life cycle between leaving home, often at around fourteen, and getting married in the mid-twenties. In service, whether domestic or farm, people entered into annual contracts, whereby they were at the beck and call of their employers at any time of day or night in return for board and lodging and a small payment. Writing on *The Chamber Maid* in 1730 Edward Phillips worried that employers' lives were being lost 'for want of momentary assistance; and a person who has just power to ring the bell, may be suffocated, whilst a maid stays to rub her eyes, light her candle, or adjust her cap'.[27] As Carolyn Steedman has put it, 'Authority over the servant's time was perpetual. The employer had obtained the day-in, day-out attentions of a servant.'[28] Of course servants might be given some time off. Eliza

Haywood in 1743 thought that servants should be allowed 'one holiday at each of the great festivals of the year, and in the time of fairs, and it is then expected that you should go to your relations, or take what other recreation you think proper'. Moreover, 'those you live with must be very unreasonable indeed . . . that would not permit you sometime to see your friends on other days than those which ought to be devoted to heaven alone'.[29] In short, servants might get some leisure time, but it was at the discretion of their employer. For women domestic service was the biggest single occupation and, proportionate to population, there were perhaps as many servants in the eighteenth century as there were in the middle of the nineteenth century. Farm servants formed a crucial element in the agricultural labour force, the disadvantages for employers, having to feed and lodge them right through the year, offset by the fact that service 'provided a central core of workers who were available throughout the year, at any time of the day or night', and this might include essential work on Sundays and Christmas Day. Farm service was in decline in the south and east in the later eighteenth century, but it held up in the more pastoral north and west, perhaps precisely because of the time demands that animal husbandry made. As with domestic service, any time off was at the employer's discretion.[30] Apprentices were similarly placed. Numbering as many as one in ten of the urban population, they ranged from those whose parents paid large premiums to secure them a training in prestigious trades to the parish apprentices, some of whom were despatched in batches to work in cotton mills. Whatever their social ranking, apprentices' time legally belonged to their masters or mistresses; indentures stated that the apprentice shall not 'from the service of his said master day nor night absent himself', and masters could bring apprentices before the Chamberlain in London if, for example, they refused to work on a Sunday. In practice, particularly as many no longer lived in the master's house and under his control, apprentices were notorious for their riotous use of leisure time.[31]

Fourth, many people lived in a degree of poverty that was itself testimony to their failure to secure regular work. The reasons for their poverty might be old age and infirmity, illness or accident, widowhood, being 'overburdened' with young children, or simply a lack of employment opportunities, but they were by definition non-participants in the regular working day or week. At the end of the seventeenth century around ten per cent of households were in receipt of poor relief, but the number of inhabitants per poor household was small, and this may not have amounted to more than five per cent of the population. A further twenty per cent of households were in some form of need as measured by exemption from paying taxes. Contemporaries thought that about one-quarter of the population lived in some form of poverty, about one-seventh in or near destitution.[32]

In the eighteenth century, Poor Law expenditure, the most accessible measure for assessing the level of poverty, suggests that between 1700 and 1750 expenditure rose by over one-third, despite falling food prices and no significant population growth until the 1740s. Thereafter the increase in expenditure was even more rapid, from £1,529,780 in 1776 to £4,267,965 by 1803, to nearly £7 million in 1814. There was a distinct regional pattern to this spending: it was far higher in the south and east than in the west and north. These increases are so stark that it might appear obvious that they provide evidence of a parallel increase in the extent of poverty. There are, however, a clutch of reasons that make it difficult to posit such a direct link. Rising food prices, for example, pushed up Poor Law expenditure, without necessarily being an indicator of an increase in poverty. The higher expenditure of the south and east might be evidence of an ability to pay higher rates of poor relief than in the north and west rather than of greater poverty there.

A different approach to assessing the level of poverty, and of changes in it over time, is, in communities for which there are good enough records, to start with numbers on poor relief, and then to add to them those in receipt of charity, paying artificially low rents, being excluded from taxes and so on. In the 1780s about 20 per cent of the population in such communities were on poor relief or in receipt of charity, and over half fell within a wider definition of poverty. By 1827–31 over two-thirds fell within this wider definition of poverty.[33]

Poverty hit families for different reasons and in different ways. In many cases it was associated with the life cycle, having too many young children, or being widowed, or being elderly. In others it was due to changes in the structure of the local economy, a decline of rural industry, for example, or the competition faced by a handcraft trade, such as weaving, when mechanisation took hold. For yet others, and increasingly, it was the outcome of the trade cycle or of regular seasonal changes in the employment market. In the second half of the eighteenth century, and particularly towards its end, the chances of escaping poverty narrowed. In four communities for which records exist, in the period 1775–99 only just over one-quarter escaped poverty altogether while 40 per cent were often or always poor; things had been easier back in the first half of the century.[34]

Poor law officials always tried to find some means of livelihood for the poor over and above the poor rate. In Leonard Schwarz's words, 'Poor relief was always linked with work. The less regular the work, the more time-consuming the alternative means of obtaining a living: the parish overseers did their best to ensure that leisure could only be available to those who could afford it.'[35] Many recipients of poor relief and many who got by without it tried desperately to maintain themselves. Their efforts are sometimes detailed in the letters they wrote in support of their claims. William James in 1822, aged sixty-nine, with a sick wife and invalid daughter to maintain, described how:

> For many weeks past, sometimes work, & sometimes none, my Earnings have been but small, not more on Average, than six Shillings, or six, and sixpence, a week, as near as I can tell – (I may say for some Months this have been my case) with which we cannot procure Necessaries, to support health, nor nature, for the want of which, I find health and strength decaying fast, so that when I have a little work to do, I find myself, through Age, and fatige, incapable to perform it, Walking into the Country five or six Miles in a morning, working the day, and returning home at Night, is a task that I cannot, but with great difficulty perform serveral times I have thought, I could not gett home, and it have been the Occasion, of my being Ill, for two or three days.[36]

James was, for a pauper, exceptionally literate, but the elements of his letter are common ones: work beyond his powers to endure it, low wages, not enough food. People like him knew all too painfully that choice in how to spend your time was a privilege of the relatively well-off.

Fifth, women's experience of time was markedly different from that of men. Knowledge of it is at best patchy. As Jane Humphries and K. D. M. Snell have written, 'We have little information about how women's time was spent over the gamut of their routines both within and outside the familial household. Gendered time schedules, their causes and their relative rewards, remain little fathomed. Yet they are of great interest in any attempt to understand how work discipline and leisure preferences have shifted over the past few centuries.'[37] The key phrase here is perhaps 'the gamut of their routines', for women in contrast to men had multiple responsibilities. As a much reprinted seventeenth-century ballad put it, 'A Woman's Work Is Never Done'.[38] The case was best put by Mary Collier, 'the washerwoman of Petersfield', in *The Woman's Labour* (1739), a poem in response to Stephen Duck's description of the life of the thresher. In harvest, after reaping and gleaning,

We must make haste, for when we home are come,
We find again our work but just begun;
So many things for our attendance call,
Had we ten hands, we could employ them all
Our children put to bed with greatest care
We all things for your coming home prepare:
You sup, and go to bed without delay,
And rest yourselves till the ensuing day;
While we, alas! but little sleep can have,
Because our froward children cry and rave;
Yet, without fail, soon as day-light doth spring,
We in the field again our work begin . . .
Were this your case, you justly might complain,
That day, nor night, you are secure from pain.

Mary Collier goes on to describe her life doing the laundry, cleaning and washing-up, brewing and fetching water, and reflects:

My Life was always spent in drudgery:
And not alone; alas! with grief I find,
It is the portion of poor woman-kind . . .
Our toil and labour's daily so extreme
That we have hardly ever *time to dream*.[39]

This lack of '*time to dream*' was in part because of the multiplicity of competing demands on women's time and the irregularity of their work. 'Leisure' time was filled up with more work. It was said of Samuel Crompton's mother, Betty, that when she was a widow the work she did in 'carding, spinning and weaving occupied every leisure hour'.[40] Looking at wage books, Steven King was struck by 'the variation in female effort that was put into the wage-earning process over the course of a month or a year'.[41] Wage-earning was only one way, and not always the best way, of sustaining and provisioning a household. Daniel Defoe met a cave-dwelling lead-miner in Derbyshire whose wife grew barley in a garden, and kept a sow and pigs and a cow.[42] Children, as Mary Collier described, needed care. Typically, for this reason, women in agriculture worked a shorter day than men. They were also perhaps less likely to work a full week of six days: at Bakewell Mill in 1786, 77 per cent of male spinners worked a full six days, but only 70 per cent of female.[43] Custom determined to a large degree, especially in agriculture, what women could and couldn't do: farm accounts show that women day labourers in the period 1790–1850 were largely employed in weeding, stone-picking, planting, picking and sorting root crops and hay making, and that most of their work opportunities were in spring and early summer. This gendered division of labour seems to date back to at least the sixteenth century.[44] Women were also more likely than men to be in or near poverty, and in Lancashire, and probably the north more generally, there was a 'seamless join between work and poor relief', with wage-earning and poor relief two different sources of livelihood.[45]

The leisure preference debate

The idea of a regular working week is further challenged by the issue that so exercised contemporary commentators, the habit for workers to work only for as many hours or days as were necessary to keep them at a standard of living to which they were accustomed. They worked the full day and the full week only when wages were low and prices high. Rather than responding to the incentive of high wages by working harder and longer, they did exactly the opposite. In short, they were addicted to idleness. Idleness had long been railed against, medieval preachers as strong against it as Puritans in the seventeenth century.[46] From the pulpit idleness was a sin against God, a heinous waste of God's time. What was new in the later seventeenth century was the insistence that idleness was an economic sin, harmful to the individual and to society. The context for this was the ending of a long period when inflation had severely affected living standards. Now things were looking better, but the workers' response to it was to reduce their labour input. The complaints were loud and prolonged.

John Houghton, for example, in 1681, wrote how 'When the framework knitters or makers of silk stockings had a great price for their work, they have been observed seldom to work on Mondays or Tuesdays but to spend most of their time at the ale-house or nine-pins . . . The weavers, 't is common with them to be drunk on Monday, have their head-ache on Tuesday, and their tools out of order on Wednesday.' Sir Josiah Child in 1693 observed how the poor in England 'in a cheap year . . . will not work above two days in a week, their humor being such that they will not provide for a hard time; but just work so much and no more as may maintain them in that mean condition to which they have been accustomed'.[47] Sir William Petty agreed: 'The poor do not labour upon average above four days in a week unless provisions happen to be very dear'.[48] For Daniel Defoe in 1704, 'there's nothing more frequent than for an Englishman to work till he has got his pocket full of money, and then go and be idle, or perhaps drunk, till 'tis all gone'.[49] Bernard Mandeville wrote in 1714 that 'EveryBody knows that there is a vast number of Journey-men . . . who, if by Four Days Labour in a Week they can maintain themselves, will hardly be persuaded to work the fifth' – or, one might add, the sixth.[50]

The people who wrote about and deplored this leisure preference tended to think that the remedy for it lay in high prices and low wages. Only this dual pressure would make workers regular. Sir Henry Pollexfen voiced the orthodoxy in 1697: 'The advances of wages hath proved an inducement to idleness; for many are for being idle the oftener because they can get so much in a little time'.[51] Arthur Young famously wrote in 1771 how 'Every one but an idiot knows that the lower classes must be kept poor or they will never be industrious'. High wages, he wrote, had the effect of making even those 'least inclined to idleness or other ill-courses' to work 'but four or five days to maintain themselves the seven; this is a fact so well known in every manu-facturing town that it would be idle to think of proving it by argument'.[52]

Edgar Furniss in 1920 described this body of writing under the heading 'The doctrine of the utility of poverty'. Poverty for the later English mercan-tilists, he said, was a necessary good, the only incentive to work.[53] Powerful as the doctrine was, it was not unchallenged. There was some questioning of the instinct to idleness of English workers. ''tis observable', wrote James Puckle in 1697, 'that where Englishmen find constant employment (as they have in the fishery), they work harder and cheaper (everything consider'd) than any in Europe: witness the labourers in our mines, and also our artificers at Birmingham'.[54] The supposed cheapness of their labour was still buying into one side of the utility of poverty doctrine, but Puckle is a rare voice suggesting that the English might be hard workers if employment conditions allowed it. More challenging was the argument, swelling in strength as the century progressed, that there might be good in high wages. Defoe thought that high wages might increase demand for goods and services, and therefore be beneficial to the economy. A rise in real wages, claimed Jacob Vanderlint in 1734, would be a stimulus to the effort put in by labourers. By the 1760s it had become widely accepted, as Nathaniel Forster put it in 1767, 'that the sure way of engaging a man to go through a work with vigour and spirit is, to ensure him a taste of the sweets of it'.[55] Adam Smith in *The Wealth of Nations* (1776) was building on a body of thought that had been growing in acceptability. His statement of his beliefs, however, was uttered with such confidence and authority that it was his challenge to the utility of poverty doctrine that would be remembered and quoted. Smith did not put an end to articulation of the doctrine, but he severely weakened its impact:

Where wages are high . . . we shall always find the workmen more active, diligent, and expeditious than where they are low: in England, for example, than in Scotland; in the neighbourhood of great towns than in remote country places. Some workmen, indeed, when they can earn in four days what will maintain them through the week, will be idle the other three. This, however, is by no means the case with the greater part. Workmen, on the contrary, when they are liberally paid by the piece, are very apt to over-work themselves, and to ruin their health and constitution in a few years . . . Excessive application during four days of the week is frequently the real cause of the idleness of the other three, so much and so loudly complained of. Great labour, either of mind or body, continued for several days together, is in most men naturally followed by a great desire of relaxation, which, if not restrained by force or by some strong necessity, is almost irresistible. It is the call of nature, which requires to be relieved by some indulgence, sometimes of ease only, but sometimes, too, of dissipation and diversion.[56]

Smith directly attacked what had passed for common sense for a century and more: workmen, he says, respond positively to high wages; the danger is that they may work too hard, so that masters may have more occasion 'to moderate than to animate the application of many of their workmen'; nature demands that work be followed by relaxation, even 'dissipation'. Moreover, a high-wage economy is a better society than a low-wage one. 'No society', he wrote, 'can surely be flourishing or happy, of which the far greater part of the members are poor and miserable'.[57]

Some historians have questioned whether the chorus of disapproval of irregular working represented what was happening on the ground.[58] The writers, it is said, had such an interest in arguing for lower wages that they would not be disinclined to exaggerate both the extent of leisure preference and its baleful consequences. Is there any way to get at how workers themselves regarded work? The answer is, only with difficulty, and more from their actions than their words. It might be expected that artisans would have been proud of their craftsmanship; they may have felt it, but historians find little evidence of their articulation of it. As Keith Thomas has put it, 'We can only guess what most people thought about their work, for they have left no record of their feelings'. Thomas's guess, entirely plausible, is that for men 'work was a primary source of self-esteem', and that 'typically, it was during the long hours of labour that individual identity was forged'.[59] The long hours, however, may have provoked that reaction against work that Adam Smith noted. Francis Place, reflecting on his life as a leather-breeches journeyman in late eighteenth-century London, sometimes working sixteen to eighteen hours a day, wrote how

> The most pains-taking, saving industrious man is not free from the desire for leisure . . . I know not how to describe the sickening aversion which at times steals over the working man, and utterly disables him for a longer or a shorter period, from following his usual occupation, and compels him, to indulge in idleness. I have felt it, resisted it to the utmost of my power; but have been so completely subdued by it, that [in] spite of very pressing circumstances, I have been obliged to submit, and run away from my work. This is the case with every workman I have ever known.[60]

If Place was right about 'every workman I have ever known', then there seems to be a ready explanation for what the commentators thought was idleness. Of course, leaving work was perhaps possible only, and certainly easier, for those who were relatively well-paid. The evidence of workers' behaviour points in this direction. Data from a small mining community in Northumberland in the late seventeenth century show that the hewers, the most skilled and highly paid section of the workforce, averaged four days' work a week. Other workers at the mine, lower paid, worked on average five and a half days.[61] A Cornish mine agent in the 1790s wrote to his employer that 'The common tinners continue to be very refractory and insolent: many of them refuse to work, and have not gone underground for three weeks past – They have no just cause for it; for their wages have been rather too high lately than otherwise; the consequence has been too much brandy drinking, and other bad practices.'[62] What the agent failed to realise was that, from the point of view of the tinners, the high wages constituted 'the just cause' for their absence from work. High wages gave them the opportunity to enjoy more leisure. In short, such evidence as we have about the behaviour of workers tends to support rather than undermine the argument that they valued their leisure.

'Leisure preference' fails fully to describe the frame of reference of workers who exercised it. Their behaviour, so baffling to employers, related directly to time and to who owned it. The workers' view was that their contract with an employer was to carry out a task, and while there might be an end time by which it had to be completed, they were free to carry it out whenever they wished: the employer had bought their labour, not their time. The notion of 'a fair day's work' linked to 'a fair day's wage' was deeply held, but workers felt it was for them to determine what a fair day's work was. In the eighteenth century hours of work were not an issue where employees were home-based and working piece-rates, but they could become so where the work was on an employer's premises; hat-finishers, saddlers and bookbinders were in the late eighteenth century demanding a limit to the day. Other workshop-based trades successfully resisted the employers' attempts to control hours. A Leicester woolcomber in 1850 told how 'we work what hours we please, but the shop is open from five in the morning until nine at night, upon Fridays until ten and upon Saturdays up to any hour we choose to stay'. Kidderminster carpet weavers frequently carried the masters' keys to open and close the workshop. The application of machinery, however, brought the hours question to the fore, for prior to factory legislation 'the employers *dictated* the hours of labor to their work-people'. In such circumstances employees lost all right to control or ownership of their time.[63]

Industrious and consumer revolutions

Some historians have argued that it is difficult to reconcile a high degree of leisure preference with evidence of increasing domestic consumption of new products that were coming on to the market. The literature on leisure preference and the literature on 'the industrious revolution', starting in the seventeenth century, or on the 'consumer revolution' of the eighteenth century don't fit easily together.

The idea of an 'industrious revolution' was proposed by Jan de Vries in the 1990s. De Vries argued that a key change becomes apparent from about the middle of the seventeenth century, and it lies in a 'reallocation of the productive resources of households'. Households decided to make more for the market and to buy more from it, reducing their own self-provisioning.[64] This involved maximising the labour resources of the household, particularly the labour of women and children, and it came at the cost of a 'reduction of leisure time'. 'Peasant and proletarian households alike', he writes, 'appear to have decided in favour of income over leisure . . . [B]y the mid-eighteenth century, such behaviour was sufficiently common to have undermined a basic feature of labour market behaviour, the backward-bending labour supply curve.'[65] De Vries does, however, admit that the greater intensity of work could lead to 'binge drinking and binge leisure', the latter exemplified by St Monday, an admission that seems to come near to some acceptance of leisure preference.[66]

The challenge of de Vries's analysis is that he places a commitment to work over leisure prior to the industrial revolution of the late eighteenth century with which it has normally been associated, and that he sees it as a choice made by innumerable and discrete households rather than the outcome of labour discipline, or legal measures, or evangelical pressure. The evidence he has for

the change lies partly in the fact, long recognised, that there was much industry in the countryside before there was a mechanised and increasingly urban
industrial revolution, and partly in evidence of changing consumption patterns. It is the latter that poses a challenge to the notion of leisure preference.

When Adam Smith wrote that 'consumption is the sole end and purpose
of all production' he was putting a seal on an argument that dated back to
the late seventeenth century when there were already signs of a shift on the
part of commentators to 'the satisfaction of wants rather than possession of
treasure as the aim of economic activity'.[67] Evidence that this reflected the
behaviour of consumers is derived from three main sources: inventories of the
possessions of the dead; figures of imports of such commodities as tea and
sugar; and studies of the growth in the number and sophistication of shops.
It has to take into account, also, what we know about the movement of real
wages and about the standard of living.

Inventories are most useful for the period up to 1725. Between 1685 and
1725 there was a rapid growth of household goods, for example clocks and
utensils for holding hot drinks. Inventories tell us mainly about the expenditure of the middling orders, evidence for consumption ending somewhere
between craftsmen and small farmers. In the industrial parish of Old Swinford
in Shropshire, 72 per cent of the adult men and unmarried women who died
in the years 1689–90 were exempt from probate because they left goods worth
less than £2.[68] Moreover it is easy to be beguiled by the number of new
products and forget that they were one-off purchases; the main expenditure
of families, 70–5 per cent, was on food. Some agricultural labourers, however, did leave inventories, and from an analysis of nearly one thousand of
them Craig Muldrew found a 'sustained and quite rapid rise' in the value of
the goods after 1650 with a special emphasis on 'better quality bedding,
furniture and kitchenware'.[69] There is, moreover, intriguing evidence from
late eighteenth- and early nineteenth-century pauper inventories from Essex.
These were normally taken when someone wanted to go on the parish in old
age, and the parish had a right to possession of the goods when the pensioner
died. These, for people who were by definition poor, show considerably higher
levels of household goods than appeared in the inventories of labourers and
husbandmen in the late seventeenth century. On the other hand they lived
in more cramped conditions than the earlier sample.[70] What these inventories
may suggest is that over the eighteenth century a variety of new kinds of good
had come to be seen as necessities in even the poorest households – and,
possibly, that some leisure had had to be sacrificed to obtain them.

The figures for the growth of imported commodities are certainly striking. Sugar imports for England and Wales, for example, worked out at about 4 lb per head of population per year at the end of the seventeenth century and had risen to 24 lb by the end of the eighteenth century. The price, which had fallen by about half in the course of the seventeenth century, fell by a further third between 1700 and 1750. Tea imports are more difficult to estimate because of the extent of smuggling. By the 1720s or 1730s roughly a quarter of the adult population was drinking one cup per day. Consumption thereafter rose and tea drinking, to a chorus of complaints, became widespread. As with sugar, falling prices were an inducement to consumption, down by a half between the 1720s and 1770s, and by a further half with the removal of tariffs in 1784.[71] By 1787 there were over 48,000 licensed, tax-paying, tea dealers, one for every 166 persons.[72] Tea and sugar had certainly become a part of most people's diet by the end of the eighteenth century, but the figures suggest that what was happening was a change in people's diets more than an increase in consumption overall. They are not enough in themselves to indicate an end to leisure preference. Indeed in some commentators' views they were an inducement to it. Thomas Alcock, for example, in a diatribe against tea in 1752 complained of the 'considerable loss of time [which] attends this silly habit . . . a circumstance of no small moment to those who are to live by their labour'.[73] Looking ahead into the nineteenth century, there is no firm upward movement in figures for per capita retained imports for sugar, tea and tobacco between the 1790s and the 1840s, and these figures, it has been argued by Joel Mokyr, are a good indicator of living standards. As Mokyr asks, 'If most workers were earning more in real terms, what were they spending it on?' – his answer is that they weren't earning more.[74]

Shops undoubtedly grew in number in the eighteenth century, though by exactly how much it is impossible to say. De Vries argues that the century between 1650 and 1750 'witnessed a retailing revolution', a key aspect of it being the production and marketing of clothing. Women, he claims, created a 'ready made clothing industry', and the sewing and stitching of clothes in the household 'shrivelled into insignificance'.[75] The evidence for this seems to me scant. Certainly many women in the nineteenth and twentieth centuries would have been astonished to hear that their sewing and stitching of clothes had long previously 'shrivelled into insignificance'. These clothes, in de Vries's analysis, were then sold in small retail shops and by travelling pedlars. Households, women to the fore, were both producing for and buying in the market. As to the number of shops, there was one for every forty-six people in 1759, with higher ratios in the south and lower in the north, but there are no strictly comparable figures to enable us to be confident of a trend, though it may well be that growth was faster in the south in the first half of the eighteenth century and in the north in the second half.[76]

The idea that eighteenth-century England witnessed 'a consumer revolution' has been put most forcefully by Neil McKendrick. A consumer boom, he argues, reached 'revolutionary proportions' in the third quarter of the eighteenth century.[77] There has been a pronounced tendency in the literature to discover in the past moments of changed consumption that seem to herald the modern world, and McKendrick's late eighteenth-century consumer revolution now has forebears. Joan Thirsk in 1978, with an emphasis on the sixteenth and seventeenth centuries, described 'the development of a consumer society in early modern England'.[78] Margaret Spufford similarly sought to 'show that the market for mass consumer goods reached the "domestic servant class" of the seventeenth century, and therefore that the "consumer revolution" of the eighteenth century had already had its forerunner'. She argued that there was conclusive evidence 'that the standard of comfort amongst the occupants of the humbler cottage, measured in terms of their linen cupboards, their clothing and their "luxuries", which were not strictly necessary to survival, like cushions and beds and window-curtains, had risen dramatically at the end of the seventeenth century'. Towels, sheets, tablecloths, napkins and wall-hangings, she claimed, were assumed by the late seventeenth century to be necessities, even to some extent for labourers.[79] Thirsk, like McKendrick for a century later, saw the money for these purchases coming from the wages earned by women and children.[80] Men might have leisure preference, but women, it might be concluded from these studies, were putting the emphasis on buying consumer goods.

It is certainly noticeable that the accusations of leisure preference made in the eighteenth century were directed at men, and never at women. Was there a gender divide, men valuing most the leisure time that their earnings could buy, women using their earnings to buy household and domestic goods? It is a tempting idea, but it encounters some undoubted difficulties. Ever since Alice Clark's *Working Life of Women in the Seventeenth Century* (1919) and Ivy Pinchbeck's *Women Workers in the Industrial Revolution, 1750–1850* (1930), the dominant motif of research on women's work has been the narrowing of work opportunities for women in the eighteenth and early nineteenth centuries. It is laid out in detail in Bridget Hill's *Women, Work and Sexual Politics in Eighteenth-Century England* (1989). Hill admits that it is 'difficult to prove' that women 'lost out in employment opportunities in the final decades of the eighteenth century', but she has little doubt that it happened.[81] Keith Snell has shown how employment opportunities for women in corn-growing eastern England were in decline over the eighteenth century, something to which contemporaries testified. David Davies, for example, in 1795 pointed to declining employment opportunities for both women and children. William Cobbett in 1822 lamented the fact that 'the land has had taken away from it those employments for its women and children which were so necessary to the well-being of the agricultural labourer'. Similarly the late eighteenth and early nineteenth centuries see a narrowing of the possibility for female apprenticeship in artisan trades – increasingly they were restricted to needlework occupations.[82] It is true that women's work in pastoral areas shows signs of holding up; true that when domestic spinning lost out to the spinning factories, there were in some areas of the country employment opportunities for women, such as glove-making in Yeovil, Woodstock and Worcester, framework knitting in the East Midlands, lace-making in Bedford-shire, Buckinghamshire and Northamptonshire; true that new opportunities for women to work opened up in the factories. Nevertheless there seems a consensus of opinion that wage-earning opportunities for women were in decline at precisely the time when the expenditure of those wages was supposed to be fuelling a consumer revolution.

It is possible, of course, that the money to buy came from children's earnings more than from those of women. But the employment market for children was as uncertain as that for women. In the South Midlands 'Eighteenth-century farm amalgamation rendered most rural women and children redundant in agriculture'. In two Essex villages in the late eighteenth and early nineteenth centuries there was a 'lack of employment opportunities for the children of the poor'.[83] Eighteenth-century commentators delighted to see children at work and if there had been a buoyant child labour market they would not have had to go to the extraordinary lengths they did to create work for children in charity schools, schools of industry and workhouses, normally with outcomes that showed all too plainly that children's work did not cover its costs.[84]

Standards of living

Standards of living shed further light on the industrious and consumer revolutions. Broadly speaking, the century from the return of Charles II in 1660 up to the 1760s was marked by a rise in real wages, and low prices for products, above all bread. In these circumstances workers could earn enough in a short time to meet their customary needs for food, housing and clothing, and have money over for the new consumer goods.[85] Indeed they might want leisure time in which to enjoy them. Leisure preference and indulgence in new consumer products were not alternatives; both could be enjoyed. It is quite plausible that people had extra money for consumption in the way that Thirsk and Spufford have described. But this does not necessarily mean that in doing so they sacrificed leisure time for more income.

In the later eighteenth century, however, the situation was entirely different. Between the 1780s and the 1850s, Charles Feinstein has calculated, the standard of living of the average working-class family improved by less than 15 per cent, and the standard had probably been dropping since the midpoint of the eighteenth century. Any rise came only after the end of the Napoleonic Wars, and it was nothing like as marked as previous, more optimistic, calculations claimed. Feinstein's standard of living is derived not simply by relating money wages to the cost of living; it also takes into account a higher dependency rate (the ratio of those in wage-earning years to those too young or too old to work), urban disamenities (the health and other costs associated with urban living), and cuts in Poor Law payments. Like all attempts to measure the standard of living it involves a degree of guesswork, a difficulty in knowing how much to add to family incomes from the work of women and children, and an assumption that hours of work per year remained unchanged between the 1780s and the 1850s. Nevertheless, even allowing for uncertainty on the details, it suggests that we need to approach with caution the idea of a consumer revolution in the late eighteenth century.[86]

Another way of measuring the standard of living is to take a basket of basic consumption goods and calculate how much work would be needed to buy it. Using data from male farm workers in southern England and from London building workers, the conclusion for the period 1750 to 1818 is that to be able to buy the basket of goods rural workers would have had to increase their days of work per year by 56 per cent, from 250 days in 1750 to an impossible 391 days in 1818, though it was down again to 285 days by 1830 – if they survived at all in 1818 it must have been due to the contributions to family income of their wives and children. London building workers, by contrast, in a different period, could have bought their basic consumption goods from 275 days of work in 1600, reduced to a mere 140 days in 1750. In actual fact it is claimed that they probably worked nearer 300 days,

suggesting that in that early period at least they were part of both an industrious and a consumer revolution. But, as for the rural workers, more work
was required to buy the basic goods after 1750.[87]

The pessimistic evidence for the standard of living for the late eighteenth
and early nineteenth centuries indicates that any sacrifice of leisure may have
been due to a desire to maintain standards of living rather than to a wish to
indulge in new consumer products. If, as happened, the cost of living rose
from a benchmark of around 100 between the 1770s and 1790s up to 182 in
1808–12, then, unless wages rose correspondingly, which with rare exceptions
they didn't, people were going to need to put in more work simply to maintain their standard of living.[88] Leisure preference became a luxury which few
could afford.

Work and leisure in the industrial revolution

The hours and the intensity of work in the classic period of the industrial
revolution between the late eighteenth century and the middle of the nineteenth varied considerably by work situation.

Artisans were best-placed to defend existing practice. Engineers, builders
and printers in the 1830s successfully reaffirmed 6 a.m. to 6 p.m. (i.e. ten
hours' actual work) as a normal day. In the London printing trade, for
example, there was clear workshop control over output and hours. According
to J. C. Hobhouse in 1825, 'ten and a half hours and in some cases eight
hours in winter, was an ordinary day's work for machine makers, moulders
of machinery, house carpenters, cabinet makers, stone-masons, bricklayers,
blacksmiths, millwrights and many other craftsmen'. In the 1840s it was
claimed that 'To talk to a mechanic or an artisan of London, Bristol or
Birmingham of working more than ten hours a day was to risk being set down
as a madman'.[89]

Control over the number of hours worked per day was not the only achievement of the better-organised trades. With varying degrees of success they also
maintained a customary irregularity of work and the right to enjoyment of
traditional holidays. Here again, each trade, each locality has to be considered
on its own. Among coal miners, for example, there was a wide variety of
experience. Staffordshire miners, it was said in 1800, were living on the pro-
ceeds of two-thirds of a week's work, and giving over the remainder of the
week to 'idleness and dissipation'.[90] In some areas there was no recognised
starting or ending time for the day's work. Normally the Monday after pay

day, itself usually fortnightly but sometimes weekly, was a holiday. Besides the regular Mondays, the amount of holiday time taken varied considerably. In Warwickshire in the 1840s a prize fight would lure the men away from the pits five or six times each summer. In Lancashire, Joseph Hatherton, an under-looker at Messrs Foster's mine at Ringley Bridge, his job as superintendent of the miners placing him in a good position to know their habits reported:

> They have a fortnight at Christmas, a full week at Whitsuntide, three or four days at Ringley Wakes, about the same at Ratcliff Wakes, and at odd times besides. The wages are paid every fortnight, and they are never expected to come on the Monday after pay . . . and when they come on a Tuesday they are not fit for their work. Christmas and New-Year's-Day are universal holidays in the district, and generally the wakes or feasts of the different villages, and the races in their respective neighbourhoods – for example, at Worsley, Eccles Wakes, at St. Helens and Haydock, the Newton Races, the Manchester Races also, which occur during Whitsuntide, attract an immense number of colliers.

Against this luxurious amount of holiday time taken by miners in Lancashire and Cheshire has to be set the much more restricted time enjoyed by miners elsewhere and, universally, the amount of enforced but probably unwelcome holiday through short time. As the 1842 Royal Commission for Inquiry into the Employment and Condition of Children in Mines and Manufactories put it, 'in general the colliers have a considerable portion of idle time, because there is not a sufficient demand for their labour to occupy them every day in the week, winter and summer'.[91]

There is little doubt that, where machinery was present, the pattern of work changed. Recruitment to the early cotton spinning mills and factories was difficult, and as late as 1800 spinners might be missing from the factory on Monday and Tuesday. The model employers at Quarry Bank Mill in Cheshire assumed that their employees would work 313 days a year, but in 1790 workers took an average of thirty unpaid days off, some perhaps because of sickness or because the mill wasn't working, but most of it voluntary, probably coinciding with Wilmslow Wakes.[92] 'Running off' at the time of wakes was a deeply entrenched Lancashire habit, and continued right through the nineteenth century. On a daily basis, however, between twelve and thirteen and a half actual hours of work became a norm. In 1849 it was reported that in Lancashire the harriers hunting hares used to be followed by

> the Ashton weavers, armed with huge leaping-sticks, by the help of which they could take hedges and ditches as well as the boldest rider of the hunt . . . The mill system has, however, utterly extirpated every vestige of the ancient sporting

spirit. The regularity of hours and discipline seem, by rendering any such esca-
pades out of the question, to have at length obliterated everything like a desire
for, or idea of, them.

The principal of Messrs Pole and Stopford's Hat Manufactory at Denton,
near Ashton, reported that the hatters used to hunt two days a week, but 'We
made it a rule that we would not employ any person who wished to be off
his two days. Now the men we employ are as regular as any set of men.'[93]

It wasn't only where 'the mill system' had taken root that work practices
changed. In Cornish tin mines, where in the late eighteenth century there
was evidence of high leisure preference, the process of erosion of holidays was
in full swing in the early nineteenth century. By 1817, according to one
observer, 'the spirit of sport has evaporated, and that of industry has supplied
its place. The occupations in the mining countries fill up the time of those
engaged in them too effectively to allow leisure for prolonged revels, or frequent festivities.'[94] Or consider forgemen in the iron industry. The technology
of their work, with simple tools and requiring strength and endurance, did
not change between 1750 and 1850. In the mid-eighteenth century there was
a maximum of one thousand forgemen in England and Wales and they were
a hereditary caste with much control over their own work processes. They
often worked a sixteen-hour shift and a regular six-day week, but their output
was much below what was possible, suggesting that they took time off during
their working hours. Their work was undoubtedly hard, though we may
wonder how long it would have been possible to sustain what a visiting
Cumbrian iron master observed of production at the Sutton forge in Shropshire
in 1754 where the forgemen 'have not more than three hours sleep in the
twenty-four'. The change in the industry followed on from the patenting of
Henry Cort's puddling process in 1783–4 which broke the power of the
forgemen and led to a significant increase in the intensity of work. The work
took its toll. 'The majority [of puddlers]', it was reported in 1864, 'die between
the ages of forty-five and fifty years'.[95] A similar process was taking place in
lead mining in the Pennines. In 1800 men there were said to 'work hard
about four days in the week, and drink and play the other three', but by the
1830s a disciplinary paternalism on the part of the London Lead Company,
a surplus of labour, and the imposition of a regime of fines, punishments and
dismissals meant that the Company could 'make its employees obey almost
any regulation it chose to lay down'.[96]

Agricultural workers were similarly vulnerable. Potential day labourers in
the late eighteenth and early nineteenth centuries retained some resources of

their own and therefore some control over their own destinies. 'if you offer them work', went the complaint in 1773, 'they will tell you that they must go to look up their sheep, cut furzes, get their cow out of the pound, or, perhaps, say they must take their horse to be shod, that he may carry them to a horse-race or cricket-match'. In Somerset in 1795, 'In sauntering after his cattle, he acquires a habit of indolence. Quarter, half, and occasionally whole days are imperceptibly lost. Day labour becomes disgusting.'[97] A survey of agriculture in Hampshire in 1813 claimed that in a good year workers could be seen leaving off work in mid-afternoon, their leisure preference still high, but such observations were rare.[98] For conditions for agricultural labourers declined in the early nineteenth century, as did the availability of alternative forms of making a living. By the 1840s in South Lindsey in Lincolnshire 'hopper feast', clipping supper and harvest supper had been suppressed, and the day labourers worked six days a week with only Good Friday and Christmas as holidays. As one official put it in 1840, 'the agricultural labourer is as much tied to regular hours as the factory labourer'.[99]

Only in workshop trades did this process of the regularisation and often increase of work not happen. As Edward Thompson argued, the pattern was one of 'alternate bouts of intense labour and of idleness wherever men were in control of their own working lives'.[100] In workshop trades, predominant, for example, in Birmingham and the Black Country and in the cutlery trade in Sheffield, Monday, 'St Monday', remained typically a day of leisure, with the pace of work increasing through the week to reach a climax on Friday, the day for finishing tasks. Handloom weavers, too, in the heyday of their prosperity in the late eighteenth century, were said to 'play frequently all day on Monday, and the greater part of Tuesday, and work very late on Thursday night, and frequently all night on Friday'.[101] But many workshop and artisan trades, not least the handloom weavers, were under severe pressure in the first half of the nineteenth century; unable to prevent an influx of labour that broke down the boundaries separating the 'honourable' from the 'dishonourable' parts of the trade, they succumbed into desperately long hours for very low pay.

Hans-Joachim Voth has made the most thorough attempt to estimate what was happening to hours between 1750 and 1850, and even he has to admit that 'The evidence on changes in hours presented here is far from certain'. His findings are, however, striking. Drawing on evidence from witness statements in court from London and from the north of England, nearly 30 per cent of the population (though his figures are for males only), he finds that labour input per member of the labour force increased by 20–3 per cent between 1760 and 1831, most of this increase happening before the turn of the century. By 1830, he estimates, men were working on average 3,232 hours per year: to put this in a wider context, the figure for 1996 was 1,732 hours. Voth found that the main way in which hours were increased was not by working longer per day (though there is some evidence for this in the north) but by ceasing to celebrate St Monday and other holidays. St Monday, he argues, wasn't evident in the north at all even in 1760, and had gone from London by 1800. This, it must be said, runs counter to much other evidence, and doubt has been cast on Voth's selection of the particularly harsh years 1799–1803 for an assessment mid-way through his period.[102]

Voth argues that people worked longer in part because of the rising pressure on living standards due to population growth, but mainly because of the attraction of the consumer market both in goods, for example clothes, and in leisure, and yet, as he also admits, and as his argument about the end of celebration of St Monday and other holidays suggests, 'Higher levels of consumption were bought at the price of a fall in leisure'. The increases in material consumption, moreover, were 'very slow': 'Improvements in living standards do not become visible before the middle of the nineteenth century, when rising consumption and increasing full-time earnings can be observed. Thus taking leisure lost into account adds further weight to pessimistic interpretations of the course of living standards during the Industrial Revolution.' For Voth, the importance of this lost leisure can hardly be exaggerated. If there was economic growth in Britain during the industrial revolution period, it was not for the reasons that economic historians have normally turned to: 'it was abstention from leisure . . . that was at the heart of economic growth'.[103]

So ingenious is Voth's research strategy, so exemplary the statistical tests to which he has subjected his data, that there has been a tendency to take his conclusions at face value. And yet, leaving aside some doubts about the strength of the data for the north of England, and the assumption that the north can stand proxy for the rest of England outside London, there is in Voth's work a narrowness of approach that perhaps blinds him to possibilities of what was happening. Voth works on the assumption that, if people were working longer hours, it was because they chose to do so. There may, however, have been factors other than the attractions of increased consumption that resulted in more hours worked. Above all, we need to look at employer strategies.

Work discipline – and its limits

E. P. Thompson's famous argument that there was a shift from task-orientation to time-discipline was not as simplistic as his critics have sometimes alleged. He was well aware that large employers before the industrial revolution had elaborate disciplinary codes for their workers. Thompson's main example of this was the Crowley iron works, where John Crowley in 1700 drew up a Law Book, running to over a hundred thousand words, to discipline the workforce. Complaining that he had 'been horribly cheated and paid for much more time than in good conscience I ought', Crowley set up a rigorous clock-disciplined work day of thirteen and a half hours of actual work, with a regulated 'account of time', 'after all deductions for being at taverns, alehouses, coffee houses, breakfast, dinner, playing, sleeping, smoaking, singing, reading of news history, quarrelling, contention, disputes or anything foreign to my business, any way loytering'.[104] We can perhaps assume that his workers prior to this had tried to 'loyter' in the ways Crowley suggested.

Crowley's regular sounding of the clock to mark out the working day, and his imposition of fines for being late or for other offences against his rules, became standard practice in the later eighteenth century. In 1780 Josiah Wedgwood, founder of the famous pottery firm, a man who aimed to 'make such *machines* of *Men* as cannot err', drew up his 'Potters' Instructions', another catalogue of rules, and associated fines for breaking them. A bell was to be rung at 5.45 or '$1/4$ of an hour before [the men] can see to work', right through until 'the last bell when they can no longer see'. Yet even Wedgwood had to admit to difficulties, his own determination to run the works in the most efficient way clashing with the potters' sense of what was appropriate and customary. Wedgwood liked to close the works for Christmas, but in 1772 he found that 'The men murmer at the thoughts of play these hard times, but they can keep wake after wake in summer when it is their own goodwill & pleasure, & they must now take a few holidays for our convenience'. Four years later, he was no nearer to weaning the workers off the wakes or accustoming them to a long Christmas holiday: 'Our Men have been at play 4 days this week, it being Burslem Wakes. I have rough'd, & smooth'd them over, & promis'd them a long Xmass, but I know it is all in vain, for Wakes must be observ'd though the World was to end with them.'[105]

Wedgwood was not alone in feeling that he was at best half-winning the battle to impose a greater regularity and intensity of working. Edward

Cave in the cotton trade wrote how 'I have not half my people come to work to-day and I have no great fascination in the prospect I have to put myself in the power of such people'. In 1806 a hosier recounted how the indiscipline of the men led to the break-up of his business:

> I found the utmost distaste on the part of the men, to any regular hours or regular habits . . . The men themselves were considerably dissatisfied, because they could not go in and out as they pleased, and have what holidays they pleased, and go on just as they had been used to; and were subject, during after-hours, to the ill-natured observations of other workmen, to such an extent as completely to disgust them with the whole system, and I was obliged to break it up.[106]

Masters might try to impose time discipline, but ingrained leisure preference in any community could defeat them.

Methodism

There is one other important aspect of the leisure preference debate. E. P. Thompson argued that the messy and only partial shift from task-orientation to time-discipline was eased and accompanied by a profound change in people's sense of their own identity. Nonconformity and in particular Methodism were the agents of change. Methodism was a religion of the heart, it demanded a total abasement of the individual in a consciousness of sin before rescue by the blood of the Saviour. It was in Methodist meetings that conversion occurred, accompanied often by people falling to the ground, speaking in tongues, ejaculating loudly. The emotional temperature was high. One account of Cornish miners in the 1840s describes how 'in the preaching-house or in the classroom . . . they let themselves go; they shouted, they wept, they groaned, they not seldom laughed aloud, with a laugh of intense excitement, a wonderful laugh'.[107] By contrast, the life of the convert was 'methodical', disciplined to a fault, aware of the dangers of back-sliding. Methodism grew rapidly in the late eighteenth and early nineteenth centuries, from 90,000 members in 1795 to 237,000 in 1827, and chiefly within the new industrial working class. When Max Weber in the early twentieth century sparked the debate on the relationship between Protestantism and the spirit of capitalism, the Protestants he had in mind were the entrepreneurial leaders of the industrial revolution. But how could there be, for capitalism, Thompson asked, any positive relationship between Protestantism and the industrial working class? The answer was that the workers developed an inner compulsion to account for the way they spent their time – the labourer, as E. Fromm put it, became 'his own slave driver'.[108]

The seeds of this inner compulsion were sown in the Sunday Schools, proliferating in the late eighteenth century, and preaching the importance to Christians of unremitting hard work.[109] 'Week in and week out', writes David Vincent, Sunday School classes 'were taught the values of order and punctuality, and once a year displayed the rewards available to those who embraced the new attitude towards time'. The annual display was the Whitsun walk. In day schools the stress on time and punctuality was equally strong.[110] But this early training needed to be reinforced. Factory discipline could do something, but if a manufacturer wanted more than 'eye-service', the 'moral machinery' of the factory had to be on a par with its mechanical machinery. This was the language of Andrew Ure in his *Philosophy of Manufactures* (1835). Ure wrote about the difficulty 'in training human beings to renounce their desultory habits of work, and to identify themselves with the unvarying regularity of the complex automaton', that is machinery. It was necessary 'to subdue the refractory tempers of work-people accustomed to irregular paroxysms of diligence'. If this was to happen, work had to be undertaken as a *'pure act of virtue* . . . inspired by the love of a transcendent Being, operating . . . on our will and affections'. Christ's sacrifice on the cross, for Ure, could have 'this transforming power': 'it excites to obedience; it purchases strength for obedience; it makes obedience practicable; it makes it acceptable; it makes it in a manner unavoidable, for it constrains to it; it is finally, not only the motive to obedience, but the pattern of it'. For Thompson, Methodist thinking of this kind amounted to 'a central disorganisation of the human personality', 'Sabbath orgasms of feeling' making possible 'the single-minded weekday direction of these energies to the consummation of productive labour'.[111] Working in submission to the pace of the machine, Methodists, it is argued, saw themselves as paralleling the submission of Christ on the cross.

Thompson's argument has been more ignored than challenged.[112] Thompson himself had no compelling evidence that anyone actually felt as Ure thought they ought to, that they came to see work in the factory as a *'pure act of virtue'*, and it seems on the face of it unlikely that anyone could sustain such a view through a life of work. He himself admits that 'There is no way in which we can quantify the time-sense of one, or of a million, workers'. But he points to evidence of changes in the structure of personality in accounts from twentieth-century societies undergoing industrialisation and to claims from western scholars, Ure-like, that such changes are necessary and desirable.

For Thompson, 'Puritanism, in its marriage of convenience with industrial capitalism, was the agent which converted men to new valuations of time; which taught children even in their infancy to improve each shining hour; and which saturated men's minds with the equation, time is money'.[113]

Conclusion

Leisure preference was not something imagined by pamphleteers with a direct economic interest in pushing for low wages. It had a reality on the ground. It had not, as is argued by those who emphasise an industrious revolution and a consumer revolution, been laid aside in favour of higher earnings and more consumption. Leisure preference, however, was not a universal value. A key feature of the labour market of the eighteenth and nineteenth centuries was variety and localism: what was true of one area was not necessarily true of another. Factories and mills in remote areas, recruiting a young workforce, and aided by machinery, may have found it easier than older industries to impose a work discipline and long hours. It may well be, too, that leisure preference was much more prevalent in industry than in agriculture.[114]

For many of those who worked, or hoped to work, leisure preference was never an issue: they would take work when it was available, but all too often it wasn't. Artisans might celebrate St Monday, but, for the labourers or journeymen who worked with them, Monday might simply be a day without work – and without pay. Women, whether or not they worked for wages, rarely if ever feature in discussions of leisure preference. For the large proportion of the population, probably somewhere between a quarter and a third, who lived in or on the edges of poverty, once again leisure preference was not an issue; they had to try to cobble together a livelihood from a variety of sources, wage labour, self-provisioning from commons or wastelands, charity, loans, perhaps the Poor Law, their time absorbed in the struggle for survival. There was, probably widespread, an ethic that suggested that a man in particular should be able to provide for himself and any dependants through his labour – it is most evident in letters written to Poor Law authorities seeking support: men stress how hard they have worked, and how old age and ill-health alone have reduced them to destitution. Leisure preference, for all the attention it received from commentators, was never enjoyed or even aspired to by more than a minority of the workforce – by and large, a masculine and well-paid minority, or one where the leisure balanced extremely long and intense hours of work in parts of the week.

Were things changing in the early nineteenth century? There are some signs of Adam Smith's message getting through. In 1820 T. R. Malthus recorded how he had 'always thought and felt that many among the labouring classes in this country work too hard for their health, happiness, and intellectual improvement': though he didn't see any possibility 'under the principle of competition, (which can never be got rid of,) to secure much more leisure to those actually engaged in manual labour'.[115] In 1830 another political economist, Nassau Senior, wrote that it was 'generally admitted, that during the last fifty years a marked increase has taken place in the industry of our manufacturing population, and that they are now the hardest working labourers in the world'.[116] This was a view markedly at odds with the chorus of complaints for much of the eighteenth century about the idleness and shiftlessness of English workers. Yet Senior went on to admit that when wages were high fewer hours were worked, that, in effect, leisure preference was still an issue. He was probably right in this double-edged view. The hours of work, and probably the intensity of work, had increased for many workers over Senior's fifty-year period, but leisure still had a high value for them. As we shall see, they had unprecedented opportunities to enjoy it in ways both new and old.

Notes

1 D. Woodward, *Men at Work: Labourers and Building Craftsmen in the Towns of Northern England, 1450–1750* (Cambridge: Cambridge University Press, 1995), p. 123.

2 J. Rule, *The Experience of Labour in Eighteenth-Century Industry* (London: Croom Helm, 1981), p. 51.

3 P. Mathias, 'Time for work, time for play: relations between work and leisure in the early modern period', *Vierteljahrschrift für Sozial- und Wirtschaftsgeschichte*, 81 (1994), 306–11.

4 Rule, *Experience of Labour*, p. 58.

5 Ibid., pp. 51, 57.

6 H.-J. Voth, 'Time and work in eighteenth-century London', *Journal of Economic History*, 58 (1998), 36; Woodward, *Men at Work*, pp. 125–6.

7 Voth, 'Time and work', 31–6.

8 M. Harrison, 'The ordering of the urban environment: time, work and the occurrence of crowds, 1790–1835', *Past & Present*, 110 (1986), 136–40.

9 Ibid., 156; Voth, 'Time and work', 34–6.

10 R. Schofield, '"Monday's child is fair of face": favoured days for baptism, marriage and burial in pre-industrial England', *Continuity and Change*, 20 (2005), 102–6;

D. A. Reid, 'Weddings, weekdays, work and leisure in urban England 1791–1911: The decline of Saint Monday revisited', *Past & Present*, 153 (1996), 145.

11 M. A. Bienefeld, *Working Hours in British Industry: An Economic History* (London: Weidenfeld and Nicolson, 1972), pp. 16–18.

12 Quoted in H. Cunningham, *Leisure in the Industrial Revolution, c. 1780–c. 1880* (London: Croom Helm, 1980), p. 145.

13 Bienefeld, *Working Hours*, pp. 28, 37–8, 51, 53–4, 57, 61, 64–6, 71; S. Peers, 'Negotiating work: absenteeism at Quarry Bank Mill, Cheshire in 1790', *Transactions of the Historic Society of Lancashire and Cheshire*, 158 (2009), 37.

14 R. Hutton, *The Rise and Fall of Merry England: The Ritual Year 1400–1700* (Oxford: Oxford University Press, 1994), pp. 232–3.

15 E. J. Bristow, *Vice and Vigilance: Purity Movements in Britain since 1700* (Dublin: Gill and Macmillan, 1977), pp. 18–22.

16 D. W. R. Bahlman, *The Moral Revolution of 1688* (1957; New York: Archon, 1968), p. 62.

17 Harrison, 'Ordering of the urban environment', 166.

18 K. Wrightson, *Earthly Necessities: Economic Lives in Early Modern Britain* (New Haven and London: Yale University Press, 2000), p. 313.

19 G. Clark and Y. Van Der Werf, 'Work in progress? The industrious revolution', *Journal of Economic History*, 58 (1998), 830–43; I. Blanchard, 'Introduction', in I. Blanchard (ed.), '*Labour and Leisure in Historical Perspective*' (Stuttgart: Vierteljahrschrift für Sozial- und Wirtschaftsgeschichte, 1994), 11–18; G. Clark, 'Farm wages and living standards in the industrial revolution: England, 1670–1869', *Economic History Review*, 54 (2001), 478–92.

20 C. Muldrew, *Food, Energy and the Creation of Industriousness: Work and Material Culture in Agrarian England, 1550–1780* (Cambridge: Cambridge University Press, 2011), pp. 282, 289–91.

21 L. Schwarz, 'Custom, wages and workload in England during industrialization', *Past & Present*, 197 (2007), 169; see also B. Reay, *Rural Englands: Labouring Lives in the Nineteenth Century* (Basingstoke: Palgrave Macmillan, 2004), pp. 38–48.

22 Woodward, *Men at Work*, pp. 133, 235.

23 Wrightson, *Earthly Necessities*, p. 318.

24 Schwarz, 'Custom, wages and workload', 171–3.

25 P. King, 'Customary rights and women's earnings: the importance of gleaning to the rural labouring poor 1750–1850', *Economic History Review*, 44 (1991), 461–76.

26 P. Borsay, *The English Urban Renaissance: Culture and Society in the Provincial Town 1660–1770* (Oxford: Clarendon Press, 1989), p. 302.

27 Quoted in A. R. Ekirch, *At Day's Close: A History of Nighttime* (London: Weidenfeld and Nicolson, 2005), p. 292.

28 C. Steedman, 'The servant's labour: the business of life, England, 1760–1820', *Social History*, 29 (2004), 5–6.

29 Quoted in Schwarz, 'Custom, wages and workload', 157.

30 D. Woodward, 'Early modern servants in husbandry revisited', *Agricultural History Review*, 48 (2000), 141–50.

31 M. D. George, *London Life in the XVIIIth Century* (London: Kegan Paul, Trench, Trubner & Co., 1930), pp. 275–86; I. K. Ben-Amos, *Adolescence and Youth in Early Modern England* (New Haven and London: Yale University Press, 1994), pp. 84–108.

32 T. Arkell, 'The incidence of poverty in England in the later seventeenth century', *Social History*, 12 (1987), 23–47.

33 S. King, *Poverty and Welfare in England, 1700–1850* (Manchester: Manchester University Press, 2000), pp. 77–140.

34 Ibid., pp. 129–34.

35 Schwarz, 'Custom, wages and workload', 170.

36 T. Sokoll, 'Old age in poverty: the record of Essex pauper letters, 1780–1834', in T. Hitchcock, P. King and P. Sharpe (eds), *Chronicling Poverty: The Voices and Strategies of the English Poor, 1640–1840* (Basingstoke: Macmillan, 1997), p. 144.

37 J. Humphries and K. D. M. Snell, 'Introduction', in P. Lane, N. Raven and K. D. M. Snell (eds), *Women, Work and Wages in England, 1600–1850* (Woodbridge: The Boydell Press, 2004), p. 2.

38 G. Porter, *The English Occupational Song* (Umeå: University of Umeå, 1992), pp. 113–15.

39 *The Poems of Mary Collier, the Washerwoman of Petersfield; To which is Prefixed her Life, Drawn by Herself* (1739; new ed., Petersfield: W. Minchin, n.d.).

40 B. Hill, *Women, Work and Sexual Politics in Eighteenth-Century England* (1989; London: UCL Press, 1994), p. 41. See also I. Pinchbeck, *Women Workers and the Industrial Revolution 1750–1850* (1930; London: Frank Cass, 1969), p. 127.

41 S. King, '"Meer pennies for my baskitt will be enough": women, work and welfare, 1770–1830', in Lane, Raven and Snell (eds), *Women, Work and Wages*, pp. 119–40.

42 Hill, *Women, Work and Sexual Politics*, p. 44.

43 P. Lane, 'A customary or market wage? Women and work in the East Midlands, c. 1700–1840', in Lane, Raven and Snell (eds), *Women, Work and Wages*, p. 112.

44 N. Verdon, 'Reassessing the employment of female day labourers in English agriculture, c. 1790–1850', in Lane, Raven and Snell (eds), *Women, Work and Wages*, pp. 190–211; P. Sharpe, 'The female labour market in English agriculture during the industrial revolution: expansion or contraction?', *Agricultural History Review*, 47 (1999), 161–81.

45 King, '"Meer pennies for my baskitt"', p. 124.

46 K. Thomas, *The Ends of Life: Roads to Fulfilment in Early Modern England* (Oxford: Oxford University Press, 2009), p. 85.

47 Quoted in E. S. Furniss, *The Position of the Laborer in a System of Nationalism* (Boston and New York: Houghton Mifflin Co., 1920), pp. 120–1.

48 Quoted in J. Hatcher, 'Labour, leisure and economic thought before the nineteenth century', *Past & Present*, 160 (1998), 70.

49 Quoted in Thomas, *Ends of Life*, p. 80.

50 Quoted in Hatcher, 'Labour, leisure and economic thought', 69.

51 Quoted in ibid., 69.

52 Quoted in Rule, *Experience of Labour*, p. 53.

53 Furniss, *Position of the Laborer*, pp. 117–56.

54 Quoted in Thomas, *Ends of Life*, p. 82.

55 A. W. Coats, 'Changing attitudes to labour in the mid-eighteenth century', *Economic History Review*, II (1958), 35–51.

56 A. Smith, *The Wealth of Nations* (1776; London: J. M. Dent & Sons, 1910), vol. 1, p. 73.

57 Ibid., pp. 70, 74.

58 For example, P. Mathias, 'Leisure and wages: theory and practice', in P. Mathias, *The Transformation of England: Essays in the Economic and Social History of England in the Eighteenth Century* (London: Methuen, 1979), pp. 148–67; J. de Vries, *The Industrious Revolution: Consumer Behavior and the Household Economy, 1650 to the Present* (Cambridge: Cambridge University Press, 2008), p. 116.

59 Thomas, *Ends of Life*, p. 108.

60 *The Autobiography of Francis Place*, ed. M. Thale (Cambridge: Cambridge University Press, 1972), p. 123.

61 Hatcher, 'Labour, leisure and economic thought', 87–90.

62 Rule, *Experience of Labour*, p. 54.

63 C. Behagg, 'Controlling the product: work, time, and the early industrial workforce in Britain, 1800–1850', in G. Cross (ed.), *Worktime and Industrialization: An International History* (Philadelphia: Temple University Press, 1988), pp. 41–58; S. and B. Webb, *Industrial Democracy* (1897; London: Longmans, Green and Co., 1920), pp. 324–35.

64 J. de Vries, 'The industrial revolution and the industrious revolution', *Journal of Economic History*, 54 (1994), 249–70.

65 J. de Vries, 'Between purchasing power and the world of goods: understanding the household economy in early modern Europe', in J. Brewer and R. Porter (eds), *Consumption and the World of Goods* (London: Routledge, 1993), p. 111.

66 De Vries, 'Industrial revolution', p. 260.

67 Smith, *Wealth of Nations*, vol. 2, p. 155; J. O. Appleby, *Economic Thought and Ideology in Seventeenth-Century England* (Princeton: Princeton University Press, 1978), p. 175.

68 Wrightson, *Earthly Necessities*, p. 319.

69 Muldrew, *Food, Energy and the Creation of Industriousness*, pp. 15, 163–207.

70 P. King, 'Pauper inventories and the material lives of the poor in the eighteenth and early nineteenth centuries', in T. Hitchcock, P. King and P. Sharpe (eds), *Chronicling Poverty: The Voices and Strategies of the English Poor, 1640–1840* (Basingstoke: Macmillan, 1997), pp. 155–91.

71 C. Shammas, 'Changes in English and Anglo-American consumption from 1550 to 1800', in J. Brewer and R. Porter (eds), *Consumption and the World of Goods* (London: Routledge, 1993), pp. 177–205.

72 H.-C. and L. H. Mui, *Shops and Shopkeeping in Eighteenth-Century England* (London: Routledge, 1989), p. 95.

73 Quoted in Hatcher, 'Labour, leisure and economic thought', 79–80.

74 J. Mokyr, 'Is there still life in the pessimist case? Consumption during the industrial revolution, 1790–1850', *Journal of Economic History*, 48 (1988), 69–92.

75 De Vries, *The Industrious Revolution*, pp. 104–5.

76 Mui and Mui, *Shops and Shopkeeping*, pp. 29–45.

77 N. McKendrick, 'The consumer revolution of eighteenth-century England', in N. McKendrick, J. Brewer and J. H. Plumb (eds), *The Birth of a Consumer Society: The Commercialization of Eighteenth-Century England* (London: Hutchinson, 1983), p. 9.

78 J. Thirsk, *Economic Policy and Projects: The Development of a Consumer Society in Early Modern England* (Oxford: Clarendon Press, 1978).

79 M. Spufford, *The Great Reclothing of Rural England: Petty Chapmen and Their Wares in the Seventeenth Century* (London: The Hambledon Press, 1984), pp. 3–4, 113–14.

80 Thirsk, *Economic Policy and Projects*, pp. 173–4.

81 Hill, *Women, Work and Sexual Politics*, p. 67.

82 K. D. M. Snell, *Annals of the Labouring Poor: Social Change and Agrarian England, 1660–1900* (Cambridge: Cambridge University Press, 1985), pp. 15–66, 270–319.

83 H. Cunningham, 'How many children were "unemployed" in eighteenth- and nineteenth-century England?', *Past & Present*, 187 (2005), 203–4.

84 H. Cunningham, 'The employment and unemployment of children in England, c. 1680–1851', *Past & Present*, 126 (1990), 115–50.

85 Wrightson, *Earthly Necessities*, pp. 326–7.

86 C. H. Feinstein, 'Pessimism perpetuated: real wages and the standard of living in Britain during and after the industrial revolution', *Journal of Economic History*, 58 (1998), 625–58.

87 R. C. Allen and J. L. Weisdorf, 'Was there an "industrious revolution" before the industrial revolution? An empirical exercise for England, c. 1300–1830', *Economic History Review*, 64 (2011), 715–29.

88 Feinstein, 'Pessimism perpetuated', 640–2.

89 Cunningham, *Leisure in the Industrial Revolution*, pp. 63–4.

90 E. Hopkins, 'Working hours and conditions during the industrial revolution: a re-appraisal', *Economic History Review*, 35 (1982), 59–60.

91 Cunningham, *Leisure in the Industrial Revolution*, pp. 64–5.

92 Peers, 'Negotiating work', 32–7, 54–7.

93 Cunningham, *Leisure in the Industrial Revolution*, pp. 60–1.

94 Ibid., p. 65.

95 C. Evans, 'Work and workloads during industrialization: the experience of forgemen in the British iron industry 1750–1850', *International Review of Social History*, 44 (1999), 197–215.

96 C. J. Hunt, *The Lead Miners of the Northern Pennines in the Eighteenth and Nineteenth Centuries* (Manchester: Manchester University Press, 1970), pp. 224–7.

97 E. P. Thompson, 'Time, work-discipline and industrial capitalism', in M. W. Flinn and T. C. Smout (eds), *Essays in Social History* (Oxford: Clarendon Press, 1974), p. 53.

98 D. Underdown, *Start of Play: Cricket and Culture in Eighteenth-Century England* (London: Allen Lane, 2000), p. 178.

99 J. Obelkevich, *Religion and Rural Society: South Lindsey 1825–1875* (Oxford: Clarendon Press, 1976), pp. 57–8, 69–70; Cunningham, *Leisure in the Industrial Revolution*, p. 63.

100 Thompson, 'Time, work-discipline and industrial capitalism', p. 50.

101 Quoted in Cunningham, *Leisure in the Industrial Revolution*, p. 66.

102 H.-J. Voth, *Time and Work in England 1750–1830* (Oxford: Clarendon Press, 2000), pp. 241, 175, 272; L. D. Schwarz, review of Voth in *Albion*, 34 (2002), 664–6.

103 Voth, *Time and Work*, pp. 210, 271, 234; H.-J. Voth, 'The longest years: new estimates of labor input in England, 1760–1830', *Journal of Economic History*, 61 (2001), 1080.

104 Thompson, 'Time, work-discipline and industrial capitalism', pp. 57–8.

105 N. McKendrick, 'Josiah Wedgwood and factory discipline', *Historical Journal*, 4 (1961), 30–55.

106 Quoted in S. Pollard, 'Factory discipline in the industrial revolution', *Economic History Review*, 16 (1963–4), 255.

107 Quoted in J. G. Rule, 'The labouring miner in Cornwall c. 1740–1870, a study in social history' (unpublished University of Warwick PhD thesis, 1971), pp. 300–1.

108 E. P. Thompson, *The Making of the English Working Class* (London: Gollancz, 1963), pp. 350–400.

109 Ibid., pp. 375–8.

110 D. Vincent, *Literacy and Popular Culture in England 1750–1914* (Cambridge: Cambridge University Press, 1989), pp. 185, 188, 315.

111 Thompson, *Making*, pp. 362, 369.

112 But see D. Hempton, *The Religion of the People: Methodism and Popular Religion c. 1750–1900* (London: Routledge, 1996), pp. 3–28, 168–72.

113 Thompson, 'Time, work-discipline and industrial capitalism', pp. 65–7.

114 Muldrew, *Food, Energy and the Creation of Industriousness*, p. 292.

115 T. R. Malthus, *Principles of Political Economy*, ed. J. Pullein, 2 vols (Cambridge: Cambridge University Press, 1989), vol. I, pp. 473, 483.

116 Quoted in Hatcher, 'Labour, leisure and economic thought', 113–14.

4

Leisure and class, 1750–1850

In the century between 1750 and 1850 there were two apparently contradictory processes at work. On the one hand, there seemed to be a concerted attack on popular leisure by the forces of authority (government, the law, the Church), egged on and reinforced by voluntary organisations and in tune with the wishes of employers. On the other, there is much evidence of a vibrant popular culture, with new forms of entertainment coming to the fore, and entrepreneurs both creating and responding to demand. Despite this there was a strong feeling, voiced within all classes, that the poorer classes had over the century been deprived, if not robbed, of many facilities and opportunities for enjoying themselves. How time outside work was spent was deeply influenced by class. 'The very essence of our laws', wrote the novelist Edward Bulwer Lytton, 'has been against the social meetings of the humble, which have been called idleness, and against the amusements of the poor, which have been stigmatised as disorder'. William Cooke Taylor agreed: 'Hitherto', he wrote in 1841, 'nearly all our legislation on the subject of the amusements of the poor has been penal and restrictive; while a sour, jealous, and selfish spirit has led to a series of encroachments on their comforts and enjoyments which has far outstripped the intentions of the legislature.'[1] It was in part in response to this kind of feeling that there was a range of attempts in the 1830s and 1840s to create, outside the ambit of entrepreneurs and the market, new institutions for the provision of facilities in leisure time where the classes might mix and new forms of civilisation emerge. The name often given to these efforts was 'rational recreation'.

The attack on popular leisure

Cooke Taylor wrote about 'legislation on the subject of the amusements of the poor' being 'penal and restrictive'. He might also have said that, at least for the nation as a whole, it was not very frequent, and was rarely the initiative of central government. Take the drink trade. The alehouse was central to many people's use of their leisure time, and alehouse-keepers were important entrepreneurs in the organisation of leisure activities. Yet in the century between 1750 and 1850 Parliament legislated in any significant way on alehouses only in 1752 and in 1830, and the 1752 Act was little more than a measure to codify existing local practice about licensing: it, for example, required clerks of the peace to keep a register of licensed alehouse-keepers.[2] But this lack of national legislative initiative did not mean that alehouse-keepers were allowed to carry on their trade unimpeded. On the contrary, at local level they were subject to an array of controls at petty and quarter sessions, and were frequently targeted in attempts to close them down. Such attempts became significantly more prominent in the 1780s, a decade that 'marked a turning point in magisterial attitudes towards the public house'. The chief feature of this new restrictiveness was an onslaught on the smaller alehouses, and an unwillingness to grant licences to new applicants even though the ratio of alehouses to population was in decline. Alehouses were linked with idleness, places where 'journeymen without numbers . . . and day labourers . . . begin and end the week'. They were also seen as a focus for political and economic unrest, and their keepers as promoters of forms of sport and entertainment that were coming under scrutiny.[3] The Rev. Henry Zouch, Chairman of the West Riding of Yorkshire Quarter Sessions, was of the opinion that 'when the common people are drawn together upon any public occasion, a variety of mischiefs are certain to ensue; allured by unlawful pastimes, or even by vulgar amusements only, they wantonly waste their time and money to their own great loss and that of their employers'.[4] In 1786 West Riding magistrates withdrew licences from those 'who had entertained tipplers, particularly on Sundays, and encouraged cockings, bull-baitings, bear-baitings, etc'. A year later, Surrey JPs prohibited skittle grounds and billiard tables.[5] At national level the Royal Proclamation for the Encouragement of Piety and Virtue in 1787 encouraged such measures. Local Proclamation Societies and newspapers gave support. In 1787 the *Bristol Journal* lamented that

> In London and other large towns diversions calculated to slacken the industry of the useful hands are innumerable; *to lessen, therefore, the number of these is the business of the magistrate* . . . Amongst the number of diversions that call for redress are those carried on in public-houses, such as cards, dice, draughts, shuffle-boards, billiards and skittles. These are the places that rob the journeymen and labourers of their time, their little property, and their less morals.[6]

It would be wrong to overplay the novelty of such a diatribe. It had precedents right through the eighteenth century. 'A Journeyman', wrote an essayist in 1757, 'can no more afford to lose, give or throw away his Time than a Tradesman can his Commodity; and the best way of preventing this useful Body of Men from this Species of Extravagancy is, to remove from their Sight all Temptations to Idleness'.[7] In short, leisure time for the lower orders should be severely restricted. But even allowing for continuity in concern about popular leisure there was undoubtedly in the 1780s a new intensity to the campaign against it.

Parliamentary debate, and occasionally action, owed most to local or individual initiatives. Bull-baiting, for example, underwent a minor revival at the Restoration, both as an ancient custom and as a practice that had long been thought to improve the quality of the bull's meat. Often there was a bull ring in or near the market square, and some towns continued to maintain them up to the 1750s. Bull-baiting continued thereafter as a plebeian sport, but by the end of the century local newspapers were condemning it, along with cock-throwing on Shrove Tuesday, as a 'barbarous' custom, fast disappearing, they claimed, as the morals of the people improved. This may have been true of some regions, but not of the West Midlands, and it was from there that there began a campaign to make it illegal.[8] A petition from 'several inhabitants' of Walsall and Wolverhampton to Parliament in 1802 described 'the Manufactories and very extensive Collieries, Iron Works, and Lime Works' and the numbers employed in them, and deplored the fact that

> for some Years past, the Practice of Bull-baiting hath prevailed amongst the lower Classes of Society in the Neighbourhood, in a very alarming Degree, to the great Prejudice of the Persons concerned therein, the Distress, and sometimes the Ruin, of their respective Families, and to the great Annoyance and Injury of the Public at large; and that such Practice is usually promoted and encouraged by Persons notorious for their Depravity; and Drunkenness, Idleness, Gaming, Swearing, and every other Species of Disorder and Riot, are the Consequences of it, and it is become highly offensive to all peaceable and well-disposed Persons.

The petition captures precisely the concerns and the tone of the attack on popular recreation. Economic change had pride of place, and bull-baiting was not consonant with the need for a regular workforce. As another petition, from Wellington and Wenlock, put it, bull-baiting 'occasions great Stagnation in the different Works and Manufactories, to the very great Injury of the Proprietors thereof'. But almost equally important was 'the great Annoyance and Injury of the Public at large'. And finally there were the predictable consequences, from drunkenness to 'Disorder and Riot'.[9] Yet powerful as the petition and others like it were, the attempt to secure legislation failed in 1800, in 1802 and in 1809. An Act of 1822 'to prevent the cruel and improper treatment of cattle' was thought to include bull-baiting, but didn't, and it was not until 1835 that bull-baiting, along with badger-baiting and dog-fighting, was explicitly outlawed, and by that date, even in the West Midlands, it had effectively been eliminated after a campaign at local level in the 1820s to prosecute bull-baiters. Parliamentary action was largely irrelevant.[10]

Parliament, too, did little to improve Sunday observance, a matter of grow-ing concern to the evangelicals who were behind the Proclamation Societies and, from 1802, the Society for the Suppression of Vice. Beilby Porteus, the evangelical bishop of London, introduced a bill aimed at preventing the opening of places of entertainment on Sundays. It won government support and was passed in 1781. But fifty years passed before there was another major phase of parliamentary activity. It stemmed from another evangelical bishop of London, C. J. Blomfield, whose pressure led to the formation in 1831 of the Society for Promoting the Due Observance of the Lord's Day (soon to be known as the Lord's Day Observance Society). Petitions were gathered urging fresh legislation, but a series of efforts through the 1830s, led by Sir Andrew Agnew, failed to win parliamentary support.[11] No one, however, could doubt that public Sunday leisure activity was under threat. In the 1830s a favourite way of spending Sunday for lower-class Londoners was to take a river trip, upstream to Richmond or downstream to Gravesend. To a non-Sabbatarian there was much that was positive in all this, certainly nothing offensive. The agent to the Gravesend Company, which ran some of the trips, described how 'you generally find that they disembark at Gravesend, walk up to the Windmill, and you generally find them spreading their little cloths, and taking their refreshments on the grass; but I must say that I have never seen anything like a tumult or anything like disorder'. But the agent was on the defensive, putting his case before the Sabbatarian 1831–2 Select Committee on the Observance of the Sabbath Day. Charles Dickens, prompted by his antagonism to the Sabbatarians to write his pamphlet on *Sunday under Three Heads* (1836), agreed with the agent in finding the Gravesend excursionists 'neat and clean, cheerful and contented', but he had to admit that 'In some parts of London, and in many of the manufacturing towns of England, drunkenness and profligacy in their most disgusting forms, exhibit in the open streets on Sunday, a sad and a degrading spectacle'. But this was not, he claimed, because of some innate immorality, but because of the lack of respectable entertainment. Open the British Museum and the National Gallery on Sunday afternoon, claimed many, and people's behaviour would improve. 'It would appear', wrote James Hogg in 1837, 'that the doors were purposely closed against the lower classes'. But it was not until 1896 that Sunday afternoon opening was achieved.[12]

It was not legislation that led to restrictions on Sunday leisure but a combination of evangelicals and magistrates. From the late eighteenth century an increasing proportion of JPs were clergymen, by 1832 about one-quarter of the total, and they tended to be the most active. A resident of East Burnham in Buckinghamshire reported what might happen. There had once been regular Sunday afternoon cricket when 'the common . . . presented a lively and pleasing aspect, dotted with parties of cheerful lookers-on, with many women and children and old persons, among whom we ourselves, and our servants, not unfrequently mingled'. But in the early 1840s some boys were brought up before the Beaconsfield magistrates for playing cricket on a Sunday and given an option of a fine or a prison sentence. That put an end to the cricket and the young men and boys thereafter spent their Sunday afternoons 'in the beershops, or played at skittles in public-houses, or prowled about the lanes looking for birds'-nests, game-haunts, hare "runs" and the like; while the common was left lonely and empty of loungers'. In Mary Mitford's village, where Sunday cricket was halted by 'an unnatural coalition between a high-church curate and an evangelical farmer', there was a happier outcome: after some years the cricket was revived under the patronage of a publican.[13]

The cricket examples point to another way in which leisure was under threat. The space in which to enjoy leisure was being reduced. Space and time were intimately linked. How time was passed was highly dependent on the space available. This was particularly so for workers without much leisure time. As a witness before the 1833 Select Committee on Public Walks argued, 'Work-people have not much spare time, and it is desirable that they should be able to get to an open space of ground to have a game of cricket or football, or whatever it might be, in a short space of time'.[14]

At the beginning of the eighteenth century town streets and especially market squares were 'legitimate places in which recreation might be organised'.[15] This was the case for bull-baiting, as it was also for the bonfires that were lit to celebrate coronations, the king's birthday, military and naval victories, and on Guy Fawkes night. In Dover, for example, until the 1730s, the chamberlain funded between five and eight bonfires a year. Football, too, was often played in the streets. James Spershott remembered that in Chichester in the early eighteenth century there was 'footballing in the streets day after day in frosty weather to the advantage of the glazier'.[16] But, and the chronology fits with that on the clampdown on alehouses, 'The final decades of the eighteenth century saw determined resolution on the part of civic leaders to clear plebeian games of all kinds out of public streets'. It wasn't always successful. In Coventry the authorities had been trying since the 1770s to control Guy Fawkes bonfires, but as late as 1814 a traveller recorded seeing 'not less, I think, than twenty very large Fires in the narrow streets of that city, around which the thoughtless rabble were at the same time throwing firebrands, discharging pistols, guns, etc.'.[17]

Clearing the streets of such activity could easily be justified, and was, in the name of safety and civic improvement. The question that arose was whether alternative space was found. Given the speed and extent of urban expansion, it would have been difficult. In London in 1801 Joseph Strutt complained that 'The general decay of those manly and spirited exercises, which formerly were practised in the vicinity of the metropolis has not arisen from any want of inclination in the people, but from want of places proper for the purpose: such as in time past had been allotted to them are now covered with buildings, or shut up by enclosures'. Giving evidence before the Select Committee on Public Walks in 1833 John Stock, magistrate, described how 'the humbler classes are now deprived of all the means of athletic exercises, from having no place to exercise themselves'. He remembered 'the fields at the back of the British Museum being covered every night in the summer by at least from one hundred to two hundred people, at cricket and other sports', and the site of the West India Docks being formerly a popular bathing place 'to which hundreds resorted every summer's evening'.[18]

Bathing, normally naked, posed problems of sex as well as of class. In London, 'from a desire to promote public decency', bathing had been prohibited, and 'the poorer classes bathe in the canal from Limehouse to Bromley at their peril, being sometimes taken into custody for it'. The police, reported a London coroner in 1833, 'drive the children now from points where they were accustomed to go, and where they understood the depth of the water; and in order to avoid them they get into deeper water and are frequently drowned; that has been repeatedly the case in sports in the river Lea'. In Manchester, Birmingham and Sheffield there were similar reports, and much concern about the annoyance caused to 'respectable females'.[19]

Land for allotments was also under pressure. In Spitalfields in London weavers had lost theirs. In Birmingham in 1833 it was the custom 'for the working men to have gardens at about a guinea a year rent, of which there are a great number round the town, and all the better parts of the workmen spend their leisure hours there', often accompanied by their families. By 1849 all had changed: 'the expansion of the town on all sides has almost swept the whole of them away, and the goods station of the London and North-Western Railway occupies the site of many scores of them'.[20]

Much of this might be explained as simply a consequence of urbanisation, rather than as an attack on the recreations of the poor. Yet, by acts of omission as well as commission, much of what J. L. and Barbara Hammond described many years ago as 'The Loss of Playgrounds' amounted, at best, to a class-based indifference to what was happening. At the heart of this was enclosure. In Oldham enclosures were carried out without any land being set aside for recreation. In Coventry land on which the weavers had been accustomed to spend much of their leisure time in 'football and quoits, and bandy, and cricket' was now enclosed and part of the property of the Marquis of Hertford. 'In Sunderland', reported D. B. Reid in the 1840s, 'as in other towns visited, a strong impression was conveyed to me that the public are deprived of rights which at former periods they have been accustomed to enjoy'. In London George Offer, a magistrate, 'often regretted the places, when I was a boy, where I used to play and amuse myself, are now [1833] entirely shut up, and devoted either to buildings or to places of promenade for the higher classes'. Great Tower-hill, for example, had been enclosed, and 'none but the aristocracy are permitted to come in'.[21]

The loss of space for recreation was as much rural as urban. In rural areas, wrote Robert Slaney in 1824, 'owing to the inclosure of open lands and commons, the poor have no place in which they may amuse themselves in summer evenings, when the labour of the day is over, or when a holiday occurs'. There were numerous examples. The enclosure at Pudsey in Yorkshire forced the feast from the nearby moor. At Ratby in Leicestershire and at Bicester in Oxfordshire, a custom of holding rural sports on common land after the hay harvest ended with enclosure.[22] At Waterbeach in Cambridgeshire, 'as the days lengthened, in the evening after our work was done, we [agricultural labourers] assembled on our village-green to spend our time in some rustic amusements, such as wrestling, football, etc.'. But this was all stopped with enclosure in 1813. In Cambridgeshire, indeed, relatively unenclosed prior to the eighteenth century, the period 1790–1837 saw 'a rapid and very real reduction in the quantity of land available for recreation', with the loss of many village greens.[23]

Footpaths were constantly under threat. An Act of 1815 allowed any land-owner who could obtain the sanction of two JPs and the confirmation of the next quarter sessions to close a path. The Manchester Footpath Preservation Society, founded in 1826 and headed by middle-class liberal radicals, fought in the courts and by direct action to keep them open. In 1833 D. W. Harvey MP complained that 'the arbitrary power lately assumed by Magistrates enclos-ing footpaths had engendered much discontent among the poorer classes who were thereby shut out from all means of wholesome recreation'. In the following year Edwin Chadwick reported how 'In the rural districts, as well as in the vicinities of some of the towns, I have heard very strong representa-tions of the mischiefs of the stoppage of footpaths and ancient walks, as contributing, with the extensive and indiscriminate closure of commons which were play-grounds, to drive the labouring classes to the public-house'.[24]

As these comments indicate, there was a distinct sense of unease about what was happening, and eventually, but too late, Parliament began to take action. The 1836 General Enclosure Act exempted common fields within a certain radius of large towns from enclosure, and in the following year Joseph Hume secured a resolution that 'in all Inclosure Bills provision be made for leaving an open space sufficient for the purposes of exercise and recreation of the neighbouring population'. This, however, left many loop-holes, some of which were tightened up in the 1845 General Enclosure Act that specifically excluded all town and village greens from land that might be enclosed.[25] But the 1845 Act by no means signalled the end of the enclosure of common land or the loss of playgrounds. The Commissioners had the power to require the appropriation of land 'for the Purpose of Exercise and Recreation for the Inhabitants of the Neighbourhood', but it did not force them to do so. Between 1845 and 1869 614,800 acres of common land were enclosed under orders approved by the Commissioners and sanctioned by Parliament, and of these only 4,000 were set aside for public purposes: 2,200 for garden allot-ments, a mere 1,742 for recreation grounds.[26]

Emma Griffin has argued that both the extent of the loss of space and its consequences have been exaggerated by contemporaries and by historians. Trespass on private land was frequent and often tolerated by the owners. In industrial areas, she argues, there was a lot of waste land, odd fields and vacant spaces that could be and were used: 'Space for recreation was rarely hard to find'. And some towns did preserve open spaces. Gateshead, for example, had a ten-acre recreation ground (Windmill Hills) preserved as a recreation ground in enclosure acts in 1809 and 1814, and this became a public park in the

1860s. In rural areas, too, she finds, landowners frequently set aside spaces for football or cricket even if village greens were less available. 'The enduring hold of paternalism and a well-entrenched tolerance for popular recreation . . . ensured the continuation of existing forms of recreation well into the second half of the nineteenth century.'[27]

There were certainly examples of this paternalism in action, but in both urban and rural areas there was now much less of a right to space for recreation. Samuel Bamford recalled how in Middleton in Lancashire a much-frequented bowling green on one side of the church 'was broken up and the games put a stop to, chiefly, it was said, because the late steward under the Suffields could not, when he resorted to the place, overawe or keep the rustic frequenters in such respectful bounds as he wished to do'.[28] It matters not whether or not this was the real reason for the end of the bowling green – it was what people in Middleton believed and told each other. What had been thought of as long-held rights and customs were now at the mercy of unaccountable and wayward authority. The police could bear down upon trespassers, a landowner could change his mind. A typical case was in Basford, a suburb of Nottingham, where common lands had been enclosed in 1793:

> There is nothing in the shape of open ground for recreation in or around the village, and this want has been very much complained of. The school-boys are consequently driven into the streets, to their own injury, and to the general annoyance of the inhabitants. The want here complained of is likewise a fruitful source of bickering and recriminations between the young men of the parish and the owners and occupiers of lands, trespasses on the part of the young men, for the purposes of cricket-playing and other games, being very common.[29]

In the 1840s in a number of towns long-running attempts to bring to an end annual customs that severely disrupted space came to a head. The best-known of these was the bull-running through the streets of Stamford. As early as 1788 the borough quarter sessions had prohibited it, and for the first and by no means the last time enrolled special constables and persuaded the War Office to send a troop of dragoons. But in this year and in subsequent ones the bullards outwitted the authorities. In the 1830s there were renewed efforts to suppress it, the magistrates, police and army now reinforced by the Royal Society for the Prevention of Cruelty to Animals, but the magistrates were disunited and the popular support for the custom still strong. Only in 1840, after an expensive and unsuccessful attempt at prohibition in 1839, did 670 inhabitants pledge personally to assist in the suppression without the intervention of outside forces, and that effectively brought it to an end.[30] In

Derby it was Shrove Tuesday and Ash Wednesday football that became the centre of controversy. As in Stamford, it was eventually, in 1845, the rallying of the clergy, tradesmen, manufacturers and a large portion of the working classes to send a requisition to the Mayor that brought an end to a game that, the petitioners claimed, gave rise 'to the assembling of a lawless rabble, suspending business to the loss of the industrious, creating terror and alarm to the timid and peaceable, committing violence on the persons and damage to the properties of the defenceless and poor', never mind its ill-effects on those who participated in the game. In Leicester another Shrove Tuesday activity, 'whipping toms', came under attack. Armed with cartwhips and preceded by a bellman, the whipping-toms set upon people in the wealthy Newark district. The practice was seen as such a threat to the business and decorum of the town that a local Act of Parliament was secured to prohibit it, but this did not prevent serious clashes between the police and those anxious to uphold the custom in 1846 and 1847.[31]

What can we conclude about the attack on popular leisure? First, with the exception of organisations like the Society for the Suppression of Vice whose own extensive self-publicity may have served to exaggerate its impact, it was rooted in a series of local initiatives which sometimes, but only rarely, sought or needed backing at the level of the nation in the form of legislation. It followed from this that its impact might vary considerably from one place to another – thus generalisations about, say, the impact of the evangelicals need to be regarded with caution: it might be considerable in some places, hardly stirring the surface in others. Second, much of it stemmed from what its progenitors saw as a concern for public order and decency, and for the creation of an environment in which business activities were not impeded by forms of leisure whose entitlement lay in custom. Thus animal baiting and running, fairs that had outlived their trade function, bonfires and football that ranged through the streets, even if only on one day in the year, were all under suspicion. Third, there is not a moment in the century between 1750 and 1850, or indeed before or after those dates, when it is impossible to find some form of popular recreation under attack. But there does appear to be in the 1780s vigour and a degree of co-ordination, previously lacking, in trying to outlaw a wide range of popular activities. Fourth, particularly with regard to space, popular recreation was under pressure because of factors that were not primarily concerned with leisure at all, above all from urbanisation and enclosure. Fifth, by the 1830s an increasing body of middle-class opinion was becoming concerned about the effects of the suppression or attempted suppression of so much popular recreation. In 1798 T. R. Malthus wrote that 'Leisure is without doubt, highly valuable to man, but taking man as he is, the probability seems to be that in the greater number of instances it will produce evil rather than good'.[32] A few years later, in 1805, Charles Hall, a critic of the dominant political economy, noted that 'Leisure in a poor man is thought quite a different thing from what it is to a rich man, and goes by a different name. In the poor it is called idleness, the cause of all mischief.'[33] Move forward thirty years, and a different tone is becoming apparent in middle-class public discourse. There was beginning to be a degree of nostalgia for bygone customs, and the need for some leisure was increasingly recognised. The Select Committee on Public Walks in 1833, for example, was of the opinion that 'The spring to industry that occasional relaxation gives, seems quite as necessary to the poor as to the rich'.[34] Leisure was still subservient to 'industry', relaxation should only be 'occasional', but at least it was gaining legitimacy. Finally, and most important, the attack on leisure has to be seen in the context of an enormous expansion of commercially provided leisure.

The expansion of commercial leisure

The English in the eighteenth century liked to think of themselves as a 'commercial people'. Commerce was the lifeblood of the economy, and there was hardly anything that could not be bought or sold. It is not surprising that people's leisure time offered opportunities to entrepreneurs. Contemporaries and historians who posit 'leisure preference' against consumption are looking at things from only one angle; for the entrepreneur, leisure quite as much as commodities offered opportunities to turn a profit. What to one person was the 'idleness' of the poorer classes, to another was a chance to make some money.

Those who were licensed to sell alcohol in alehouse, tavern or inn were best-placed to take advantage of any opportunities. It is difficult to find any form of popular leisure with which publicans had no connection at all. Sometimes they were initiators, sometimes they latched on to ongoing activities, at yet others they developed an activity beyond the bounds of the pub. From back in the seventeenth century they had tried to boost custom by offering packs of cards, billiard tables, shove-halfpenny boards, bowling and skittle alleys, all with associated gambling. They also organised outdoor sports, wrestling and boxing matches, cricket, cock-fights, horse races.[35] In Bristol, for example, as public space for leisure in the city centre was lost through building programmes, 'entrepreneur publicans' re-established sports 'as part of the facilities of public houses'. And in Bristol as elsewhere they tacked on commercial elements to traditional holidays.[36] The Bell Inn at Great Cheverell, near Market Lavington in Wiltshire, for example, was certainly not unusual in sponsoring cudgelling contests on its premises on Whit Monday and Tuesday in 1751, nor was the Bell at South Newton in Wiltshire which offered 'riding for geese' (riding a horse at the gallop and pulling off the neck of a goose) on Whit Monday in 1764 and bull-baiting and cock-fighting at Easter and Whitsun 1760.[37] In 1767 Hampshire JPs complained of the 'pernicious practice' which allowed publicans 'to advertise and encourage revels and such like unlawful meetings of idle and disorderly persons . . . for their private gain and advantage', thus leading 'the lower sort of people' to be 'seduced from their respective labours and employments'. It was precisely the 'private gain and advantage' that was so attractive to the publicans.[38] The Hampshire magistrates reissued this order in 1781 and, as we have seen, there were vigorous efforts in the later eighteenth century to disentangle recreation from the alehouse, but success was difficult to achieve. In 1833 the Liverpool merchant and temperance advocate John Finch complained how publicans and beer house-keepers

> institute clubs of various kinds, benefit societies, political societies, money clubs, clothing clubs, watch clubs, clock clubs, furniture clubs, building, or a hundred other clubs; they also get up what they call in the country wakes; once in the year, bull-baiting is also resorted to, for the purpose of increasing the sale of intoxicating liquors; also quoit-playing, bowling, wrestling, running, boxing, horse-racing, gaming, card-playing, etc.[39]

No one pub doubtless managed the full range of activity outlined by Finch, but the pub remained a key provider of commercial leisure.

Publicans were not alone as entrepreneurs in the commercialisation of popular leisure. The opportunities lay in two main spheres of activity, sport and, in the widest possible sense, theatre. In both there was a substantial element of upper- and middle-class patronage, for example in horse racing and in the development of circus, but both developed in ways that outran the intentions of patrons.

The sports that were most affected by commercialisation were horse racing, cricket, prize-fighting, pedestrianism, wrestling and rowing. Football, by contrast, 'played in all parts of the land throughout the eighteenth century' remained 'firmly rooted in the lower ranks of society'.[40] The marks of commercialisation were gambling, the presence of large numbers of spectators and opportunities for participants to become 'professionals', a word in use by the 1830s to indicate someone earning money from sport.[41] Many of these commercialised sports had some form of national organisation, such as the Jockey Club or the Pugilistic Club and its successors after its demise in 1824: these came to have a role as adjudicators of disputes and setters of the rules, essential where gambling was involved.

Horse racing was the sport that developed earliest and had the most money involved in it. By 1740 there were over 130 race courses. An Act in that year was designed to prevent the smaller races, which 'have contributed very much to the Encouragement of Idleness'; it had a dramatic effect, reducing the number to forty-seven by 1749, but thereafter there was recovery. In 1781 over fifty small towns had a race meeting.[42] Race courses were for the most part, however, used only once a year; in 1823 eight-seven out of ninety-five race courses had only one meeting a year.[43] Horse racing had the highest patronage from the monarch downwards, and the races were often the focal point of local seasons – and money spinners. At York in 1708 the corporation claimed that 'the making of a yearly horse-race . . . may be of advantage and profit to the . . . city'.[44] At national level, Newmarket, linked with the Jockey Club from 1752, was the sport's centre of gravity. The classics of flat-racing, the St Leger, the Oaks and the Derby, were all established between 1778 and 1780.[45]

It is difficult to exaggerate the dominance of horse racing in the sporting world. Between 1793 and 1804 over 80 per cent of sporting stakes reported in the sporting press were for horse races, a percentage which exceeded 90 in the following decade.[46] But horse racing was not exclusively a high-status sport. In London in 1738 there were races at Belsize, Finchley, Hampstead, Highgate, Kentish Town and Tothill Fields, 'frequented chiefly by apprentices, servants, and the lowest sort of tradesmen'.[47] These were the kind of races that the 1740 Act was aimed at, but in the early nineteenth century Londoners could see horse racing at Kentish Town, Bayswater and Sadler's Wells.[48] As Dickens's description of a race meeting in *Nicholas Nickleby* or W. P. Frith's famous painting of Derby Day in 1858 richly demonstrated, racing could attract people of low social rank, many of them either spending money or hoping to make some. 'By 1850', writes Adrian Harvey, 'almost all of the 40,000 crowd at Manchester's race meeting paid admission money, the lowest cost being one shilling'. They were, he is confident, predominantly working-class.[49]

Cricket also acquired the patronage of the rich. It was in origin, and still very largely in the early eighteenth century, a southern and 'peasant sport which was taken up by the aristocracy and gentry, and in the process transformed and professionalized'.[50] London became a magnet, and by the 1740s matches were advertised and spectators were paying. Soon the best players from the villages were attracted there. Crowds could be large. Nearly twenty thousand watched Hambledon play 'Surrey' (actually the Caterham Club) at Guildford in 1769, and there were twenty thousand spectators, largely working men and their families, when Nottingham played Sussex at Nottingham in 1835.[51]

Prize-fighting was another sport attracting large sums of money, patronised at the highest level. Its supporters saw it as a promoter of manly courage, no harm at all at a time of almost constant warfare. As Pierce Egan put it, 'the manly art of Boxing, has infused that true heroic courage, blended with humanity, into the hearts of Britons, which has made them so renowned, terrific, and triumphant, in all parts of the world'. No one could doubt its ability to attract crowds – there were upwards of thirty thousand at the fight between Tom Spring and John Langan at Worcester Race Course in 1824.[52]

Wrestling traditionally had two main centres, the north-west and the south-west, publicans perhaps taking over patronage from the gentry. Spectators were again numerous, twenty thousand for a match at Devonport in 1826, up to ten thousand in the Lake District in the mid-nineteenth century. In the 1820s the sport took a hold in London, the chief promoter Thomas Rouse of the Eagle Tavern in the City Road. William Howitt reports eight thousand spectators watching Westmorland wrestling at Chalk Farm in London in 1837.[53]

All these sports, and others – rowing and pedestrianism perhaps the chief among them – offered opportunities to gamble, and all became to a greater or lesser degree corrupted. 'By 1800 the London game [of cricket] was being seriously corrupted by professional gamblers.' By the 1820s 'criminal machinations' were affecting most sports.[54]

Theatre, or more broadly popular drama, spectacle and entertainment, had a more tense relationship with government and the law than did sports. There was a long history of censorship and control of performance outlets. The Licensing Act of 1737, passed at a time when government was anxious about the use of the stage for political purposes, reasserted a monopoly of legitimate drama (five-act plays) for the two London patent theatres, Covent Garden and Drury Lane, and for places where 'his Majesty, his Heirs or Successors, shall in their Royal Persons reside, and during such Residence only'. This legislation withdrew the right of magistrates in the provinces and in London to grant theatrical licences. There was some amelioration for London from 1752 onwards, but none for the provinces until the Theatrical Representations Act of 1788. For more than fifty years anyone performing drama in the provinces was liable to be treated as a 'Rogue and Vagabond', and there was a fine of £50 for anyone performing 'any Interlude, Tragedy, Comedy, Opera, Play, Farce or other Entertainment of the Stage'. The bark of the 1737 Act, however, was worse than its bite: many theatrical troupes toured well-established circuits in the country, knowing which magistrates were likely to turn a blind eye to their activities.[55] And the larger towns simply ignored the law. The first major wave of investment in purpose-built auditoriums dates from the 1750s. Sheffield, for example, had a theatre and assembly rooms built by public subscription in 1762 and rebuilt in 1773.[56] So neglected had the 1737 law become that the 1788 Act was intended, as part of the Proclamation Society's campaign to stiffen the spines of magistrates, to give them back some power under strict limits; they were to be allowed to license theatrical performances. Immediately the better-off touring companies, with the permission of the magistrates, began to build permanent theatres. In East Kent, for example, Sarah Baker's company soon had purpose-built theatres in Canterbury, Rochester, Maidstone and Tunbridge Wells. Between 1736 and 1760 there were about ten purpose-built theatres erected in the English provinces, between 1760 and the 1820s at least one hundred and probably as many as one hundred and fifty.[57]

In London, too, the late eighteenth and early nineteenth centuries were a period of growth. Average nightly attendance at Covent Garden and Drury Lane rose from about a thousand at each in the mid-eighteenth century to fifteen hundred in the 1790s. At the same time seating capacity expanded, to over three thousand at Covent Garden in 1792 and to just short of four thousand at Drury Lane in 1794. The so-called minor theatres in London had to wait until 1843 before an Act removed the monopoly of the two patent theatres, but they had by that date already encroached on it to a considerable degree.[58]

This nationwide expansion of the supply of theatre was associated with a decline in the social status of audiences. When actors and proprietors gave evidence before the 1832 Select Committee to Inquire into the Laws Affecting Dramatic Literature they were almost unanimous in claiming that the Surrey and Coburg theatres on London's south bank and the Pavilion in the east attracted audiences from their neighbourhoods. The proprietor of the Coburg, with seating for 3,800, explained how 'On Monday nights I conceive we have the working classes generally, and in the middle of the week we have the better classes, the play-going public generally'. The behaviour of audiences was in tune with this. At the Old Price Riots at Covent Garden in 1809 the audience for sixty-seven nights not only demanded the older and cheaper prices but also protested against the increase in the number of private boxes at the expense of the gallery. And it was to the gallery that actors had to pay special attention. Joseph Mather described how in Sheffield,

> To ger reit into't gallera, whear we can rant an' roar,
>   Throw flat-backs, stooans, an' sticks,
>   Red herrins, booans, an' bricks.
> If they dooant play Nanca's fanca, or onna tune we fix,
> We'll do the best at e'er we can to braik sum o' ther necks.

The consequences were predictable: the respectable withdrew from patronage of theatres, the gallery was an insufficient financial basis for successful theatrical management and from 1820 there was decline in the prosperity of provincial theatre.

Popular entertainment, however, in a huge diversity of forms, was flourishing. Circus was an invention of the late eighteenth century. There had been rope-dancers and vaulters at Sadler's Wells and Vauxhall Gardens from the late seventeenth century but, leaving aside some minor pretenders, modern circus with its equestrian emphasis was founded by Philip Astley in the 1760s. By the early nineteenth century circus, and the hippodrama that was derived from it, had begun to make a major impact on the entertainment world, to be seen at Covent Garden for the first time in 1811, and frequently thereafter, and well known in the provinces through Astley's winter tours.

Soon there were rivals. By about 1830, according to Thomas Frost, 'the northern and midland counties were travelled . . . by Holloway's, Milton's, Wild's, and Banister's; the eastern, southern, and western by Saunder's, Cooke's, Samwell's and Clarke's'. These were small affairs with rarely more than three or four horses, the first elephant appearing at a circus in 1828. But big or small, the visit of the circus was a memorable event in the life of any community. When the American lion tamer Van Amburgh visited Redruth in Cornwall in July 1842 he headed a procession of forty horses and carriages, drove eight horses in hand himself, and attracted a crowd of over seven thousand. At the other end of the country, in Hartlepool in 1843, there was a public holiday to watch Van Amburgh's entry.[59]

The flourishing state of circus in the 1840s owed much to Andrew Ducrow, whose triumphant debut at Covent Garden in 1823 gave circus an enormous boost. By 1828 the Royal Family was patronising Astley's. There were permanent circus buildings in the provinces even before Ducrow rose to fame, in cities as diverse as Bath and Liverpool, but Ducrow in the 1830s embarked on a major building programme. In Bristol James Ryan's 1826 Olympic Circus was rivalled by the National Olympic Arena built by Ducrow in 1832, itself followed by a new permanent building erected by Ryan in 1837 and by Price and Powell's New Circus Royal in the early 1840s.[60]

Annual fairs and wakes welcomed travelling entertainers of all kinds. Pantomimes and shortened versions of Shakespearian plays (*Richard the Third* twenty times in seven hours was perhaps the record) were ever-popular; freaks of nature, conjurors, sword-swallowers, wild animals, all drew an audience. Travelling menageries were especially popular, none more so than that of George Wombwell who gained nationwide fame with tours that started in the first decade of the century and continued until his death in 1850. The exterior alone of the menageries was enough to excite; Thomas Frost recalled at Croydon Fair 'the immense pictures, suspended from lofty poles, of elephants and giraffes, lions and tigers, zebras, boa constrictors, and whatever else was most wonderful in the brute creation, or most susceptible of brilliant colouring'. So well known was Wombwell, so universal his presence, that the song, 'The Rigs of the Fair', specially adapted for use at any fair, contains the lines:

> Wombwell's wild beast is come again
> Where works of nature's art is seen;
> Lions, tigers, panthers, apes and bears
> Are all to be seen at - - Fair.[61]

Looking ahead to the second half of the nineteenth century there is one narrative that suggests that it was only with the increased per capita wealth of that period that a commercialisation of leisure for the mass of the people was possible. In this narrative, music hall starts in the 1850s, sports begin to spread from public school origins and initiatives in the 1860s and 1870s. It is clear, however, that this does less than justice to the extent of commercialisation before 1850. With regard to sport, Adrian Harvey has argued that 'between 1793 and 1850 a substantial, essentially homogeneous, commercial sporting culture grew up in Britain, servicing a mass-public'.[62] True, that culture had become corrupted, and it required an 'interlude' of amateur dominance in the 1860s and 1870s before the commercial culture could resume its growth. But the evidence is very strong that there was a working-class spectatorship for sport and entertainment in the first half of the nineteenth century.

How can this evidence be squared with that set out in the previous chapter which suggests an increase in working hours and, at least until the second quarter of the nineteenth century, no substantial or sustained rise in living standards? First, a close attention to chronology indicates that the 1830s and 1840s, despite the known hardships, especially the depression in 1842, saw a rise in the scale and regularity of commercially provided entertainment. Second, entrepreneurs were able to benefit from the massing of the people into the new industrial cities such as Manchester and Birmingham. If these on the one hand deprived people of old entertainments and sports by building over the space on which they took place, on the other they provided a potential audience or spectatorship on a scale previously unattainable. There may have been less an increase in leisure time or leisure expenditure, more a different way of spending time and money.

Class reconciliation through leisure?

The attack on popular leisure between 1750 and 1850 lends itself to a class interpretation. As both the language and the actuality of class became in the early nineteenth century the way in which people imagined social structure, so the upper and middle classes bore down upon the recreations of the people who were themselves increasingly thought of as working-class. That was how many people who lived through these years experienced what was happening and it has informed much historical interpretation. But on its own it fails to do justice to some of the nuances and complexities of the period.

First, the popular commercial entertainment culture had critics from within the working classes. From the later eighteenth century there was a largely secular and mainly urban strand within the working classes that distanced itself from aspects of what might be seen as hangovers from a pre-industrial past. In Birmingham, for example, such people were not to be found among the bull-baiters or cock-fighters. Rather, they formed tavern and debating societies, read the new newspapers, patronised the theatre.[63] Arising out of this culture, there was in the first half of the nineteenth century a more radical and improving culture. As Robert Colls has argued, 'Those radicals who pushed for working-class "improvement" in all its guises, Teetotalism, Owenism, Chartism, Trade Unionism, Benefit and educational clubs, social-ism, secularism, they all had their own particular sincerities, but equally they all also had the destruction of the old popular culture as integral to their ends'.[64] That popular culture, they believed, patronised as it was by the rich, was destructive of working-class self-esteem.

The commercial entertainment culture was also under attack from religious radicals. The Wesleys had confronted the old popular culture from the moment they started open-air preaching in 1739. As Charles Wesley reported in 1744 from Cornwall, 'At the last revel, they had not men enough to make a wor-thy match all the Gwennap men being struck off the devil's list, and found wrestling against not for him'. Starting as a minority culture, Methodism in the course of a century grew to become one which could set the tone and standards for a community. It achieved this because at one and the same time it both confronted the older popular culture and retained links with it. Methodism's success owed not a little to its ability to impart excitement and in its blatant poaching, especially in its music, from secular traditions. Open-air preaching was deliberate spectacle, with processions through towns rivalling those of the showmen. Methodism offered its adherents an alternative form of recreation, but one which retained the sense of community, of drama and of participation that had been part of the old. Methodist miners in Cornwall in the 1840s, it was said, 'had given up the public-house . . . they felt no need and had no thought of theatre or dancing room. All the relief, the refresh-ment, the congenial excitement of their underground life they found in the preaching-house or in the classroom.' William Clowes, an early nineteenth-century Methodist, was 'occasionally told to cease my noise in the lovefeasts, as by my shouts of glory I made the chapel like a cock-pit'.[65]

A simple class-conflict interpretation of the history of leisure in this period is further complicated by the support for a variety of forms of popular leisure by the upper and middle classes. William Windham, Tory Secretary for War between 1794 and 1801, was vocal in support of the older sports that were coming to be denominated as cruel. 'The common people', he said, 'may ask with justice, why abolish bull-baiting, and protect hunting and shooting?' Whigs were as likely as Tories to elaborate on this point. Sydney Smith in 1809 in the archetypal Whig journal, the *Edinburgh Review*, argued that 'Any cruelty may be practised to gorge the stomachs of the rich, – none to enliven the holidays of the poor'. Lord Brougham, again on the Whig side, opposed a bill to prohibit bull-baiting in 1823 'because it tended to draw a distinction between the lower and higher classes of his Majesty's subjects, with respect to amusements in which there was equal cruelty'.[66]

The stakes at issue were claimed to be immense. Sports like boxing, racing, cock-fighting, hunting, it was said, brought together people from all ranks of society, 'peer' and 'peasant' meeting on equal ground. Further, they promoted 'manliness' and were a guard against a much-feared 'effeminacy'. And to cap it all, they were fundamentally British or English. To the Tory *Blackwood's Magazine* in 1827, worried about impending legislation, 'cock-fighting has been part of the system under which the country has become the terror, and envy, and admiration of the world . . . One rash enactment may destroy, in a few years, that manly spirit which it often requires centuries to generate in a nation.' In 1832 the *Sporting Magazine*, fearful of the future, said of field sports that 'with their decline we may expect the fall of that spirit of manly independence for which the English people are remarkable'.[67]

Support for manly rural sports sometimes took the form of patronage of events that seemed to offer hope for the future even while they harked back to an imagined past. From the early seventeenth century there were the Cotswold Games. In 1819 the Games, held on Thursday and Friday in Whit week, 'now patronised and esteemed by all noble, brave, and liberal minded Men, who have a sincere and true regard for their native Country', included backswords, wrestling, jingling, bowling, leaping, running in sacks, a horse race, cock-fighting and the Steward's Ball on the Friday evening with tickets costing 5s for Ladies and 10s 6d for Gentlemen, prices which suggest that the patronage for the Games was indeed coming from the well-off. But by 1846, apparently, the games had become 'the trysting place of all the lowest scum of the population which lived in the districts lying between Birmingham and Oxford'. The year 1851, when some thirty thousand attended, was the last celebration, the Rural Dean securing an Act of Parliament to abolish them.[68] There were other games of this kind, the St Ives Games in Cornwall, Col. Mason's Necton Sports from 1817, and the so-called Uffington Olympics and Much Wenlock Olympics.[69] At Necton in Norfolk, Col. Mason had instituted a 'guild', 'entirely distinct from a fair', held on Whit Monday and Tuesday, and featuring an elaborate procession of constables, beadles, May pole dancers, morris dancers, the Mayor and the 'Principal tenantry on horse-back, two and two' to a park where they were greeted by Mason. Rustic games of the usual kind ensued, the evening ending in dancing and singing of the national anthem. 'The greatest harmony prevails throughout', the occasion attended by 'numerous, respectable, and fashionable companies'.[70] Lord John Manners, one of Disraeli's associates in the Young England movement which sponsored the Eglinton Sports in Scotland, published in 1843 *A Plea for National Holy-Days*, a pamphlet whose old-fashioned spelling of holidays was deliberately pitching for a romantic version of the past, something which would in time be called 'Merrie England'. In this imagined England of 'the olden times' the gentry patronised sports and their social inferiors happily participated in them.

A different response to the feeling that the classes had drifted apart and that leisure might bring them together again was voiced by the Liberal Whig Unitarian MP William Smith, a man close to but not of the evangelical Clapham Sect. In the debates on bull-baiting he argued that the belief that the poor 'were entitled to their own amusements . . . arose from a contempt for the lower class of people . . . if they wished to make them rational beings, let them not educate them with one hand, and with the other turn them loose to sports like these'.[71] The rationality that education might impart should be carried through into rationality in leisure time.

The middle classes themselves had since the middle of the eighteenth century promoted their own leisure as 'rational'.[72] From the 1820s they began to promote 'rational recreation' for the working classes. Central to this was the creation of space for leisure outside the commercial ambit and under middle-class control. Public parks were the most visible aspect of this. Prompted by the Report of a Select Committee on Public Walks in 1833, government money was made available, achieving quite considerable results in London and rather less elsewhere. Private philanthropy, entrepreneurial development schemes and local government initiatives were more important than central government in providing urban space for recreation.

At the heart of these projects, as for all rational recreation schemes, was a desire to educate – it was 'relentlessly didactic'. Josph Strutt's Arboretum in Derby, for example, was laid out by J. C. Loudon in 1840 with careful display of individual trees, shrubs and plants, nature in harmony with order. Visiting it would be a learning experience. Arboreta and public parks were deliberately differentiated from the commercially run pleasure gardens, many of which were opening at much the same time, in London the Eagle Tavern Gardens in 1825, the Royal Surrey Gardens at Walworth in 1831, the Cremorne Gardens in 1843. Dickens described one of these tea-gardens in *Sketches by Boz*: 'What a dust and noise! Men and women – boys and girls – sweethearts and married people – babies in arms and children in chaises – pipes and shrimps – cigars and periwinkles – tea and tobacco'. To Dickens the people seemed 'all clean and happy, and disposed to be good-natured and sociable', but to the stricter kind of rational recreationist there was too much hearty vulgarity and open flirtation in such a scene. The 'due regulations to preserve order' that the 1833 Select Committee had insisted on were imposed in the parks. *The Times*, commenting on a move to open up Regent's Park in London, thought it an encouraging move in 'the redemption of the working class through recreation' and, perhaps tongue in cheek, saw no reason why they should not enjoy 'the liberty of taking a walk in the more plebeian portions of the park, provided they have a decent coat on'.[73]

Mechanics' institutes, lyceums, art galleries, museums and concerts were the other chief ways in which it was hoped to elevate the working classes and promote class harmony. There was, thought Bishop Blomfield, one important precondition, public bathhouses, for 'before the needful recreations of the people can be attained, before museums and public places could be made available, habits and cleanliness must be diffused throughout the whole community'. Many working-class people recoiled from this kind of language and the assumptions built into it. As Henry Mayhew angrily noted in the early 1850s, 'we strive to make true knowledge and true beauty as forbidding as possible to the uneducated and the unrefined', so that it was hardly surprising 'that they fly to their penny gaffs, their two-penny hops, their beer shops and their gambling grounds for pleasures which we deny them, and which we, in our arrogance, believe it is possible for them to do without'.[74]

Music exemplifies the hopes vested in these schemes. Here there was a base to build on. Handel was reported to be popular among northern factory audiences as early as 1788; employers simply had to encourage and foster, and this they did. In Belper the Strutts, in Yorkshire and Durham the London Lead Company, and in Cheshire the Greggs all encouraged music amongst their employees. Of the cotton-spinners of Cresbrook in Derbyshire it was said in 1824 that 'their highest species of enjoyment, the highest that man can enjoy, is music; this delightfully intellectual source of pleasure is improved, encouraged, and scientifically taught at Cresbrook'. In the Committee of Council on Education in 1840–1 J. P. Kay argued that 'The songs of any people may be regarded as an important means of forming an industrious, brave, loyal and religious working class'. They might 'inspire cheerful views of industry', 'associate amusements . . . with duties' and 'wean the people from vicious indulgences'. Taught by the new Tonic-Sol-Fa method of J. Curwen and J. P. Hullah, one which 'more especially addresses itself to the working class', there were soon mammoth working-class choirs and working-class audiences. Leon Faucher's Mancunian annotator in 1844 claimed that 'of the various styles of music, Sacred music has always enjoyed the especial preference of the working classes. The oratorios of Handel and of Haydn, are as household words, familiar to them from childhood; and no difficulty is ever found in selecting from amongst the factory operatives, choirs capable of doing justice to these immortal compositions.'[75]

Conclusion

In 1850, in contrast to 1750, most people in the upper and middle classes accepted that the working classes had an entitlement to some time for leisure. Some of them strenuously tried to provide space and facilities for forms of leisure that they approved of, public parks, public museums and public libraries being the most notable example. Such people wanted to reverse the trends towards the privatisation of all leisure facilities and towards the market as the sole provider – they were all too aware of the attraction to the working classes of what the entrepreneurs of leisure were offering. On the ground, the results of these efforts were rarely visible before mid-century. But the impulse to do something suggests that William Cooke Taylor's worries that opened this chapter were widely held. The faith they put in rational recreation was testimony to the unease they felt about a society where in leisure, as much as in work, the classes were divided. Leisure time became the focus of the deepest hopes and fears – the hope that in leisure time class division might be stilled, the fear that the stability and order of English society was threatened by the gambling, the drunkenness, the disorder that to the upper and middle classes seemed to characterise 'the amusements of the people'.

Notes

1 Lytton quoted in P. Bailey, *Leisure and Class in Victorian England: Rational Recreation and the Contest for Control, 1830–1885* (London: Routledge and Kegan Paul, 1978), p. 35; W. Cooke Taylor, *Notes of a Tour in the Manufacturing Districts of Lancashire* (1841; London: Frank Cass, 1968), p. 133.

2 P. Clark, *The English Alehouse: A Social History 1200–1830* (London: Longman, 1983), p. 179.

3 Ibid., pp. 255–8.

4 Quoted in E. Moir, *The Justice of the Peace* (Harmondsworth: Penguin, 1969), pp. 107–8.

5 S. and B. Webb, *The History of Liquor Licensing in England, Principally from 1700 to 1830* (1903; London: Frank Cass, 1963), pp. 59, 61.

6 Ibid., p. 160.

7 Quoted in R. W. Malcolmson, *Popular Recreations in English Society 1700–1850* (Cambridge: Cambridge University Press, 1973), p. 98.

8 E. Griffin, *England's Revelry: A History of Popular Sports and Pastimes 1660–1830* (Oxford: Oxford University Press, 2005), pp. 41–3, 59–69, 124–9, 223–49.

9 *House of Commons Journals*, vol. 57 (1801–2), 344, 364, 371, 380.

10 Griffin, *England's Revelry*, pp. 223–49.

11 W. B. Whitaker, *The Eighteenth-Century English Sunday: A Study of Sunday Observance from 1677 to 1837* (London: Epworth Press, 1940), pp. 155–270.

12 H. Cunningham, *Leisure in the Industrial Revolution c. 1780–c. 1880* (London: Croom Helm, 1980), pp. 85–6.

13 Malcolmson, *Popular Recreations*, p. 105; M. R. Mitford, *Our Village*, ed. E. Rhys (London: Scott, 1891), p. 171.

14 Quoted in Griffin, *England's Revelry*, p. 173.

15 Ibid., p. 57.

16 Ibid., pp. 75, 107.

17 Ibid., pp. 108–12.

18 Cunningham, *Leisure in the Industrial Revolution*, p. 81.

19 Ibid., p. 79.

20 Ibid., pp. 81–2.

21 Ibid., p. 82.

22 Malcolmson, *Popular Recreations*, pp. 107–8.

23 Griffin, *England's Revelry*, pp. 198, 201–8.

24 H. Taylor, *A Claim on the Countryside: A History of the British Outdoor Movement* (Edinburgh: Keele University Press, 1997), pp. 19–32; Cunningham, *Leisure in the Industrial Revolution*, p. 81.

25 Griffin, *England's Revelry*, pp. 209–10.

26 Cunningham, *Leisure in the Industrial Revolution*, p. 96.

27 Griffin, *England's Revelry*, pp. 167–89, 222.

28 Quoted in Cunningham, *Leisure in the Industrial Revolution*, p. 77.

29 Malcolmson, *Popular Recreations*, p. 110.

30 Ibid., pp. 126–33.

31 Cunningham, *Leisure in the Industrial Revolution*, pp. 78–9.

32 Quoted in A. Harvey, *The Beginnings of a Commercial Sporting Culture in Britain, 1793–1850* (Aldershot: Ashgate, 2004), p. 63.

33 Quoted in Cunningham, *Leisure in the Industrial Revolution*, p. 12.

34 Ibid., p. 92.

35 Clark, *Alehouse*, pp. 233–4.

36 P. Glennie and N. Thrift, *Shaping the Day: A History of Timekeeping in England and Wales 1300–1800* (Oxford: Oxford University Press, 2009), pp. 121–2.

37 D. Underdown, *Start of Play: Cricket and Culture in Eighteenth-Century England* (London: Allen Lane, 2000), pp. 28, 30; Clark, *Alehouse*, p. 234.

38 Underdown, *Start of Play*, p. 23.

39 Cunningham, *Leisure in the Industrial Revolution*, p. 84; see also Bailey, *Leisure and Class*, pp. 9–11.

40 Griffin, *England's Revelry*, p. 43.

41 Harvey, *Commercial Sporting Culture*, p. 205.

42 P. Borsay, *The English Urban Renaissance: Culture and Society in the Provincial Town 1660–1770* (Oxford: Clarendon Press, 1989), pp. 183–5; P. Clark, 'Small towns 1700–1840', in P. Clark (ed.), *The Cambridge Urban History of Britain, vol. 2 1540–1840* (Cambridge: Cambridge University Press, 2000), p. 764.

43 W. Vamplew, *The Turf: A Social and Economic History of Horse Racing* (London: Allen Lane, 1976), p. 25.

44 Borsay, *English Urban Renaissance*, p. 219.

45 R. Mortimore, *The Jockey Club* (London: Cassell, 1958), pp. 10–18.

46 Harvey, *Commercial Sporting Culture*, p. 13.

47 Borsay, *English Urban Renaissance*, p. 302.

48 R. Longrigg, *The Turf* (London: Eyre Methuen, 1975), pp. 39–40.

49 Harvey, *Commercial Sporting Culture*, p. 180.

50 Underdown, *Start of Play*, p. 72.

51 Ibid., pp. 89–90, 110, 153; Cunningham, *Leisure in the Industrial Revolution*, p. 27.

52 Cunningham, *Leisure in the Industrial Revolution*, pp. 25–7.

53 Ibid., p. 27.

54 Underdown, *Start of Play*, p. 163; Harvey, *Commercial Sporting Culture*, p. 165.

55 J. N. Baker, 'Theatre, law and society in the provinces: the case of Sarah Baker', *Cultural and Social History*, 1 (2004), 162–6; S. Rosenfeld, *Strolling Players and Drama in the Provinces 1660–1765* (1939; New York: Octagon Books, 1970), passim, esp. pp. 8–9.

56 Borsay, *English Urban Renaissance*, pp. 118–20, 148, 329–31; M. Reed, 'The transformation of urban space 1700–1840', in Clark (ed.), *Cambridge Urban History*, p. 630.

57 Baker, 'Theatre, law and society', 167–78; C. W. Chalklin, 'Capital expenditure on building for cultural purposes in provincial England, 1730–1830', *Business History*, 22 (1980), 51–70.

58 Cunningham, *Leisure in the Industrial Revolution*, p. 28; J. Moody, *Illegitimate Theatre in London, 1770–1840* (Cambridge: Cambridge University Press, 2000).

59 A. H. Saxon, *Enter Foot and Horse* (New Haven and London: Yale University Press, 1968); Cunningham, *Leisure in the Industrial Revolution*, pp. 33–5.

60 A. H. Saxon, *The Life and Art of Andrew Ducrow and the Romantic Age of the English Circus* (Hamden, Conn.: Archon Books, 1978); K. Barker, *Bristol at Play* (Bradford-on-Avon: Moonraker Press, 1976).

61 Cunningham, *Leisure in the Industrial Revolution*, pp. 30–3, 35.

62 Harvey, *Commercial Sporting Culture*, pp. 1, 180.

63 J. Money, 'Birmingham and the West Midlands 1760–1793: politics and regional identity in the English provinces in the late eighteenth century', *Midland History*, 1 (1971), p. 16.

64 R. Colls, *The Collier's Rant: Song and Culture in the Industrial Village* (London: Croom Helm, 1977), p. 94.

65 Ibid., pp. 76–96; J. G. Rule, 'The labouring miner in Cornwall c. 1740–1870, a study in social history' (unpublished University of Warwick PhD thesis, 1971), pp. 300–1; D. Erdozain, *The Problem of Pleasure: Sport, Recreation and the Crisis of Victorian Religion* (Woodbridge: The Boydell Press, 2010), p. 69.

66 Cunningham, *Leisure in the Industrial Revolution*, p. 46.

67 Ibid., pp. 47–50.

68 E. R. Vyvyan (ed.), *Cotswold Games: Annalia Dubrensia* (London: The Tabard Press, 1970), esp. pp. iii–x.

69 D. Brailsford, *Sport, Time, and Society: The British at Play* (London: Routledge, 1991), p. 12.

70 W. Hone, *The Every-Day Book*, 2 vols (London: William Hone, 1826–7), vol. 2, pp. 670–5.

71 Quoted in Cunningham, *Leisure in the Industrial Revolution*, p. 50.

72 Ibid., pp. 90–1.

73 Ibid., pp. 92–7; Bailey, *Leisure and Class*, pp. 50–5.

74 Bailey, *Leisure and Class*, pp, 51, 55.

75 Cunningham, *Leisure in the Industrial Revolution*, pp. 102–3; D. Russell, *Popular Music in England, 1840–1914: A Social History* (Manchester: Manchester University Press, 1987), pp. 21–4.

5

Work time in decline, 1830–1970

From the 1830s hours of work, which increased over the period from 1750 onwards, began a long decline that lasted through to the 1970s. The decline began with daily hours, first for children, and then more widely. The pattern of the week began to be reshaped with St Monday losing out to Saturday afternoon. Towards the end of the nineteenth century, and with much greater impetus in the twentieth, annual holidays with pay became a possibility and eventually a norm. It was in the twentieth century, too, that retirement became institutionalised. Less of the life course was spent working. Life began in an ever lengthier childhood free of paid work and ended in a retirement that was prolonged as life expectancy rose. In the intervening years a smaller proportion of time was spent working. In the mid-nineteenth century many people spent half of their hours working; by the 1970s it was down to one-third. This chapter will both trace these developments, which were by no means even, continuous or universal, and attempt to explain why they happened.

Factories and mines

Children were initially at the heart of campaigns to reduce hours. Throughout the eighteenth century and into the nineteenth there was a tension between the fear of the consequences to children of idleness and a growing concern that too much work could harm the development of their physique, and leave little time for the inculcation of moral values. On top of this, inspired by the Romantic poets, came a belief, by no means universally shared, but powerful nonetheless, that work in factory or mine was incompatible with the kind of childhood that nature had ordained for all children.[1]

In 1784 there was an outbreak of fever at the Radcliffe cotton works. The Lancashire magistrates set up an investigation, led by Dr Thomas Percival.

The report spoke of 'the injury done to young persons through confinement and too long-continued labour', noting that, especially for those under fourteen, 'the active recreations of childhood and youth are necessary to the growth, the vigour and the right conformation of the human body'. In response the Manchester Justices refused to apprentice anyone to cotton mills and other works where children were obliged to work at night or for more than ten hours a day. Other doctors reiterated Percival's opinion, and it soon became a commonplace. In *The State of the Poor* (1797) Sir F. M. Eden, in general in favour of the acquisition at a young age of 'habits of industry and perseverance', noted that 'Intense application to any kind of bodily labour is generally admitted to be peculiarly injurious to children'. Medical opinion continued to assert the danger to children of work. 'The employment of young children in *any* labour is wrong' asserted Dr Thackrah in 1831. A colleague at St Thomas's Hospital agreed: 'Children were not designed for labour'.[2]

This body of opinion was in some ways simply utilitarian. On a simple calculation of gain and loss, society lost, as did many individual children, by the kind of work that children did in cotton mills and factories. But there was more to it than utilitarianism. Childhood in the late eighteenth century took on new meanings. Some still held to the belief that children were born in sin, and that the prime parental duty was to lead them towards God and salvation, but William Wordsworth's belief that children came 'trailing clouds of glory', direct from heaven, was gaining ground. If Wordsworth was right, childhood should be cherished and prolonged, children's playful activities should be encouraged. Hard work in a cotton mill, or perhaps anywhere, was a denial of such a childhood. Where Daniel Defoe in the 1720s had delighted to find children of three or four earning their own keep, for a poet in the 1830s 'Ever a toiling *Child* doth make us sad'. Childhood, an indeterminate stretch of human life, but one which was progressively stretched and lengthened, was beginning to be thought of as a time without work. Otherwise you would have, as a critic put it in the 1840s, 'children without childhood'.[3]

The medical profession and those imbibing a Wordsworthian view of childhood were up against the political economists whose instinct was to avoid any interference in the labour market. In addition they argued that in mechanised factories there was an inescapable logic to long hours of work. In Nassau Senior's words, 'The great proportion of fixed to circulating capital . . . makes long hours of work desirable . . . The motives to long hours of work will become greater, as the only means by which a large proportion of fixed capital can be made profitable.' On top of this, it was claimed, improvements in machinery had a tendency 'as steady in their operation as a physical law' to replace adult with child labour. It was a bleak outlook. Karl Marx pointed to 'that remarkable phenomenon in the history of modern industry, that machinery sweeps away every moral and natural restriction on the length of the working day'.[4]

On the other hand, many who were sympathetic to the arguments of political economists recognised the absurdity of applying their views too rigidly to children. Lord Liverpool, the prime minister, thought it 'preposterous to talk of these poor children as free agents'.[5] If they were not, how much protection should they get? And up to what age? Attempts to answer these questions preoccupied those trying to frame legislation, starting with the 1802 Health and Morals of Apprentices Act that concerned parish apprentices and then in the debates in Parliament on so-called 'free labour' in textile mills and factories.

The impulse and pressure for shorter hours, however, had its roots in factory experience in Lancashire and Yorkshire, and its foot-soldiers were working men, women and children. It was the first and perhaps most significant moment in a history stretching over three centuries when there was mass agitation in pursuit of shorter working hours. Lancashire, the original home of the factory, led the way, the first short-time committee being formed in Manchester in 1814 in close association with the operative fine spinners' union. John Doherty, the trade union leader, never ceased to push for shorter hours and, together with Thomas Foster, brought numerous cases for infringement of the law against employers, but obtained convictions in only twenty-four out of 187 cases.[6] Witnesses were intimidated, magistrates hostile. Doherty was keen, wherever possible, to work with employers who were sympathetic to shorter hours, but he was constantly depicted as a union agitator. He may, too, have had some difficulty in persuading the operative spinners of the case for shorter hours. Colonel Fletcher in 1823 reported to the Home Office that he had not found among the journeymen cotton spinners 'any very lively interest' in the subject, and feared that many of them 'would prefer working at those mills where they work the greatest number of hours, and have the opportunity of making the most money. There may be, however, and doubtless are, many exceptions in this respect.'[7]

After fifteen years of agitation for shorter hours, mostly in Lancashire, and with Acts passed in 1819, 1825 and 1831, none of them effectively enforced, the movement for shorter hours was rekindled by Richard Oastler's 'Yorkshire slavery' letters in the *Leeds Mercury* in 1830. The ten hours movement was born. Ten hours of work was the norm of the past, and campaigners urged that it should be restored to the present. Some, however, looked much further back than living memory to good King Alfred who had divided the twenty-four hours into three equal divisions, eight for work, eight for sleep, and eight for recreation. Alfred became a popular hero, his name given to radical newspapers and public houses.[8] A demand for an eight-hour day became popular after the 1833 Factory Act had limited children's hours to eight. The National Regeneration Society, inspired by Robert Owen, and with support from Doherty, urged adult factory workers to ignore the parliamentary route to factory reform and simply refuse to work more than eight hours from 1 March 1834. It was a proposal that attracted more comment than support.[9]

The prominent leaders remembered in the history books are Michael Sadler, Lord Ashley, Richard Oastler, George Bull, John Fielden. Their role was vital, but it would have had no resonance and power without the impetus from below. John Fielden told the House of Commons in 1844, that the working people had 'got it into their heads that they work too hard'. The *Northern Star* urged in 1847 that 'the people' should not forget 'that they mainly owe to outdoors agitation the support they have met with in the House'. For Karl Marx the passing of the Ten Hours Act in 1847 signalled that 'the political economy of the middle class succumbed to the political economy of the working class'.[10] Looking back in 1867 it was acknowledged that 'the credit of this arduous conflict – ending as it did triumphantly – belongs, in the sacrifices it called for, as well as in the blessings it has brought to the community, to the working men of England'.[11]

A contemporary account of the County Meeting, presided over by the High Sheriff, and held in the Castle Yard in York on 24 April 1832, gives some idea of the working-class pressure. Leeds, the nearest factory town, was 24 miles distant, but thousands from there and from much more distant factory communities walked to York in weather 'the most inclement within memory', stood for five hours listening to speeches, and then embarked on the long road home. The emphasis was on the need to rescue children from the long hours, many banners inscribed 'Father, is it time?' in reference to the story of a factory girl, worn to death, whose last words these were, even in death an anxiety about being late for work uppermost in her mind. But if children were prominent in the propaganda, few could doubt that campaigners were intent on a maximum ten hours day for all workers.[12]

The 1833 Factory Act, the first to have a significant impact, was in many ways a defeat for the Ten Hours campaign. The Whig government had set up a Royal Commission to examine the issue, and it focused entirely on children. No legislation throughout the nineteenth century controlled the hours of work of adult males. The Commission concluded that at the age of fourteen childhood ended; at that age, they said, 'They usually make their own contracts, and are, in the proper sense of the word, free agents'.[13] The Act did not entirely follow this logic. It forbade any work in factories for those under nine, limited it to a maximum of eight hours for those under thirteen, and to a maximum of twelve hours for those aged thirteen to eighteen. In some ways the Act, in limiting to eight hours work for those under thirteen, went further than the campaigners were demanding, but its deliberate failure to respond to the extra-parliamentary agitation meant that the issue was by no means settled.

The 1833 Act set in motion a process of government action to shift young children from paid work in factory or mine to unpaid schoolwork. The two hours of compulsory schooling a day for children working in factories that became law was no more than a first step, but it opened a space for those concerned about low levels of education. When Lord Ashley moved in 1840 for a Children's Employment Commission he was resolute that 'My *first* grand object is to bring these children within reach of education'.[14] This concern had its roots in a worry about the consequences of an uneducated proletariat at the mercy of mob orators. The content and purpose of education were therefore central issues: 'no plan of education', wrote J. P. Kay, a man at the heart of government thinking, 'ought to be encouraged in which intellectual instruction is not subordinate to the regulation of the thoughts and habits of the children by the doctrines and precepts of revealed religion'.[15] Political economy was in fact as important to the educationists as revealed religion.

The Children's Employment Commission's most notable investigations concerned children working in coal mines. Ashley wanted to exclude all children under thirteen from the pits and to send them to school, but he had to make a series of concessions under pressure from the coal owners, so that the 1842 Act excluded only children under ten from working and didn't enforce schooling – though coal owners did come quickly to appreciate the desirability of schooling.[16]

After the passage of the 1842 Act attention switched back to the factories, and it was in 1844 that there came to the fore a solution that for nearly half a century found favour amongst a wide range of opinion, from Charles Dickens to Karl Marx: the half-time system whereby children would spend half their time at work and half at school. The long hours which manufacturers insisted were necessary for profitability could be maintained by employing children for shorter hours in relays. Schooling, too, would benefit, or so it was argued, children learning more half-time than full-time. The half-time system became the default solution to the issue of child labour in the major enquiries into it in the 1860s and beyond. It was only in the 1880s that there began to be heard a chorus of complaint from teachers that half-time children came to school tired and with language and behaviour that disrupted the classroom and demoralised the full-time children.[17]

From the mid-1840s factory agitation was building towards its second climax. In parliamentary debates, reflecting the pressure from without, there was a 'shift in emphasis from the need to protect children to the need to protect *labour*'.[18] John Fielden promoted a Ten Hour bill in 1846, and it was defeated by only ten votes. Reintroduced in 1847, and benefiting from the split in the Tory Party after the repeal of the Corn Laws and from economic recession, it became law. The economic argument in favour of change was one that would resonate through debates about shorter hours from that time onwards. It was that shorter hours would increase employment oppor-tunities, and reduce overproduction; or, put another way, that it would help prevent unemployment. Fielden had made this point in 1833, and Ashley in the coal mine debates had argued that 'shortening the hours of labour' would 'call into action those who were unemployed'.[19] It was significant that over nine hundred textile firms petitioned Parliament in favour of the Act – owners could see the dangers of continuing cut-throat unregulated competition.[20]

The passing of the 1847 Act was a significant achievement, bringing fac-tories into line with what had from back in the eighteenth century been regarded as a normal working day. Poor drafting of the Act allowed manu-facturers to maintain a twelve- or fifteen-hour day, while the young and women worked no more than ten hours, but were kept in the factory in what Marx called 'hours of enforced idleness'. The situation was remedied only by a concession that in 1850 increased hours up to ten and a half and ended relays. As Disraeli put it to Parliament, 'You take advantage of a flaw in an Act of Parliament, and are about to deprive the people of an agitation of thirty years'. It was not until 1874 that ten hours was restored.[21] Nevertheless, from 1847 the principle that ten hours was a maximum length of the work-ing day was there to be appealed to in the many work situations where it was not yet in place.

Towards eight hours

The symbolic importance of Acts of Parliament in the reduction of daily hours of work is undeniable. By the early twentieth century a narrative had become established that placed factory legislation at the heart of a process whereby children in particular, but also the factory workforce as a whole, had been rescued from excessive hours of labour by a legislature that had wisely seen the need for intervention in the free workings of the market. Industry by industry, it could be claimed, shorter hours and improved conditions of work had been introduced. This narrative, however, was not without its problems.

First, legislation was difficult to apply in all work situations. It was relatively easy to do so in large factories, much less so in small workshops. It was even more difficult to do so in those growing sectors of the economy that relied on what came to be called 'casual labour', where the problem was not overwork but too little work. Just as in the eighteenth century, regular year-long work was the preserve of a minority. The seasons continued to exert their influence, whether through weather conditions or through shifts in the level of demand by consumers. In London in the late nineteenth century it is estimated that over 285,000 male workers, at least one-third of the male workforce, were affected by seasonal slackness in January. There were other factors leading to casualisation, deskilling and a constant surplus of available labour chief amongst them. Henry Mayhew in mid-century London thought that 'there is barely sufficient work for the regular employment of half our labourers, so that only $1\frac{1}{2}$ million are fully and constantly employed, while $1\frac{1}{2}$ million are employed only half their time, and the remaining $1\frac{1}{2}$ wholly unemployed, obtaining a day's work occasionally by the displacement of some of the others'. These were rough and ready figures, but they indicate the scale of the problem which was by no means alleviated later in the century. If casualisation left many people short of work, it was associated with exceptionally long hours for those who did find work, especially those in the sweated industries; in homes and workshops in London's East End men, women and children made clothes, footwear, furniture and a host of other goods in conditions that shocked contemporaries.[22] There were too, as periodic scandals of overwork exposed, many people who continued into the twentieth century to work way beyond ten hours a day.

Second, there remained many sectors of the economy where workers had no need of Acts of Parliament to control their working hours – they exercised the control themselves. There were many kinds of work, in quarrying, mining and mineral work, for example, where a piece of work was contracted out to a group of workers, often family-based, for a set sum, the hours of work determined by the workers themselves. In coal mining, the hewers normally paid by the piece, employers found it no easier than it had been in the eighteenth century to control hours. When Thomas Burt started work at Cramlington colliery in the 1850s, 'the coal-hewers went into the pit and came out when they liked'. A Wigan miner in 1866 reckoned to work 'about five days a week, or ten a fortnight': 'Sometimes I work 11, sometimes eight or nine days'. Absenteeism was endemic, at its height on Mondays, the workforce most regular on Fridays and Saturdays.[23]

Third, there was an alternative narrative, one that told how the reduction of hours of work in the second half of the nineteenth and the first half of the twentieth was due much more to trade union pressure on employers than to legislation.

In the years between 1850 and 1970 reduction in hours of work were concentrated in four periods, the early 1870s, in 1919–20 immediately after the First World War, in 1947–8 after the Second World War, and in the first half of the 1960s. Broadly speaking, the nine-hour day was achieved in the first period, and the eight-hour day in the second; in the third period 'normal' working hours fell from 47.1 in 1945 to 44.6 in 1950, but overtime eroded half this gain. In the 1960s the forty-hour week became a norm, but actual hours (counting overtime) were often longer than this. In the long intervals between these short bursts of reduction, changes in hours of work were slight. Between the 1880s and 1914, for example, the average reduction in all industries was in the range of 2.5–5 per cent.[24] Averages of this kind, as the Royal Commission on Labour in 1890 demonstrated, smoothed out a huge range of actual experience, from the forty-two hours worked by hewers in the mining industry to the ninety-six hours of restaurant waiters. Overtime, moreover, which dominated much public discussion in the period after the Second World War, was well entrenched in the late nineteenth century.[25]

The campaign for the nine-hour day started in the building trades in the 1840s. New large-scale builders winning contracts for major projects, for example building the new Houses of Parliament, wanted more control over their workforce. Disputes centred on attempts to introduce piecework and overtime. The workers resisted, campaigning for shorter hours. For the masters in 1859 'the demand [for nine hours] . . . was only . . . a further development of the arbitrary and extravagant demands which the building operatives of London had been forcing on their employers during recent years'. At issue were power, authority and control. As one master builder put it, if it had been simply a matter of wages, 'I will be one of the first to yield', but the issue was 'the republican notion of controlling the labour market'. Employers in 1859 and in subsequent disputes saw hours reduction as amounting to a loss of managerial power, and for this reason they were always reluctant to concede to it – and in this instance successfully.[26] In the economic boom of the early 1870s, however, employers were in a weaker position. In 1871 a successful six-month strike by engineering workers for a nine-hour day, initiated and sustained at grass-roots level, was a critical breakthrough, and in its wake most organised trades secured a fifty-four-hour week.[27]

The campaign for an eight-hour day started in the late 1880s. From the outset it had an international dimension. Workers across Europe campaigned for eight hours and there was strong pressure for it on the first May Day in 1890. Some engineering firms introduced the eight-hour day in 1891, but there were many reservations amongst trade unionists. At the Trades Union Congress a proposal for eight hours legislation was defeated in 1887, and only narrowly passed in 1890. Government works at Woolwich and elsewhere accepted eight hours in 1894, but private employers were determinedly against giving way and, the 1908 Mines Act apart, there were few successes to notch up until the First World War and its immediate aftermath.[28]

The situation in that period was transformed in two ways. First, the suspension of factory legislation and introduction of longer hours in 1914 led to a worrying decline in productivity and rise in bad time-keeping. Investigators who in the prewar years had been promulgating a science of work, claiming that there was only so much work a human body could do, now seized their moment on the newly established Health of Munitions Workers Committee. H. M. Vernon, for example, inquiring into the productivity of women workers in shell production, found that both hourly production and weekly output were higher with a shorter working week. Long hours, it was asserted, were having dangerous political consequences: the Committee of Enquiry into Industrial Unrest of 1917 claimed that fatigue and consequent nervousness were a prime cause of the unrest.[29] The second transformative feature was the heightened fear of revolution after the Bolsheviks seized power in Russia in 1917. The Bolsheviks themselves had proclaimed an eight-hour day in 1917, and this spread to Finland and Norway in 1918, then to Germany in November 1918, to Poland, Czechoslovakia, Austria and Switzerland by December, and to Italy in February. In these circumstances it was hardly surprising that between December 1918 and March 1919 major industries, headed by the railways and engineers, conceded the eight-hour day. As the prime minister, Lloyd George, told his cabinet, 'It is not a question of whether the men can stand the strain of a longer day, but that the working class is entitled to the same sort of leisure as the middle class'. In short, this was class war, and it was a war that the workers won: some seven million workers achieved reductions averaging six and a half hours a week, and the normal working week was reduced from fifty-four hours to forty-eight. For the most part this was achieved by starting work later, at 8.30 rather than 7.30.[30]

Many shop stewards had campaigned for an even shorter week, forty-four or forty hours, and the miners did win a seven-hour day, but from the summer of 1919 employers felt strengthened by the surplus of labour, and a backlash began. The government's promise to introduce eight hours by legislation was dropped in 1920, and in 1921 it refused to ratify the attempt to secure international commitment to eight hours as agreed at the 1919 Washington Hours Convention. In the mid-1920s crisis in the coal industry the employers wanted to end the seven hours agreement, something which the government-appointed Samuel Commission was against. Nevertheless the miners' slogan of 'not a penny off the pay, not a minute on the day' was defeated on both counts. They suffered a wage cut and a return to the eight-hour day.[31] Reflecting on these reverses, and fearing further loss of the gains made in 1919–20, the Trades Union Council in 1923 saw reduced hours as 'the principal advantage secured by over sixty years of trade union effort and sacrifice . . . the most important achievement of industrial organization'.[32]

In 1947 and 1948 there was a decrease of about three hours a week, mostly achieved by moving to a five-day week – and returning to longer hours on the days that were worked. In 1960–1 a reduction of those daily hours was agreed, though the implementation was in many cases achieved only in 1964–6: an eight-hour day on five days in the week became the standard, though actual hours, including overtime, were often longer.[33]

Explanations for these changes give scant weight to parliamentary legislation. Acts of Parliament did do something to achieve shorter hours. In 1874 factory textile workers' hours were reduced to fifty-six and a half, in 1902 there was a further reduction of one hour for textile workers, in 1908 workers underground in coal mines were restricted to eight hours, and the 1934 Shops Act and the 1937 Factories Act also limited hours. But in the overall pattern these changes had marginal impact. Trade union pressure was the key factor in the reduction. From 1833 onwards the builders realised that 'the main question to fight about was the shortening of hours'. In coal mining 'hours had been at the centre of industrial relations since at least 1831'.[34] The reductions happened at times of economic boom when union bargaining power was strong. What motivated the unions? First, they took the opportunity to press for shorter hours in times of boom because they had an underlying anxiety that bust might be round the corner with the unemployment that would accompany it. Reduce the hours of those in employment, went the argument, and there would be more hours of work for those who might be unemployed. Second, leisure normally took second place to maintaining or increasing wage levels, not least because employers were more inclined to concede to wage demands than to reductions in hours.[35] These factors were unquestionably important, but they tend to underplay the evidence for leisure preference. When the factory inspector Leonard Horner examined the returns of a questionnaire he had issued on the effects of the 1847 Ten Hours Act he found that the vast majority of respondents welcomed the shorter hours even if they implied lower wages. South Wales miners, of whom it was said in 1873 that 'they want short hours and more leisure', do seem to have taken out some of their higher wages in increased leisure in the succeeding half-century.[36] In 1891 Sidney Webb and Harold Cox were confident that

> The demand for shorter hours of labour has arisen among the working classes, not so much from the conviction that their present hours are injurious to health – though that in many cases is the fact, – not so much from the theory that shorter hours mean higher wages – though that theory is in the main sound, – but from the strongly-felt desire for additional opportunities for recreation and the enjoyment of life.

Reviewing the experience of factory workers S. J. Chapman in 1914 concluded that 'The first step towards improvement of welfare is not in the direction of goods, food or clothing, but towards leisure'.[37] In the interwar period trade unions certainly never considered increased leisure if it meant a fall in wages, but some did campaign for more leisure in preference to higher wages.[38] In short, there is evidence for a continuation of the leisure preference that so marked the eighteenth century.

In the years after the Second World War the decline in hours was also in part fuelled by leisure preference. The situation in this period was complicated by significant changes in the structure of the labour force, particularly the growth in the number of married women working and, for both men and women, but especially for women, the growth of part-time working. A further change in the labour force was the trend towards clerical and professional work with shorter hours than traditional heavy industry or service work. It is estimated that between 30 and 40 per cent of the reduction in hours between 1951 and 1973 was accounted for by this trend, but the trend itself may have 'reflected an increasing reluctance of workers to take on jobs with long hours, and in this way gave expression to the increase in leisure-preference associated with the long-term rise in income'.[39] Another feature of the labour market after the Second World War was a marked increase in overtime work. This reflected the tendency of unions to try to obtain higher wages by increasing the proportion of the working week classified as overtime and therefore paid at a higher hourly rate. Overtime in many cases become habitual, but even so the actual hours worked decreased; for full-time manual workers in production industries, transport and communications, and public administration from 47 hours per week in 1955 to 43.9 in 1973.[40] Put another way, if hours of work inclusive of overtime were in decline, the fact that many worked overtime may be entirely consistent with leisure preference. The higher income that overtime brought made it more possible to seek a reduction in hours of work.

The hours of work of the middle classes resist easy and straightforward documentation or explanation. Among businessmen there had been some heroically long hours in the late eighteenth and early nineteenth centuries. Isambard Kingdom Brunel, working on the Great Western Railway line, confessed that 'Between ourselves it is harder work than I like. I am rarely much under twenty hours a day at it.' But this was never the norm, and certainly by the later nineteenth century, in both the private and public sectors, hours were, compared with those of manual workers, relatively short and indeed imprecise. In 1875 daily hours in the civil service were 'generally from 10 to 4 or from 11 to 5'. In the early 1890s 'a few phenomenally active lawyers or City men may be at work by nine o'clock, but at present ten is certainly the more usual hour, and quite a large proportion of business men do not reach their offices before eleven'. Lower down the middle-class scale, clerks worked rather longer hours, in the London and North-Western Railway Company, for example, from nine to five, and we can perhaps assume a gradual normalisation of a nine to five day. In the early twentieth century the elite of Manchester's middle class, both businessmen and the professions, travelled in from Alderley Edge by the 8.25, 8.50 or 9.10 train, returning home by the 5.07 or 5.45.[41] But old habits died hard. On the eve of the Second World War, as an expert observer in Whitehall noted, the lower ranks of the civil service – typists, junior executives, clerical officers – arrived at work by 10 a.m., the higher clerical and executive officers between 10.05 and 10.15, and between 10.15 and 10.45 the Principals, 'the potentates of the Service may usually be seen walking briskly, but without undignified haste, to their places of power'.[42]

At the lower end of the middle classes, amongst shop-workers, hours were notoriously long and remained so. High hopes entertained in the 1840s and 1850s that shops could be persuaded to reduce their hours overall and in particular to close early on Saturdays had dimmed by the mid-1880s when the Early Closing Association admitted that only a minority of shops in London accepted the half-holiday. In 1881 the Shop-Assistants Twelve Hours' Labour League had been formed, the name itself indicative of the situation: in the cotton factories they had been campaigning for ten hours back in the 1830s. In 1901, after over half a century of effort to curtail hours, a House of Lords Select Committee could only confirm that many shops were working eighty to ninety hours a week. For shop-workers the downward trend in hours from the mid-nineteenth century, so prominent elsewhere, seems to have had little reality. There was a succession of enquiries, bills before Parliament and permissive Acts of Parliament, but only snail-like progress towards a reduction of hours.[43]

The reduction of the hours of workers between 1830 and 1970 can seem to have about it a degree of inevitability. That would be seriously to underestimate the difficulties of achieving it. Employers were much more willing to give wage rises than to agree to shorter hours. It required sustained political action to secure the passage of the Ten Hours Act in 1847, to push through nine hours agreements in the 1870s, and above all to make the breakthrough to eight hours in 1919, thirty years after the demand was first articulated. It was no accident that the successes of 1847 and 1919 occurred at a time of widespread international workers' agitation when the established order had reason to be fearful. The achievement of shorter hours wasn't solely due to workers' pressure. They needed allies in other classes, parliamentary spokesmen in 1847, science of work advocates in 1919, but without worker pressure it is difficult to see how shorter hours could have been achieved. The motives that drove workers certainly included a concern to spread jobs and avoid unemployment, but there was also a simple wish to have more leisure time. In the eighteenth century leisure preference displayed itself in irregular working habits. In the nineteenth and twentieth centuries, workers wanted to know in advance when their work ended and their leisure began.

Re-shaping the week

In the second half of the nineteenth century St Monday was slowly, and incompletely, replaced by a Saturday half-holiday. This looks like a loss of leisure, a whole day on Monday being surrendered for a half day on Saturday. But St Monday was not universally observed. There was pressure for a Saturday half-holiday from three different groups.

First, and in many ways most vocal, were the Sabbatarians who wanted a Saturday half-holiday so that everyday concerns did not intrude on Sunday observance. The focus was on hours of work in offices, shops and warehouses. For employees here, Sunday was the only day of leisure, and in food shops in particular they would often be at work until late on Saturday evening as working-class consumers did their shopping for Sunday dinner. Organisation to remedy this situation started in the late 1830s, with Sabbatarian concerns to the fore. The Metropolitan Drapers' Association, formed in 1838, evolved in the 1840s into the Early Closing Association, but its impact was marginal. Its strength lay in the wealth and influence of employers who backed it, its weakness in the lack of pressure from below, from employees or small shopkeepers.[44]

Manufacturers, and especially those who used steam power, were a second force behind a Saturday half-holiday. They had every reason to want a regular workforce committed to strict daily, weekly and annual hours. In some parts of the country and in some industries this proved exceptionally difficult to implement. Factory Inspector J. E. White reported the situation in the Birmingham metal industries in 1864:

> An enormous amount of time is lost, not only by want of punctuality in coming to work in the morning and beginning again after meals, but still more by the general observance of 'Saint Monday', which is shown in the late attendance or entire absence of large numbers on that day. One employer has on Monday only about 40 or 50 out of 300 or 400, and the day is recognized by many masters as an hour shorter than others at each end. On Mondays I found few works fully and some but very partially employed; and in a large well-conducted foundry the casters were getting to work for the first time in the week towards midday on Tuesday. Masters complain much of this, but say that it cannot be helped.

White believed that it could be helped. Employer firmness and use of steam power would improve the situation.[45] Yet in Birmingham and the West Midlands the transition from St Monday to the Saturday half-holiday was drawn out over many years, apparent success at the negotiating table often failing to be followed up on the factory floor. In 1876 John Hampton, the manager of a firm of engineers and iron and brass founders in West Bromwich, complained that 'when the hours of labour were reduced to fifty-four, our men agreed to work on Mondays if we would consent to them leaving at 2 on Saturdays, but we find more difficulty in getting them to work on Monday than before the alteration, in fact as wages have been advanced less time has been made'.[46]

In the West Midlands or in Sheffield, another redoubt of St Monday, the Saturday half-holiday might, for a time at least, be simply added to Monday absenteeism. In Sheffield the United States consul reported in 1874 that 'large numbers of the workmen, stopping work on Saturday noon, do not commence again until the following Wednesday', suggesting a three and a half day week, a degree of leisure preference generous even by eighteenth-century standards. In Sheffield St Monday and even Holy Tuesday remained popular into the twentieth century, one manufacturer in 1907 claiming that he 'lay awake at night devising ways of circumventing them and getting them to work'.[47] He sounds like Josiah Wedgwood and his struggles with his pottery workers in the eighteenth century. In London, too, as Charles Booth discovered in the late 1880s, there were many workers who retained the habit of working to achieve a certain level of income and then opted for leisure. Booth found this among match factory workers; as for piano workers, 'hard work and large earnings succeeded by idleness and hard drinking make exactly the life that suits them'.[48]

Monday was in many areas, certainly in the third quarter of the century, the preferred day for excursions and entertainment. It was often spent respectably. As one witness before the 1854 Select Committee on Public Houses put it, Monday was now 'a legitimate holiday. It was a holiday then of a depraving, bad character, now it is a holiday spent with their families, and benefiting both their health and minds.' Thomas Wright, an engineer who wrote extensively about the working classes in the 1860s, described the sporting and drinking types enjoying St Monday in the old ways, but also families sedately taking a day out at the seaside. It was a Monday that the Hartlepool Temperance Society chose for its excursion to Middlesbrough Polytechnic.[49] Monday was also a day to get married on. There were distinct local customs. In Blackburn, for example, in 1821 nearly half of all weddings were on Monday, but by 1861 it was down to 14 per cent. The reason was that the early nineteenth century handloom weaving economy was replaced by factory spinning, an example of how steam power, as factory inspector

J. E. White had claimed for Birmingham, could help eliminate St Monday. But elsewhere Monday weddings remained popular, nearly one-quarter of those in Lambeth in 1864, high in Birmingham until the 1880s, one-fifth of all weddings in Manchester up to the 1890s, and in Bristol the same proportion into the early twentieth century. If Monday was in decline as a wedding day, it tended to be replaced by Sunday rather than Saturday. This was in part because until 1886 it was impossible to get married on Saturday after noon, so the spread of the Saturday half-holiday initially did nothing to facilitate marriage on that day.[50]

Workers were the third group pressing for a Saturday half-holiday. When the Factory Act of 1850 legislated a Saturday half-holiday from 2 p.m. for factory workers it was almost certainly building on a tradition of early Saturday stopping. In 1816 stopping work at 4 p.m. on Saturdays was reported as general in the cotton districts. Short-time committees pushed for shorter working on Saturdays, and a limit of nine hours work on that day was included in the 1825 Factory Act.[51] In 1843 there was short Saturday working in Lancashire, in paper mills and in parts of the west of England, but even in these areas and trades it was by no means universal. The way that Saturday was spent was in fact subject to as much regional or local variation as Monday. The 1850 Act, however, provided an incentive for other workers to push for a Saturday half-holiday. Builders had already been doing so since 1847, and in London by the late 1850s they had gained the half-holiday but in return for accepting payment by the hour. Other builders began to achieve success in the 1860s, the engineers by the early 1870s, Nottingham lace workers also in that decade. It is a confused story, not least because one person's half-holiday might begin at 1 p.m., another's at 5 p.m.[52]

Non-manual workers seem to have achieved the Saturday half-holiday on much the same time-scale as manual workers. The Stock Exchange started early closing on Saturdays in 1843. By the end of 1848 closure at 4 p.m. on Saturdays had been achieved in City of London and West End banks; in Manchester banks, solicitors' offices, local government offices and warehouses also closed at that hour. By 1857 there was 2 p.m. closure for workers in solicitors' and other law offices. The Bank of England's Saturday closing hours changed from 3 p.m. in 1860 to 2 p.m. in 1886 to 1 p.m. in 1902.[53]

At national level the Saturday half-holiday had become a norm by the early 1890s with enormous consequences for the spread of competitive sport. For the first time it could be assumed that matches and competitions could be organised across the country at a set time in the week. Many workers, however, failed to benefit from the Saturday half-holiday, most of all shop-workers, for Saturday afternoon and evening became a key shopping time. For shop-workers the solution was to be a half-holiday in mid-week, on a Wednesday or Thursday – a goal achieved in the 1912 Act which gave shop assistants one weekday free from 1.30 p.m.[54] Unpaid workers, mainly women, were also much less than men beneficiaries of the Saturday half-holiday. But, as the enormously successful weekly magazine *Ally Sloper's Half-Holiday* suggested, the idea of a weekly half-holiday had taken root in the national psyche.[55]

Sunday, basically a day of recuperation and rest for most of the nineteenth century, began to be opened up for recreation. In 1855 the National Sunday League was formed, encouraging brass bands playing in parks and campaigning for Sunday afternoon opening of museums and art galleries. Early signs of modest clerical rethinking of strict sabbatarianism in the 1860s became much more open by the 1880s. In a symposium of 1889, *Sunday and Recreation*, the vicar of All Saints, Highgate, wrote that he 'would not make it a sin that a young man, wearied with the work of "the city", should take his bicycle and go for a "spin" on Sunday afternoon'. The assumption was that in the morning the clerk would be in church or chapel. From the non-religious side, this began to be challenged, sport being said to have a higher value than church-going. In the words of Lieutenant-Colonel R. W. Osborn in 1880, 'there is no question that, as a moral discipline, lawn tennis on a Sunday afternoon is very superior to sermons'. In the seclusion of their suburbs and gardens the middle classes were certainly turning to sport on Sunday afternoons. Such sport became a problem only when it was played in public. Golf was often the test case, there being many disputes especially in the 1890s, the arguments sometimes at the level that 'a man who would play golf on a Sunday would not be very particular whether he paid his debts or not'. Sometimes the compromise was that Sunday golf would be allowed but without caddies, so allowing teenage boys, desperate for extra cash, an unwanted holiday. By 1914 getting on for half of English courses advertised Sunday play. Other sports and activities, particularly boating and cycling, had also by then colonised Sunday, the more advanced clergy sometimes offering special services, shorn of a sermon, for cyclists. By 1914, concludes John Lowerson, 'for many middle-class men, particularly in southern England, organised religion had become one of a number of possible ways of employing non-work time'. Sunday sport had the attraction for them of being 'an additional refuge from onerous domestic obligations, of which churchgoing was one'.[56]

In the 1880s Frederick Temple, bishop of London, had seen the way things were going: 'There was a serious danger of the day being seized by the pleasure-lovers; and the money-lovers were sure to follow'.[57] Golf caddies might initially be banned from Sunday work, but others seized the opportunities for money-making that lay in Sunday recreation. Town by town, battles were fought, many of them in the interwar years over cinemas opening on Sundays. Most shops up to the 1970s remained closed on Sundays, but in other respects the Victorian Sunday had becoming a thing of the past.

By the late nineteenth and early twentieth century the shape of the week had taken on a form that would endure to the present. Residues of St Monday remained and remain, higher absenteeism on that day than on others, and often a later start to the working day. Saturday working time diminished, the start of the half-holiday creeping earlier and earlier, and after the post Second World War, especially from the 1960s onwards, a whole holiday coming to replace the half-holiday. By that date Saturday and Sunday formed a weekend leisure counterpoint to a working week that stretched from Monday to Friday.

Holidays

Holidays in the first half of the nineteenth century were always unpaid and were measured in particular days rather than weeks. Only in Lancashire did the wakes weeks survive and take root in the new industrial economy. A localised attachment to particular days was a much more common pattern. The Factory Acts of 1867 and 1874 extended to much larger groups of workers those clauses from the 1833 Act which ruled against work on Christmas Day or Good Friday. But Good Friday in particular remained an unpopular and often unobserved holiday. In 1876 the Royal Commission on the Factory and Workshop Acts heard how among Sheffield cutlers Good Friday is 'against the custom and feeling of the workpeople'; a scissors manufacturer there employed women who took no fewer than forty half-holidays in the year but wanted to work on Good Friday. The same message came from the Midlands: 'with the men all through South Staffordshire', claimed an ironfounder and hollow-ware manufacturer from West Bromwich, 'Easter has been as great a holiday as Whitsuntide is in Manchester and that district', but Easter Monday, not Good Friday. 'Good Friday is no use to the hands', said a cape manu-facturer from Tamworth, 'and they do not like forced play on that day . . . There are during the year certain popular holidays, such as the statute fair, club days, and occasional extra demonstrations, excursions, etc.' The customary holidays continued to be celebrated, in new ways perhaps, but at the old times and as a consequence there was very little national uniformity. For to the regional differences – Manchester's preference for Whitsun against that of the Midlands for Easter Monday – must be added trade particularities: the custom in clothing factories, for example, of giving two or three weeks' holiday after the busy season.[58]

Holidays were often geared to the needs of employers. Just as in the eighteenth century Josiah Wedgwood had tried to force his workforce into taking holidays when he wanted to close the works, so in the nineteenth century holidays often smacked of unemployment. In Cheshire saltworks, for example, where trade was often dull between Christmas and Easter, whenever the warehouses were full, the employers declared a 'holiday'. In the 1890s the Winsford Saltmakers' Association regularly wrote to the employers asking them to 'give as little holidays as possible'.[59]

Beginning around mid-century there is evidence of workers saving in anticipation of a holiday. It happened widely in the build-up to the Great Exhibition of 1851 which attracted many working-class visitors who came to London in organised trips. For annual holidays Lancashire took the lead with the celebration of Wakes Weeks transferring from mill town to the seaside, the finance for it coming from worker-organised Wakes Savings or Going-off Clubs. At Werneth Spindle Works, for example, from the 1850s onwards employees saved for fifty weeks at 6d a share for 25s per share pay out just before the wakes. In Oldham the amount paid out by such clubs rose from £1,000 in 1871 to £175,000 in 1900. Such savings made possible and reflected the existence of annual week-long holidays in most Lancashire textile towns by the end of the nineteenth century. The clubs continued as long as holidays remained unpaid, in Leicestershire the earliest mention of them in 1930. There is some evidence that they were most often to be found where women were employed in local industries, women being more inclined than men to save for holidays than for immediate consumption of, most probably, beer.[60]

Towards the end of the third quarter of the nineteenth century there are indications that some success was being achieved in the attempt to 'rationalise' holidays. From the mid-1860s there were efforts made to bring some order to the multitude of different wakes weeks in the Potteries, and this led in 1879 to the Great Stokes Wakes, one annual festival for the whole district. At national level the 1871 Bank Holiday Act was a significant step taken by the state in the recognition and regularisation of leisure. Its innovation was the August Bank Holiday on the first Monday in August. The immediate effects were limited, but its extension in 1875 to cover docks, customs houses, inland revenue offices and bonding warehouses made it much more likely that the parliamentary holidays would be nationally observed; as R. Baker, Factory Inspector, noted in 1876, 'the bank holidays are now becoming universal. People are shutting up their shops on those days, generally.'[61]

There is some very limited evidence that for the middle classes holiday time contracted in the early nineteenth century. It is based on the fact that the Bank of England closed on forty-four days in 1808 and on only four in 1834. By 1845, however, the trend had been reversed, and Bank workers were getting six to eighteen days' annual leave, depending on their length of service. Evidence given to the Civil Service Commission of 1875 indicated that clerks working for insurance companies, solicitors, banks, railway companies and the civil service were all getting at least two weeks' holiday a year. They had achieved this some three-quarters of a century before the bulk of manual workers. In the private sector advance was patchier than in the public, but by 1932 the General Secretary of the National Union of Clerks and Administrative Workers was confident that 'in regard to clerical and administrative workers, paid holidays are the rule rather than the exception'.[62]

In the late nineteenth and early twentieth centuries larger employers increasingly conceded holidays to all their workers, and trade unions demanded them. Brunner Mond, Lever Bros, the Gas Light and Coke Company, the London and North-Western Railway Company and the Royal Dockyards had all done so by the 1890s. These concessions were generally tied to stipulations that holiday entitlement was dependent on good conduct and minimal absence in the course of the year.[63] In 1897 the Amalgamated Society of Railway Servants negotiated one week's paid holiday after five years of service. Other unionised workers, in coal and iron, for example, were putting forward similar claims before the First World War, and in 1914 cotton employers and unions agreed the equivalent of 136 and a half hours' work (or roughly a fortnight) holiday per year – but it was without pay.[64]

The First World War made holidays with pay a national issue. The Ministry of Reconstruction discussed the question in 1917, somewhat indecisively, and nearly all industries put forward claims. By the beginning of the 1920s general and district agreements covered an estimated one million manual workers. The next major advance came in the late 1930s when union pressure by April 1938 had raised the number of manual workers with holiday pay agreements to three million (out of a total occupied population of 18.5 million of whom a further 4.75 million non-manual workers had secured agreements). By September 1938 the number of manual workers with holiday pay agreements was up to four million, and by 1945 it had reached ten million, most of whom had a two-week holiday. The Departmental Committee on Holidays with Pay of 1937, and the Act which followed in 1938, were more a reflection of union pressure than a major factor in securing the advance.[65]

The period after the Second World War was marked by a further increase in holiday time. Indeed holiday time seemed to advance faster than reduction in daily and weekly hours. By 1951 many manual workers had two weeks plus public holidays. By 1964 all had at least two weeks, and some had more, and by 1973 about three-quarters had three or more weeks. Non-manual workers had longer holiday breaks. As with hours of work, improvements in holiday entitlement were discontinuous, focused on the two World Wars and on 1968–73 during which years the average amount of holiday time rose from 3.8 weeks to 4.7 weeks.[66]

It is difficult to interpret the advance of holiday time as anything other than an indication of leisure preference. Crucial to it, however, was the issue of payment for holidays. This required a change in attitude, as much on the part of workers as of employers. The assumption was that you should be paid only for work. George Potter of the London Working Men's Association argued in 1868 for national holidays, but couldn't see them coming until 'a man will have more money for his labour, in order that he may be able to lose his time'.[67] Even just before the First World War, in 1911, it was said that if paid holidays were asked for 'in the cotton trade we should be heartily laughed at'. It was probably the awareness that white-collar employees were getting paid holidays that helped change the trade union attitude. Without payment, a holiday was, in the words of the Manchester and Salford Weavers Association in 1938, 'enforced collective unemployment'.[68] Many people in the interwar years had holiday entitlement but without pay were unable to go away, and even with pay might not be able to afford the extra costs that holidays entailed. For women in poorer working-class families, holidays simply increased the difficulty of making ends meet. This issue was very much to the fore in the discussions within the Committee on Holidays with Pay, and the popular press took up the cause of the 'poor British housewife' and of her need for a holiday as much as one for her husband. The solution was a paid holiday for the male worker spent in one of the rapidly emerging holiday camps run by Butlin and Warner where 'his wife can enjoy rest and recuperation and freedom so far as possible from arduous household duties'.[69]

A holiday – or at least a 'real holiday' – became defined as time spent away from home, 'relaxation and rest' the prime consideration.[70] As one housewife put it in a competition on 'How I would like to spend my holidays', 'I am hoping to go to the North of Blackpool all being well. Just to leave the washing of dishes and clothes and baking and all the little jobs that make each day full. Just to be able to sit and knit or read, and watch my kiddies play in the sands and gaze right out to where the sea and sky seem to meet each other will make my holiday just OK.'[71]

Work in the life course

Reduction of working hours, as we have seen, first focused on children, and children remained at the centre of attention up to the 1970s. From the mid-nineteenth century the concern became less that they were put to work too young and for too long hours, and more that they needed education. Preventing children working at a young age was never easy and never fully accomplished, but from the mid-nineteenth century there was general agreement as to the means by which it could be achieved. George Smith, who in the 1860s and 1870s campaigned vigorously on behalf of children working in brickyards, expressed a common opinion when he urged that such children needed to be brought under 'the benign aegis of LAW'.[72] If trade unionism secured a reduction of daily working hours and fought for holidays, legislation played a much more significant role for children, both legislation forbidding them from working and legislation enforcing school attendance.

Work and school, however, were often at odds, and work seemed to many the priority. This was true not only of working-class parents, who were fully aware of the contribution that children's earnings could make to family budgets, but also to middle- and upper-class commentators. The Newcastle Commission of the late 1850s argued that 'if the wages of the child's labour are necessary, either to keep the parents from the poor rates, or to relieve the pressure of severe and bitter poverty, it is far better that it should go to work at the earliest age at which it can bear the physical exertion rather than it should remain at school'. Forty years later, Seebohm Rowntree's study of *Poverty* in York at the turn of the century demonstrated all too clearly how children's wages or the absence of them determined the category within the working class to which a particular family would belong. Those who advocated compulsory schooling or a raising of the school leaving age knew that there would be opposition from the parents and often children who would be affected by it, and saw the need, as Helen Bosanquet put it, to 'proceed slowly' in extending protective legislation.[73]

The half-time system remained for many years the preferred solution to this tension between work and school. Educationists, however, began to question the impact of half-timers on school, and were looking to keep children in school longer, at least up to ten in the 1870s.[74] The 1880 Education Act, which made schooling compulsory, did so from the ages of five to ten. Education Acts and Factory Acts were often thereafter in some disharmony if not conflict, no one quite certain which held priority, but the effect of Education Acts, with exceptions and numerous local variations, was to raise the school-leaving age from ten in 1880 to fourteen in 1918. It was, on the face of it, a decisive lengthening of childhood, a reshaping of the time of childhood.

In practice, however, the shift from work to school was much less clear-cut than the introduction of compulsory schooling suggested. In the first place, schooling changed the nature and location but not the fact of work; in the 1880s anxiety about overwork in schools replicated earlier worry about work in factories. 'Absorbing and explosive', writes Gillian Sutherland, debates about 'over-pressure' raged. Suicide, 'brain-fever' and numerous other ills were blamed on it by psychiatrists and teachers. In 1884 the death certificates of two London School Board children referred to 'over-taxed brainwork'. Sir William Jenner, President of the Royal College of Physicians, was convinced by evidence that there was 'over-brainwork in Board schools'. Ministers and civil servants responded by casting doubts on the motives and evidence of alarmists. Malnutrition, they contended, was a much more serious health issue than notional overwork.[75]

Second, the half-time system, despite the volume of criticism directed at it, refused to die away, especially in its heartlands of Yorkshire and Lancashire. It was eventually legislated against in the 1918 Education Act, but until then it was normal for children in factory districts, at the age of twelve or thirteen, to start work part-time. It was not only parents who supported it. 'Given the choice', concluded James Pressley, 'children expressed a distinct preference for work'.[76]

Third, from the end of the nineteenth century there was growing awareness of the paid work that notionally full-time schoolchildren did, either before or after school or, especially girls, kept at home to help their mothers. An Employment of Children Act in 1903 tinkered with the issue but had little effect and on the eve of the First World War it was estimated that over quarter of a million full-time schoolchildren were also in employment.[77] The

Home Office instinctively downplayed the issue, the Education Department talked it up. In the interwar period and after, there was much denial that schoolchildren were in employment, but the evidence for it is compelling.[78] The raising of the school leaving age to fifteen in the 1944 Education Act and to sixteen in 1973 further tipped the balance away from work towards education for the young, but the reality remained that most children were doing some form of work before they left school.

Childhood over the period from 1830 became defined as a time that should be free of work. Positively, it came to be seen, especially in early childhood, as a time for play. Even at the age at which school became compulsory it was interrupted by periods of holiday much longer than any claimed in the adult world of work. Children in the twentieth century, much more than those before them, often had time on their hands. Boredom became a characteristic feature of childhood, the world of work denied them. For some campaigners in the early 1970s, childhood was not a garden of delight but a prison – and in prison people serve time, waiting for the end, for release.[79]

Time was also restructured for the old. In the eighteenth and for most people throughout the nineteenth century there was no sense of a universal or even appropriate time for something called 'retirement'. As a word 'retirement' was in common use from the mid-eighteenth century, but it meant retiring to the country as much as retiring from a job or employment.[80] The eighteenth century saw the development of numerous, mostly male, benefit clubs that were, amongst other things, designed to provide funds to members in sickness, to help with funeral expenses and provide aid for widows. By the early nineteenth century there were nearly ten thousand societies and over seven hundred thousand members, these figures, in Poor Law returns to Parliament, almost certainly an underestimate. In one 'friendly and mechanical society' in Halifax, all members reaching sixty received two shillings a week in benefit. In Bradford, the pension didn't begin until you were seventy.[81] Generally, however, clubs resisted committing themselves to the expense that regular pension-paying involved. The assumption was that wage-earners would continue to work and earn until they became too sick or ill to continue, and then they would become eligible for sick payments.

These eighteenth-century benefit clubs were individual clubs, in towns generally run by the trades, in the countryside often patronised by the wealthy. In the 1830s and 1840s nationally organised friendly societies began to offer benefits that were actuarially sounder, and the membership of them became considerable. But they, like the earlier benefit clubs, hesitated to offer regular pensions or annuities to members, and without that there could be no wide-spread notion that at a certain age you might retire.[82]

Saving for a pension made little sense. It was not unreasonable for the Friendly Societies Act of 1875 to define old age as 'any age after 50'; even in the early twentieth century the average trade union member (i.e. the better-off members of the working class) lived to barely more than fifty years of age.[83] In the eighteenth century three-fifths of males aged twenty-five died before they were sixty-five, and in the nineteenth century there was little improvement in these figures.[84] People could expect to be dead before they reached the age at which a pension would be payable. Without a pension the pressure was on to continue working for as long as possible. Manual wages peaked at around the age of forty-five, and thereafter, as physical strength waned, there was a decline in earnings, but only incapacity ended work.[85] In 1881 73 per cent of males aged sixty-five and over were in employment, a century later, in 1980, only 13 per cent.[86] It was a dramatic change. How was it that, as health improved dramatically over the twentieth century, the age at which people stopped working fell?

Improving life expectancy, and a consequent shift in the demographic profile of society as a whole, was at the heart of the issue. In England and Wales it is estimated that in 1766 just under one person in twelve was sixty or over, falling to one in fifteen by 1826, but thereafter rising to reach over one in thirteen by 1911, nearly one in eight by 1931, and almost one in six by 1951.[87] In friendly societies an increasing proportion of members were over sixty-five. In 1846–48 only 0.2 per cent of the total sickness risk in the Manchester Unity of Oddfellows represented members over sixty-five, but by 1893–97 this had increased to 4.66 per cent. The pressure was mounting to face up to the pension problem. One idea was to offer sickness benefits only up to sixty or sixty-five, help to be offered after that age by way of an annuity. But the problem so much debated was how to finance it. No one could doubt, however, that old age was the most potent cause of dependence on the Poor Law. As Charles Booth showed, in 1890 the percentage of paupers to population under the age of sixty was 4.6 per cent, and for those over sixty-five 38.4 per cent. After 1870 the Poor Law had put increasing pressure on family members to contribute to the welfare of ageing parents, but it was a contribution that many were unable to make. At least 40 per cent of those who died over the age of sixty-five required Poor Law relief in their final years. Most of them were women. As Leslie Hannah put it, 'Poverty in old age was pre-eminently a problem for women'.[88]

The eventual, and partial, solution in the 1908 Old Age Pensions Act was to pay up to five shillings a week to those over the age of seventy, financed out of general taxation. Entitlement was hedged around with clauses that excluded anyone earning over £26 (or £39 for married couples), who had a criminal record during their sixties, or who had wilfully failed to maintain themselves or their families.[89] The state pension did something, but not much, to introduce a notion of retirement: no one could live on the pension alone. 'A pension', writes David Vincent, 'would just about feed and clothe a parsimonious couple, but would not stretch to meet any housing costs.'[90] Even after the 1925 Pensions Act reduced the starting age to sixty-five, over half of all state pensioners continued in employment.[91]

Occupational pensions were more important than the state pension in 'inventing retirement'. The 1891 census was the first to classify the retired as a separate category, and the proportion so classified rose census by census, initially heavily concentrated amongst those with occupational pensions.[92] Those employed by the state (in 1891 less than three per cent of all employees) were the first to benefit. Earlier schemes stretching back into the eighteenth century were systematised in 1859 with the introduction of a non-contributory scheme to provide a pension from the age of sixty of one-sixtieth of final salary for each year of service. In the 1890s retirement at sixty-five was made compulsory. Large employers in railways and gas introduced similar schemes in the later nineteenth century, usually confined to their managerial and clerical grades. Here compulsory retirement ages were less common. The reason employers introduced these schemes were varied. In smaller firms there was often a tradition of *ex gratia* payments to long-serving staff. For larger employers there were obvious benefits in systematising this through a funded pension scheme. Some acted out of a sense of paternal responsibility for their employees, but most also came to see benefits in tying employees into their companies and trying to develop in them a sense of belonging to the company – the pensions were not transferable. Pensions, therefore, can be seen as one element in a labour strategy. If a compulsory age of retirement was then built into them, as tended to happen in the twentieth century, this could help remove promotion blockages and prevent having to pay large salaries to older employees whose productivity was in decline. Whatever the motive, occupational pensions increased in number – in 1936 they covered only 13 per cent of the workforce, in 1956 33 per cent.[93]

These occupational schemes were much more prevalent in salaried than in waged employment. They had in the first half of the twentieth century resulted in the development of a practice of retirement at age sixty or increasingly sixty-five in white-collar and managerial posts. Developments in the state pension scheme built on this practice. The 1946 National Insurance Act made state pensions available to all, at a level of 26 shillings for a single man and 46 shillings for a married couple, with the National Assistance Board from 1948 paying supplementary means-tested pensions. The pension rates were hardly generous, but were rising: in 1953 a single person's pension was equivalent to 16 per cent of the average male manual worker's wage, up to 26 per cent by 1979.[94] The incentive to carry on working was certainly still there, as nearly one-quarter of men sixty-five or over continued to do in the 1960s.[95] Barbara Castle's Social Security Act of 1975 was 'the first serious British state earnings-related pension scheme', substantially increasing retirement income, and especially beneficial to women.[96] Retirement thereafter became concentrated in a narrow age range, between sixty and sixty-five, earlier for women than for men. There was a history to this. Cadburys, for example, rare in allowing women into occupational schemes prior to the First World War, had a retirement age of sixty for men, fifty for women. Why this was the case is not at all clear. It can have had little to do with marriage or child-bearing as there was a marriage bar on many occupations. There is evidence that women were pressed into retirement at younger ages than men. When in 1940 the pension age for women was set at sixty, it was building on this tradition of early retirement for women, and was being pushed for by trade unions anxious to preserve jobs for men and by unmarried women who argued for early retirement on the grounds that they had home-keeping as well as employment jobs.[97]

The 1940s and 1950s inaugurated what Pat Thane has called 'mass retirement'. Middle-class men's expectation of retirement, funded by occupational pensions, had grown through the first half of the twentieth century. Only in the middle decades of the century did working-class men also gain that expectation. What caused it is a matter of dispute, some emphasising the demands and expectations of employers, others the understandable wish of older men to live off a pension, inadequate as it might be, rather than struggle on in work where they were marginalised. There is evidence that the first generation of mass retirees did so reluctantly or felt disoriented by the experience, but by the 1960s and 1970s retirement at pensionable age had become the norm, and it came to be thought of as a time of freedom and independence.[98] Put another way, and as the move to even earlier retirement spread, it seems plausible that leisure preference had resonance provided that standards of living in retirement could be maintained.

Conclusion

The decline of work time between 1830 and 1970 transformed the time of life for the bulk of the population. Working hours, whether by day, week or year fell. The extension and redefinition of childhood and the emergence of a period of life called retirement further reduced the amount of the lifespan taken up by paid work. These changes were most marked for men. Women, most of whose work was unpaid, were much less likely to experience the change, particularly as their domestic responsibilities rarely diminished as they got older. By the 1970s, however, paid work for both sexes had become concentrated between the ages of sixteen and sixty or sixty-five. Outside this work band there were childhood and schooling at the beginning of life and, as life expectancy rose, an increasingly elongated retirement at its end. Work, which had previously been most people's expectation and experience from about ten until death or incapacity, was now a much smaller proportion of the total life course. The causes of this change remain a matter of debate, but there is much evidence that people wanted and campaigned for a different balance between work and leisure.

Notes

1 H. Cunningham, *The Children of the Poor: Representations of Childhood since the Seventeenth Century* (Oxford: Blackwell, 1991), pp. 8–96.

2 Ibid., pp. 65–6, 89.

3 Ibid., pp. 51, 90, 96.

4 Senior and Marx quoted in S. and B. Webb, *Industrial Democracy* (1897; London: Longmans, Green and Co., 1920), p. 328; Cunningham, *Children of the Poor*, p. 84.

5 Cunningham, *Children of the Poor*, p. 71; K. O. Walker, 'The classical economists and the factory acts', *Journal of Economic History*, I (1941), 168–77; M. Blaug, 'The classical economists and the factory acts – a re-examination', *Quarterly Journal of Economics*, 72 (1958), 211–26.

6 R. G. Kirby and A. E. Musson, *The Voice of the People: John Doherty, 1798–1854, Trade Unionist, Radical and Factory Reformer* (Manchester: Manchester University Press, 1975), pp. 353–61.

7 Ibid., p. 349.

8 G. Langenfelt, *The Historic Origin of the Eight Hours Day: Studies in English Traditionalism* (New York: Greenwood Press, 1974).

9 Kirby and Musson, *Voice of the People*, pp. 272–301; for a revival of support for eight hours in the 1840s, see S. A. Weaver, *John Fielden and the Politics of Popular Radicalism, 1832–1847* (Oxford: Clarendon Press, 1987), p. 268.

10 Quoted in Weaver, *John Fielden*, pp. 251, 266–7.

11 Cunningham, *Children of the Poor*, p. 12.

12 Alfred [S. H. G. Kydd], *The History of the Factory Movement*, 2 vols (1857; New York: Augustus M. Kelley, 1966), vol. I, pp. 235–54.

13 Quoted in Cunningham, *Children of the Poor*, p. 94.

14 Quoted in A. J. Heesom, 'The Coal Mines Act of 1842, social reform, and social control', *Historical Journal*, 24 (1981), 81.

15 Quoted in R. Colls, '"Oh Happy English Children!" Coal, class and education in the North-East', *Past & Present*, 73 (1976), 87.

16 Ibid., 93–5.

17 H. Silver, 'Ideology and the factory child: attitudes to half-time education', in P. McCann (ed.), *Popular Education and Socialization in the Nineteenth Century* (London: Methuen, 1977), pp. 141–66; Cunningham, *Children of the Poor*, pp. 169–70.

18 Weaver, *John Fielden*, p. 260.

19 Quoted in Heesom, 'The Coal Mines Act of 1842', 268.

20 Weaver, *John Fielden*, pp. 296–7; Alfred, *Factory Movement*, vol. II, p. 255.

21 Weaver, *John Fielden*, pp. 275, 282–7.

22 G. Stedman Jones, *Outcast London: A Study in the Relationship between Classes* (1971; Harmondsworth: Peregrine, 1976), pp. 53–126, quoting Mayhew, p. 53.

23 R. Samuel, 'Mineral workers', in R. Samuel (ed.), *Miners, Quarrymen and Saltworkers* (London: Routledge & Kegan Paul, 1977), pp. 50–5.

24 R. C. O. Matthews, C. H. Feinstein, and J. C. Odling-Smee, *British Economic Growth 1856–1973* (Oxford: Clarendon Press, 1982), pp. 70–1; M. A. Bienefeld, *Working Hours in British Industry: An Economic History* (London: Weidenfeld and Nicolson, 1972), esp. pp. 145–7; J. Arrowsmith, 'The struggle over working time in nineteenth- and twentieth-century Britain', *Historical Studies in Industrial Relations*, 13 (2002), 83–117.

25 G. Cross, *A Quest for Time: The Reduction of Work in Britain and France, 1840–1940* (Berkeley, Los Angeles and London: University of California Press, 1989), p. 235; Webbs, *Industrial Democracy*, pp. 329–33; S. Webb and H. Cox, *The Eight Hours Day* (London: Walter Scott, 1891), pp. 153–64.

26 R. Price, *Masters, Unions and Men: Work Control in Building and the Rise of Labour 1830–1914* (Cambridge: Cambridge University Press, 1980), pp. 39–54.

27 Bienefeld, *Working Hours*, pp. 106–18; Arrowsmith, 'Struggle over working time', 94.

28 Cross, *Quest for Time*, pp. 52–78.

29 Ibid., pp. 111–24.

30 Ibid., pp. 129–42; Matthews, Feinstein and Odling-Smee, *British Economic Growth*, p. 71.

31 Cross, *Quest for Time*, pp. 145–6, 162–70.

32 Quoted in Arrowsmith, 'Struggle over working time', p. 101.

33 Arrowsmith, 'Struggle over working time', 83; Bienefeld, *Working Hours*, pp. 162–78.

34 R. W. Postgate, *The Builders' History* (London: The National Federation of Building Trade Operatives, 1923), p. 113; R. Church, *The History of the British Coal Industry, Vol. 3, 1830–1913: Victorian Pre-eminence* (Oxford: Clarendon Press, 1986), p. 251.

35 Bienefeld, *Working Hours*.

36 H. Cunningham, *Leisure in the Industrial Revolution c. 1780–c. 1880* (London: Croom Helm, 1980), p. 149; W. J. Hausmann and B. T. Hirsch, 'Wages, leisure and productivity in South Wales coal mining, 1874–1914: an economic approach', *Llafur*, 3 (1982), 58–66.

37 Webb and Cox, *Eight Hours Day*, p. 1; Chapman quoted in B. McCormick and J. E. Williams, 'The miners and the eight-hour day, 1863–1910', *Economic History Review*, 12 (1959), 223.

38 S. G. Jones, *Workers at Play: A Social and Economic History of Leisure 1918–1939* (London: Routledge and Kegan Paul, 1986), p. 15.

39 Matthews, Feinstein and Odling-Smee, *British Economic Growth*, pp. 72–3.

40 Ibid., pp. 69–70.

41 H. Cunningham, 'Leisure and Culture', in F. M. L. Thompson (ed.), *The Cambridge Social History of Britain 1750–1950*, 3 vols (Cambridge: Cambridge University Press, 1990), vol. II, pp. 286–7; Webb and Cox, *The Eight Hours Day*, p. 145; Brunel quoted in N. McKendrick, 'Josiah Wedgwood and factory discipline', *Historical Journal*, 4 (1961), 51.

42 K. Thomas (ed.), *The Oxford Book of Work* (Oxford: Oxford University Press, 1999), p. 240.

43 W. B. Whitaker, *Victorian and Edwardian Shopworkers* (Newton Abbot: David and Charles, 1973).

44 Cunningham, *Leisure in the Industrial Revolution*, pp. 143–4.

45 Ibid., p. 144.

46 D. Reid, 'The decline of Saint Monday', *Past & Present*, 71 (1976), 84–90; Cunningham, *Leisure in the Industrial Revolution*, pp. 144–5.

47 S. Barton, *Working-Class Organisations and Popular Tourism, 1840–1970* (Manchester: Manchester University Press, 1995), p. 85.

48 Quoted in ibid., p. 108.

49 Cunningham, *Leisure in the Industrial Revolution*, p. 147.

50 D. A. Reid, 'Weddings, weekdays, work and leisure in urban England 1791–1911: the decline of Saint Monday revisited', *Past & Present*, 153 (1996), 135–63; J. Boulton, 'Economy of time? Wedding days and the working week in the past', *Local Population Studies*, 43 (1989), 38–40. For evidence of hewers in Northumberland working a full day on the day of marriage, see P. Kirby, 'Attendance and work effort in the Great Northern Coalfield, 1775–1864', *Economic History Review*, 65 (2012), 975–6.

51 Kirby and Musson, *Voice of the People*, pp. 350–2, 364.

52 Bienefeld, *Working Hours*, pp. 71, 86–116; Reid, 'The decline of Saint Monday', p. 86.

53 Cunningham, 'Leisure and culture', p. 287.

54 Cross, *Quest for Time*, p. 89.

55 P. Bailey, *Popular Culture and Performance in the Victorian City* (Cambridge: Cambridge University Press, 1998), pp. 47–79.

56 J. Lowerson, *Sport and the English Middle Classes 1870–1914* (Manchester: Manchester University Press, 1993), pp. 268–77.

57 Quoted in J. Wigley, *The Rise and Fall of the English Sunday* (Manchester: Manchester University Press, 1980), p. 151.

58 Cunningham, *Leisure in the Industrial Revolution*, p. 142.

59 B. Didsbury, 'Cheshire saltworkers', in R. Samuel (ed.), *Miners, Quarrymen and Saltworkers* (London: Routledge & Kegan Paul, 1977), pp. 158, 164.

60 R. Poole, 'Oldham Wakes', in J. K. Walton and J. Walvin (eds), *Leisure in Britain 1780–1939* (Manchester: Manchester University Press, 1983), pp. 71–98; Barton, *Working-Class Organisations*, pp. 76–9.

61 Cunningham, *Leisure in the Industrial Revolution*, pp. 142–3.

62 Cunningham, 'Leisure and culture', pp. 287–8; Barton, *Working-Class Organisations*, p. 109.

63 S. G. Jones, 'Trade-union policy between the wars: the case of holidays with pay in Britain', *International Review of Social History*, 31 (1986), 41–2.

64 Barton, *Working-Class Organisations*, pp. 79, 110.

65 Jones, *Workers at Play*, pp. 17–20.

66 Matthews, Feinstein and Odling-Smee, *British Economic Growth*, pp. 75–6.

67 Quoted in Barton, *Working-Class Organisations*, p. 107.

68 S. G. Jones, 'The Lancashire cotton industry and the development of paid holidays in the nineteen-thirties', *Transactions of the Historic Society of Lancashire and Cheshire*, 135 (1985), 103–4.

69 S. T. Dawson, *Holiday Camps in Twentieth-Century Britain: Packaging Pleasure* (Manchester: Manchester University Press, 2011), pp. 10–41.

70 W. Beveridge and A. F. Wells (eds), *The Evidence for Voluntary Action* (London: George Allen and Unwin, 1949), pp. 62–4.

71 G. Cross (ed.), *Worktowners at Blackpool: Mass Observation and Popular Leisure in the 1930s* (London: Routledge, 1990), p. 42.

72 Cunningham, *Children of the Poor*, p. 173.

73 Ibid., pp. 168–9.

74 Silver, 'Ideology and the factory child', pp. 141–66.

75 G. Sutherland, *Policy-Making in Elementary Education 1870–1895* (Oxford: Oxford University Press, 1973), pp. 245–57; *The Times*, 27 June 1884; 29 Oct. 1884.

76 J. Pressley, 'Childhood, education and labour: moral pressure and the end of the half-time system' (Lancaster University PhD thesis, 2000), esp. pp. 91–5.

77 Cunningham, *Children of the Poor*, pp. 180–2.

78 S. Cunningham, 'The problem that doesn't exist? Child labour in Britain 1918–1970', in M. Lavalette (ed.), *A Thing of the Past? Child Labour in Britain in the Nineteenth and Twentieth Centuries* (Liverpool: Liverpool University Press, 1999), pp. 139–72.

79 J. Holt, *Escape from Childhood: The Needs and Rights of Children* (1974; Harmondsworth: Penguin, 1975).

80 *Oxford English Dictionary.*

81 P. Clark, *British Clubs and Societies, 1580–1800: The Origins of an Associational World* (Oxford: Clarendon Press, 2000), pp. 350, 361.

82 L. Hannah, *Inventing Retirement: The Development of Occupational Pensions in Britain* (Cambridge: Cambridge University Press, 1986), pp. 6–7.

83 P. H. J. H. Gosden, *Self-Help: Voluntary Associations in Nineteenth-Century Britain* (London: B. T. Batsford, 1973), p. 266; D. Vincent, *Poor Citizens: The State and the Poor in Twentieth-Century Britain* (London: Longman, 1991), p. 27.

84 M. Anderson, 'The emergence of the modern life cycle in Britain', *Social History*, 10 (1985), 72.

85 Hannah, *Inventing Retirement*, p. 7; J. S. Quadagno, *Aging in Early Industrial Society: Work, Family and Social Policy in Nineteenth-Century England* (New York: Academic Press, 1982), p. 154.

86 P. Thane, *Old Age in English History: Past Experiences, Present Issues* (Oxford: Oxford University Press, 1990), p. 386.

87 M. Anderson, 'The social implications of demographic change', in Thompson (ed.), *Cambridge Social History of Britain*, vol. II, p. 46.

88 Gosden, *Self-Help*, pp. 262–3, 268; Hannah, *Inventing Retirement*, p. 118.

89 Gosden, *Self-Help*, pp. 280–1; Vincent, *Poor Citizens*, pp. 24, 26.

90 Quadagno, *Aging*, p. 152; Vincent, *Poor Citizens*, p. 41.

91 Hannah, *Inventing Retirement*, pp. 17, 159.

92 Quadagno, *Aging*, pp. 151–2.

93 Thane, *Old Age*, pp. 236–55; Hannah, *Inventing Retirement*, pp. 9–40, 130, 135–6.

94 Hannah, *Inventing Retirement*, pp. 53–4.

95 Matthews, Feinstein and Odling-Smee, *British Economic Growth*, p. 564.

96 Hannah, *Inventing Retirement*, pp. 61–3.

97 Ibid., p. 128; Thane, *Old Age*, pp. 284–6, 331–2.

98 Thane, *Old Age*, pp. 385–406.

6

Men, work and leisure,
1850–1970

Time spent at work, daily, weekly, annually, declined over the period 1850 to 1970. Correspondingly, time for leisure increased. At a simple level this suggests a consistent preference for leisure time over work time. Other factors, however, affected the balance of how time was spent: concerns about employment opportunities and threats to them; rising standards of living; changes in the nature of work; a huge expansion of leisure facilities. Between them work time and leisure time gave men a sense of who they were, of their identity. Did they think of themselves first and foremost as a miner or a clerk or a factory worker, with leisure time flowing out of that as a primary identity, or did football or cinema or Blackpool or enjoying home life or chapel membership or a hobby loom larger for them, work being a necessary means for the enjoyment of them? How did these ways of forming an identity mesh with others such as social class, family, neighbourhood, or nation? The focus is on men – women's experiences are considered in Chapter 8 – because experience of time was thoroughly gendered. For men time came to be thought of as 'work and leisure'. In this chapter these issues will be discussed in relation to that three-quarters or more of the male population who made up the working and lower middle classes.

The gospel of work

Work is what we associate with Victorian England; not only long hours and grinding toil, but also a dominant work ethic, a belief that work was the most important and most rewarding aspect of life. 'Except for "God"', wrote the historian Walter Houghton, 'the most popular word in the Victorian vocabulary must have been "work".'[1] Thomas Carlyle was the most fervent advocate of the merits of work. Writing in the midst of the social and political crisis of the 1840s, an outspoken critic of his society as it was, he still found 'a perennial nobleness, and even sacredness, in Work . . . In all true Work, were it but true hand-labour, there is something of divineness. Labour, wide as the Earth, has its summit in Heaven.' For Carlyle work was a defence against doubt and despair:

> in Idleness alone is there perpetual despair . . . a man perfects himself by work-ing . . . even in the meanest sorts of Labour, the whole soul of a man is composed into a kind of real harmony, the instant he sets himself to work! Doubt, Desire, Sorrow, Remorse, Indignation, Despair itself, all these like helldogs lie beleaguer-ing the soul of the poor dayworker, as of every man: but he bends himself with free valour against his task, and all these are stilled, all these shrink murmuring far off into their caves. The man is now a man.

'Work', said Carlyle, 'and therein have wellbeing.'[2]

Such was Carlyle's reputation that when Ford Madox Ford's painting of *Work* was exhibited in 1865, Carlyle was included in the picture, looking on approvingly at a navvy digging up a road to lay a water pipe. In assessing his influence, W. R. Greg wrote how he 'preached up the duty and the dignity of WORK, with an eloquence which has often made the idle shake off their idleness, and the frivolous feel ashamed of their frivolity'.[3] Carlyle and others like him were claiming that only through your work could you be fully human.

Neither Carlyle's prose style nor some of his attitudes endeared him to all. But his belief in the importance of work runs through many other Victorian texts, perhaps most famously in Samuel Smiles's *Self-Help*, a bestseller in 1859, and reprinted fifty-two times in the following fifty years. Addressed initially to young men, Smiles wanted 'to re-inculcate these old-fashioned but whole-some lessons – which perhaps cannot be too often urged, – that youth must work in order to enjoy, – that nothing creditable can be accomplished with-out application and diligence'. 'Labour', wrote Smiles, 'is not only a necessity and a duty, but a blessing: only the idler feels it to be a curse'.[4]

Beneath the tide of praise of work in Victorian England there lay a disturb-ing undercurrent. It was 'true hand-labour' to which Carlyle looked for salvation, not 'industrial work, still under bondage to Mammon'.[5] Karl Marx shared with Carlyle a belief that work was what distinguished men from animals and gave them their humanity. But Marx thought that in the world of the nineteenth century, and under conditions of wage labour, work alien-ated man from his true nature:

> Work is external to the worker . . . it is not part of his nature . . . ; consequently, he does not fulfil himself in his work but denies himself, has a feeling of misery

rather than well-being, does not freely develop his mental and physical energies but is physically exhausted and mentally debased. The worker, therefore, feels himself at home only during his leisure hours, whereas at work he feels homeless.[6]

This sense of alienation, Marx believed, was the outcome of the worker having no sense of ownership in what he produced, and of a division of labour which removed any satisfaction in craftsmanship.

Marx was by no means alone in the nineteenth century in thinking that work was not what it ought to be. John Ruskin was a persistent critic of the dominant political economy and of the damage that it inflicted on any sense of worth in work. In the 1850s he wrote about 'the degradation of the operative into a machine', and went on to describe its consequences:

> The foundations of society were never yet shaken as they are at this day. It is not that men are ill fed, but that they have no pleasure in the work by which they make their bread, and therefore look to wealth as the only means of pleasure . . . they feel that the kind of labour to which they are condemned is verily a degrading one, and makes them less than men.[7]

William Morris agreed – but he had hopes for the future. In what he called 'Useful Work' as distinct from 'Useless Toil', there was hope, hope of the rest to come after work, hope of the value of the product, but perhaps above all

> The hope of pleasure in the work itself: how strange that hope must seem to some of my readers – to most of them! Yet I think that to all living creatures there is a pleasure in the exercise of their energies . . . a man at work, making something which he feels will exist because he is working at it and wills it, is exercising the energies of his mind and soul as well as of his body . . . as a part of the human race, he creates.[8]

Morris spoke from experience. He knew what it was to create. He had trained himself in an astonishing range of skills, in furniture-making, in fabric design and manufacture, in pottery, in metalwork, and knew at first hand of the three hopes embedded in 'useful work'. But he also thought that most of those who lived in the late nineteenth century would find it 'strange' to talk of there being pleasure in work. If that strangeness was to be removed, society would have to be transformed; there would have to be some kind of socialist revolution.[9]

Carlyle, Ruskin and Morris had a huge influence on the early labour movement and on circles way beyond that. In 1906 the first big intake of Labour

MPs were asked which authors and books had most influenced them; Ruskin and Carlyle were in the first four, along with Charles Dickens and the Bible.[10] After the First World War, R. H. Tawney reiterated their arguments for a new generation, writing of 'the degradation of those who labour' that arises out of there being no proper purpose for industrial production, too much of it being directed towards making 'trivialities' for the rich.[11] This body of writing held out a hope of a society in which work would be individually fulfilling and socially necessary.

These hopes may sound inspiring on the one hand or unrealistic on the other. They were also thoroughly gendered. Work ideally was going to make a man a man or, in nineteenth-century circumstances, less than a man. Masculinity and work cannot be separated. Jan de Vries has argued that for a century or more after 1850 'the breadwinner-homemaker household' was the ideal, with the husband as breadwinner, and the wife as homemaker. He argues that this form of household was not a consequence of women being forced out of the labour market, or of the needs of capitalists, or of patriarchy: it was freely chosen by households as the best way of utilising their labour resources. As homemakers women could enhance the health and comfort of the family in ways otherwise unattainable.[12] The male breadwinner ideal rarely transmuted into reality – adult male earnings were supplemented by those of children and by the usually part-time earnings of mothers – but it shaped and defined 'work' and 'leisure' in a deeply gendered way for over a century.

The reality of work

The utopia that Morris and others imagined and hoped for has never come near to realisation. Indeed, there is a powerful argument that, despite shorter hours and in some ways because of them, the experience of work deteriorated. Surveying the enormous amount of sheer physical toil in the nineteenth century, Raphael Samuel was in no doubt that there was 'an enormous deterioration in working conditions' and a 'momentous transformation . . . imposed on working pace'.[13] Contemporaries agreed. Towards the end of the nineteenth century Robert Blatchford, in his letters to 'John Smith, of Oldham, a hard-headed workman', wrote of his work that 'You are employed in a factory for from 55 to 70 hours a week. Some of your comrades work harder, and longer, and in worse places. Still, as a rule, it may be said of all your class that the hours of labour are too long, that the labour is monotonous, mechanical and severe, and that the surroundings are often unhealthy, nearly always disagreeable, and in many cases dangerous.'[14]

Employers were under pressure to increase productivity – output per worker – and thereby effectively to reduce labour costs. There were various options open to them. One option, common in factory areas in Lancashire in the middle years of the nineteenth century, was to try to tie the employees by both self-interest and affection to the firm through paternalism: to provide housing, recreational facilities and outings to employees. A whole way of life, leisure as much as work, became centred on the mill.[15] Effective as this was, it became difficult to sustain in the later nineteenth century as the size of firms increased and family control diminished. Nevertheless paternalism remained a force through the period. Large employers, epitomised by the Quaker chocolate manufacturers Cadburys and Rowntrees, and public organisations such as the police, the prison service and the post office were its keenest practitioners. Edward Cadbury, for example, in 1911 declared that for Cadburys 'The supreme principle has been the belief that business efficiency and the welfare of employees are but different sides of the same problem'. In the police, extensive provision of leisure facilities by the employers from the 1860s onwards was a strategy of control and discipline, sometimes resented, more broadly accepted.[16]

The First World War spawned welfare institutions attached to war industries and in its aftermath, with great fear of worker unrest, employers in engineering saw advantages in pursuing this path. Paternalism in the interwar period might start slowly with a company magazine and proceed to a social club and sporting facilities. In the mid-1930s the Coventry Works Sports Association ran leagues for thousands of workers, headed by thirty football and swimming teams. Employers, however, encountered opposition from some workers who saw these enterprises as entirely dominated from on top. Most workers used employer-provided facilities instrumentally. They enjoyed the sport or the excursions or the Christmas parties, but they did not buy into the sometimes explicit hope that employer and employee would begin to have a shared understanding of the aims of the enterprise and a common loyalty to it. In fact, the more work-based leisure there was, the more social divisions became entrenched. When the Coventry-based Armstrong Siddley works closed for a day in September, management and office staff took a river trip to Oxford, the Inspection Department visited Warwickshire villages and many others went to watch Coventry City play Blackpool away, giving them the added advantage of time to enjoy by the beach or in

Blackpool's many other attractions.[17] Work and leisure for them remained separate spheres.

A second employer option was to shift from work paid by time to piece-work, and hope thereby to increase the effort expended in work. There was nothing new in the concept or practice of paying by piece. Adam Smith had pointed to both the practice – workers, he thought, were 'generally . . . in manufactures' paid by the piece – and the dangers associated with it. 'Workmen', he wrote, '. . . when they are liberally paid by the piece, are very apt to over-work themselves, and to ruin their health and constitution in a few years.'[18] In the mid-nineteenth century more and more employers seemed to be moving to payment by piecework, often in conjunction with the spread of machinery. In London's docks, for example, the replacement of sail by steam, and the increased capital value of ships, made it 'necessary that they should earn profits without waste of time'. In consequence, from the 1870s, payment by the day was replaced by piecework by the hour, time off for beer in the mornings and afternoons ended, and 'work became harder'.[19] Piece-work methods of payment were introduced in cotton, mining, woodworking, printing, ironfounding, boot and shoe manufacturing, and above all in engineering. Whereas only 5 per cent of engineering workers were paid by results in 1886, 70 per cent were in 1950. The aim was, as was argued in 1921, to remove 'the tendency to limited effort which was characteristic of flat rate remuneration'.[20] In a Swindon railway factory in the early twentieth century the introduction of piece rates led to a slight improvement of wages, but at the cost of almost doubling the amount of work each man did.[21]

A third option was to simplify work processes, thereby undermining the position, status and high pay of skilled workers. In boot and shoe making in the 1860s riveting the sole to the upper replaced sewing: 'Skill was reduced, labour costs fell, and there was a sharp increase in productivity'. In this case and in others it was the division of labour rather than machinery that changed work.[22] But the introduction of machinery could also deskill people and lead to a 'degradation' of work. An engineer in the 1890s wrote that 'All mechanics will agree with me that the introduction of machinery has not raised the standard of skill among workmen. Nay, on the contrary, it has enormously increased the monotony of their toil, and limited the scope for the exercise of their ingenuity.' A study of mining in the mid-twentieth century reported that

An old miner took pride in his work . . . the getting of coal by hand, with all the cutting, shovelling, ripping, packing, drawing off, etc., was a craft, an art, while now all the jobs are specialised, and have become monotonous . . . The collier of today in a mechanised colliery is doing practically nothing but shovelling – shovelling all the time. How can you expect him to take an interest in his job? An old collier could take his time; there was not such a rush and strain as there is now, with the conveyor and the twenty four hours' cycle.[23]

This 'rush and strain' was, from the employers' point of view, a fourth option, and probably the most significant one, for increasing productivity. Workers might work shorter hours but work harder. Marx was quickly alert to this likelihood. 'As soon as the working day has been legally restricted', he wrote, 'the intensification of labour . . . becomes much more marked.' Machinery became speeded up so as to squeeze more labour out of the worker in a given time. In 1858 factory inspectors reported that

The great improvements made in machines of every kind have raised their productive power very much. Without any doubt the shortening of the hours of labour . . . gave the impulse to these improvements. The latter, combined with the more intense strain on the workman, have had the effect that, at least as much is produced in the shortened working days as was previously during the longer one.[24]

Marx foresaw the consequences:

It is absolutely indisputable that the tendency of capital, as soon as a prolongation of the working day is once for all prohibited, to compensate itself by systematically increasing the intensity of labour, and the tendency of capital to make of every improvement in machinery a more effective means of getting the utmost out of labour power, will ere long lead to a state of things that will make a further reduction in the hours of labour inevitable.[25]

In short, there was a price to be paid for shorter hours and more leisure, an intensification of work on the job.

The intensification of work was widely felt, sometimes, but not always, associated with the introduction of new machinery. When the eight-hour day was introduced in the Royal Ordnance Factories and Royal Docks, it was linked to the introduction of clocking in and out and the employment of 'workchasers' to ensure there was no idling. There was much dissatisfaction. A Portsmouth dock worker in 1894 described how 'The men find that they really have to work all their time in the yard. Much of the idling has been stopped, and it is probable that more work is being turned out per man than ever before.'[26] In a Swindon railway factory just before the First World War, it was reported, 'The speeding-up of late years has been general and insistent . . . I am not exaggerating when I say that the actual exertions of the workman have often been doubled or trebled.'[27] In the depressed industries in the interwar period, the speed-up of work was much noted. 'Speed is the essence of present-day industry', noted the 1935 Factory Inspector's Report. There was, argued a 1937 study, a 'terrific drive for increased output through speed-up . . . Every nerve has to be concentrated under modern conditions on the keeping up of the output.'[28]

The effects on health of the intensification of work were widely deplored. It says much that there was an Industrial Fatigue Research Board between 1918 and 1928, succeeded by an Industrial Health Research Board, these building on the First World War Health of Munitions Committee, set up in the face of declining productivity and chronic fatigue in munitions work. Fatigue, doctors had been saying since the late nineteenth century, stunted growth, increased insomnia, contributed to liver, lung and digestive disorders, and led to nervous diseases.[29]

The increasing sub-division of work processes and the speeding-up of machinery became in the early twentieth century linked to a quest for 'scientific management' as preached by F. W. Taylor in America. Time and motion studies, followed by a restructuring of labour processes, were at the heart of this, and were almost certain to imply a shift of supervision from foremen, at the peak of their powers in the later nineteenth century, to those in managerial roles. Large manufacturing companies, especially in the newer industries, adopted parts of the new management ideas; overall, however, in 1939 only one in ten firms had done so.[30]

These four options for increasing productivity were not mutually exclusive. An employer might, for example, introduce new machinery, switch to piece-work and build recreational facilities. Or equally some employers might do very little to change their managerial practices. Overall, however, 'Workers were more directly managed, monitored and controlled at the point of production by 1950 compared to 1880'.[31]

There were two other factors that did little to allay the overall pessimism about the experience of work. The first, strongly articulated in the first half of the twentieth century, was that the work available for teenage boys on their entry into the labour market had particularly deleterious effects. Fred Williams started work at Tizer's mineral water factory in Oldham in 1935:

The work was mind-numbing, lasting long hours on a conveyor belt performing repetitive tasks: putting corks into bottle necks, grasping two bottles and inverting them, slapping a label on each bottle. Charlie Chaplin conveyed it humorously in *Modern Times* but the reality was no laughing matter . . . I moved through a succession of youthful blind alley jobs, each of them dominated by the frustratingly slow impatient passage of time.[32]

Such work had no training element and led nowhere, its results widely deplored. 'Work which is monotonous kills development', wrote Cyril Jackson, 'and work which is intermittent destroys perseverance and power of concentration.' 'Continually', confirmed C. E. B. Russell in 1913, 'the employment offered to youths is becoming more monotonous', leading to 'the deadening of the intelligence and the atrophy of many of the finer qualities of youth'. Writers in this vein wanted to bring back some modernised form of apprenticeship, but were not optimistic, hardly hoping, as Arnold Freeman put it in 1914, 'that in the near future boys or men can be educated or elevated *through* their labour as to some extent they were in the days of handicraft'.[33]

A second feature of work was its danger. According to official figures, which almost certainly understate the case, in the period 1880–1914 150,000 workers in the United Kingdom were killed by injuries sustained at work, transport, shipping and mines having particularly high rates. In 1914 a miner was killed in Britain every six hours and severely injured every two hours. Things, it's true, were getting better, both in the years up to 1914 and subsequently, partly owing to legislation, itself the outcome of campaigning by trade unions and others, partly to a shift in the occupational structure towards safer white-collar jobs.[34] There remained, however, huge disparities in safety at work, a feature even more evident if the scope is widened from deaths and injuries in accidents to occupational diseases. As Dr Thomas Oliver, a pioneer in the field, noted in his *The Diseases of Occupations* (1908), 'There is scarcely any trade or occupation that is not attended by some risk or other'. Take, as one of many possible examples, mortality from lung and respiratory diseases: in the 1880s earthenware workers were five times more likely to die from these than were agricultural workers.[35] Improvements, by no means universal, were often halted in the depressed industries in the interwar years, and then by overworking in the Second World War. Moreover, the nature of work seemed to many observers to be introducing new kinds of illness. As the Senior Medical Inspector of Factories noted in 1931

the pleasure of the craftsman is being crushed by the steady increase in mechanised processes, the result of which is seen in the tendency to rise of sickness rates for 'nervous disabilities' . . . Vastly more days are lost from vague, ill-defined, but no doubt very real, disability due to *ennui* than from all the recognised industrial diseases put together.[36]

There is, then, a powerful argument that the experience of work worsened in the period after 1850 despite or because of increased leisure time. In the 1860s an observer of Lancashire factory workers said of them that 'the omni-present and probably the strongest sentiment of this people is an inveterate repugnance to factory work, and a constant desire to get away from it'.[37] The shift towards factory work, however, was ongoing. Some of it in the twentieth century industries that concentrated in the south undoubtedly had better conditions than those in Lancashire in the 1860s, but that had to be counterbalanced by the speed-up of machinery. Initiatives like 'Music While You Work', on air between 1940 and 1967, were desperate attempts to relieve the awfulness of it.

A consistent pattern of evidence from the 1960s and 1970s about work suggests that then also a negative feeling about work was dominant. A factory worker, making cigarettes, wrote how 'Time, rather than content, is the measure of factory life. Time is what the factory worker sells: not labour, not skill, but time, dreary time. Desolate factory time that passes so slowly com-pared with the fleeting seconds of the weekend.' Mechanisation, he thought, 'has led to jobs that are both dull and monotonous'. For a print-worker, 'there is little interest in the job other than getting your money on Friday and get-ting out of the building as fast as you can to your family and the questionable cult of the television and the "leisure" it provides'.[38] A worker for Ford, on the assembly line, thought that 'A robot could do it. The line here is made for morons. It doesn't need any thought. They tell you that. "We don't pay you for thinking" they say.' Another Ford worker said that 'It's the most boring job in the world. It's the same thing over and over again. There's no change in it, it wears you out. It makes you awful tired. It slows your think-ing right down . . . You just endure it for the money. That's what you are paid for – to endure the boredom of it.'[39] As Jack Jones, the trade union leader, summed it up in 1973, 'Life in the factories is drab, monotonous, uninspiring'.[40] When the American Marxist Harry Braverman wrote about *Labor and Monopoly Capital: The Degradation of Work in the Twentieth Century* (1974), it's not surprising that it received a ready response.

This bleak picture of the worsening of the work experience needs to be balanced by evidence of different experiences of work and of work time. Not all manufacturing processes had undergone the rationalisation of work processes associated with Taylorism. Take the pottery industry which Josiah Wedgwood had struggled to reduce to order in the eighteenth century. He would have been alarmed to find how shallow a root his changes had taken, for in the 1920s there was virtually no reference to clock time in the organisation of work. As a moulder wrote in 1920, 'We have no set time for stopping and starting here, that is in regards to moulded work, should any job be given out, a piece-work rate is at once fixed on. So the Boss troubles no more about one's coming and going.' The intricate division of labour meant that there were small occupational groupings with workshops of four to eight people, working to quite different time schedules, slipware taking two to three hours, the firing department's oven work spread over two days. 'Management' was distant, work divided up by the workpeople themselves.[41] There remained opportunities in some work for scavenging or pilfering materials at work, and for using work time to make them up. In engineering shops, for example, an 'itinerant mechanic' recalled in 1935, supervision was often lax in the pre-breakfast period, during which

> Sets of fire-irons and dogs, toasting-forks, kitchen shovels, and ornaments of novel design and ornate handles, brass, copper, bronze, and gunmetal candlesticks, photo frames and mantelpiece ornaments, door-knockers, model engines for the son, were some of the 'foreign orders' executed in the bosses' time.[42]

In ship-building, too, it was difficult to impose 'close managerial control of work'. In consequence there was an 'occupational culture' which allowed for considerable leisure in work, with regular groups for cards, dominoes or crosswords in different parts of the shipyard meeting both in and out of work time.[43]

Many occupations didn't lend themselves easily to greater intensification of work. As late as 1931 the percentage of the workforce employed in manufacture, mining and quarrying was just under 40 per cent, leaving the majority, 60 per cent, in other occupations. These included agriculture, with over one million employees throughout the first half of the twentieth century and slow to introduce mechanisation prior to the Second World War; building where, in the 1930s, half of the workforce remained 'skilled tradesmen'; and the service sector with 40 per cent of the total workforce in 1931. The service sector included transport, where small-scale enterprise continued to be prevalent – of the 6,486 bus operators in 1931 over 80 per cent owned fewer than five buses; and retailing where again, despite the growth of multiple or chain stores, the overwhelming majority of outlets were single shops run by their owner.[44]

These qualifications are important, but they do no more than dent the dominant pessimistic discourse about work. That pessimism is reinforced by the word that was adopted to describe work: 'labour'. In the crucial political sphere where workers represented themselves, they did so as 'labour': the Labour Representation Committee, the Independent Labour Party, the Labour Party, the labour movement. Labour in this discourse was opposed to capital, and the word had value and resonance in that it pointed to the fact that without labour capital was useless. But whereas 'work' might carry with it some connotations of pride or skill, 'labour' gave off nothing positive with respect to the activity itself. Even skilled workers, 'the aristocracy of labour', were content to present themselves as no more than toilers.

Leisure as a problem

There was an equally pessimistic discourse about leisure. Worn out by work, in the hours they had for leisure, men, it was said, all too often stuck to the old pleasure of drinking or whittled away their time as spectators in the new commercial world of leisure – at the music hall, or later the cinema, at the newly professionalised football, at Bank Holiday entertainments. Work at least provided some discipline, man's use of time dictated by the machine or the supervisor. 'It may well be doubted', thought John Ruskin, 'whether more distressful consequences may not have resulted from mistaken choice in play than from mistaken direction in labour.'[45] 'No man goes wrong when he is at work', wrote Frederick Atkins in 1890.[46] Lady Bell in Middlesbrough in the early twentieth century, wife of an ironmaster, was equally insistent that the danger lay in leisure: 'The resources provided for a man's leisure matter incomparably. It is during these that he may be ruined and dragged down, and not in the hours of his work.'[47]

In the 1890s people began to write about 'the Leisure Problem'. The problem was that workers didn't know how to spend their time in purposeful and uplifting ways. One observer in the 1890s wrote of factory workers that 'They believe that they are born to work; they do not see that work is but a means to live'.[48] Attempts to uplift the quality of living were rarely successful. 'Is it possible', asked the writer Walter Besant in 1884, 'that, by any persuasion, attraction, or teaching, the working men of this country can be induced to aim at those organized, highly skilled, and disciplined forms of recreation which make up the better pleasure of life?' Besant put his faith in the People's Palace, a cultural and entertainment centre in London's East

End, but he knew that he was acting against the grain, and the Palace hardly bore out his hopes.[49] Commentators, particularly those on the left, inherited the presuppositions of rational recreation, and worried that the leisure provided by private enterprise was 'invariably cheap, tawdry and demoralising'. As Robert Blatchford, editor of the *Clarion*, lamented in 1907, 'the majority of our people do not know how to enjoy themselves'.[50]

The anxiety in the upper and middle classes and in sections of the working class about the way leisure time was spent in no way abated. Take stock in the interwar years. Constance Harris in a survey of *The Use of Leisure in Bethnal Green* in the mid-1920s was almost unreservedly pessimistic, painting, as the writer of the Preface was unable to deny, 'a dismal picture'.[51] 'Leisure', wrote *The Times* in 1929, 'has become that serious thing, a "problem"; especially if it is other people's leisure'. The leader went on to describe how a speaker at the recent Industrial Welfare Conference had claimed that 'leisure does as much harm to the worker as anything else . . . Too much money may be spent on devices for killing time during the hours of leisure, or amusements are not such as to make for real bodily and mental refreshment. No sooner have work and its demands been reasonably, even scientifically, adjusted to the individual's power, than leisure proves to be an enemy.'[52] J. B. Priestley in his *English Journey* of 1934 was similarly alert to the danger that 'robot employment will alternate with robot leisure, passive amusement as standardised and impersonal as the tasks at the machines . . . The trouble is that a man does not want to work at something he despises in order to enjoy his ample periods of leisure.'[53] The title of Henry Durant's book of 1938, *The Problem of Leisure*, announced its thesis. Why, asked Durant, is leisure seen 'as a problem, one almost said a danger?' The answer lay partly in work, about which Durant was typically pessimistic: 'The main forms of work are characterized by monotonous, repetitive operations, wearying to the body and stultifying to the mind'. Without more fulfilling work, the prospects for leisure were bleak, the importance of them vital: 'On all sides educationalists and social workers say that the important questions are what people do with their spare time, how to guide their activities into the "right" channels'. The assumption here seemed to be a top-down organisation of leisure, though Durant was in fact critical of much philanthropic provision of leisure, arguing that those who took part in leisure activities should organise them.[54]

Particular forms of leisure came under the critical hammer. In 1932 a Home Office report on the impact of American films wrote about how 'this mentality of turbid showmanship, operating through the screen by shoddy conceptions of art and a glossed materialism, saps the traditional culture and disposition of this country'. They were, in the words of a Metropolitan Police magistrate, 'fouling civilisation'. As to literature, many librarians had a mission to raise taste, wanting to 'eliminate from the library the mere butterflies of fiction, the three volume novels here to-day and forgotten to-morrow', some even believing of working-class readers that 'if they have not enough energy left to read anything but trash, we should be doing them a real service if we could prevent them from reading at all'.[55]

William Beveridge in 1948 found it 'difficult to imagine any standard by which transfer of time from even the dullest form of earning by work to the filling in of a football coupon in hope of unearned wealth can be regarded as progress'. He had in mind a much higher purpose for 'the increased leisure of the democracy': the first call on that time, he wrote, 'should be the fitting them for the responsibilities of democracy in choosing leaders and deciding on public issues'.[56] But that was not what was happening. The Labour Minister of Education, George Tomlinson, in that same year, 1948, summed up a century of comment when he lamented that 'In place of real interests and worth-while amusements, people drugged themselves with constant visits to the cinema, football pools, fun fairs and all the rest of the meaningless paraphernalia of commercial entertainment'.[57] It was all thoroughly depressing and insubstantial, a 'candyfloss world' as the critic Richard Hoggart was to call it in the 1950s.[58]

Work, leisure and identity

The pessimistic evaluation needs to be set against evidence that men's sense of their own identity was intimately linked to, and shaped by, the overlapping worlds of work and leisure. That identity itself was enmeshed in notions of masculinity. 'A man, to be a man, has to work and earn his living' was how one man felt about himself in the mid-twentieth century, but masculinity could also be formulated and asserted in the pub or in sport or in a hobby.[59]

However alienating it might be in many respects, work gave many men a sense of who they were, an identity which they could be proud of and comradeship. Some workers – it is impossible even to estimate the proportion – had taken to heart the idea that had taken root by the 1830s, that, in contrast to the leisure preference eighteenth century, English workers worked harder than anyone else. As the *Mechanics Magazine* put it in 1860, 'There is no doubt whatever that the people of England work harder, mentally and physically, than the people of any other country on the face of the earth'.[60] Hard work, physical strength and endurance had become a constituent element of national pride.

Many workers also took a pride and interest in their skills and in machinery. Trade union banners present striking evidence. As Gwyn Williams wrote, the banners 'invest . . . labour with dignity and worth . . . they celebrate a craft'. They picture men at work, proud of their skills, often tracing them back to ancient sources: the Amalgamated Society of Carpenters' banner features Joseph of Nazareth, 'the most distinguished member of the craft on record'.[61] Men also liked to talk of their work. In the 1860s Thomas Wright wrote of his fellow-engineers that

> Those who when in their cups talk 'shop' – and many do, since work is the only subject on which many of them *can* talk – will begin to display their knowledge now. With no other tools or materials than the stem of a pipe, beer sloppings, and a public-house table, they will in a few minutes erect stupendous palaces, construct locomotives and steamers capable of unheard-of speed, design ordnance of hitherto undreamt of destructive powers.[62]

Engineers could only dream about the locomotives they could build, but many other workers could carry their work skills into their leisure. A carpenter in the early twentieth century 'prosecutes his craft at home and manufactures furniture and decorations for himself and family'.[63] There was pride in the skill, and often enough pride in the product. A retired engineer who had worked for Boulton and Watt in London used to encourage his grandson to play truant from school so that he could show him his workplaces – what he wanted to pass on, the grandson told me in the 1980s, was, first, a tradition of craftsmanship, and close behind it a sense of a proper masculinity. Occasionally encountering the School Attendance Officer, his grandfather would, he wrote, 'roundly abuse his impertinence and lack of masculinity for earning a dishonourable pittance as a low grade servant doing a woman's job of chasing children'.[64]

Songs suggest that work lay at the heart of people's sense of who they were. About half of the traditional songs between the seventeenth and nineteenth centuries mention the occupation of at least one of the protagonists. There were rhythmic songs to accompany work and labour songs to sing in pub or at home. Many of them link work with sexual prowess. In the nineteenth century there was a widespread song about a young man who visited his girlfriend wearing, depending on the version, a billycock, a cattle-smock, a leather apron, navvy boots and so on; whatever happened to the hero he never removed the badge of his standing or trade. The last verse of the miners' version runs:

> Come all you young maidens wherever you be,
> Beware of them colliers who are single and free,
> For their hearts do run light and their minds do run young,
> So look out for the fellow with the pit boots on!

'Songs', concludes Gerald Porter, 'integrate life and work'.[65] Or rather they used to – it's difficult to imagine a twenty-first-century work song. Pubs may still bear names like the Carpenters' Arms or the Bricklayers' Arms, but it would be surprising to find them still the resort of carpenters or bricklayers.

Leisure in the nineteenth century was often organised around the social contacts that derived from work. In the mid-nineteenth century Henry Mayhew described how the chief recreations of fancy cabinet-makers seemed to be 'card-playing, dominoes, and games that are carried on without bodily exertion'. By contrast, coopers 'are generally fond of manly exercises, such as cricket. There are very few skittle-players among them. Cards are played sometimes in the public-house on Saturday night, but not generally . . . The theatre and the public gardens, I am told, are, however, the principal recreations of the coopers.' Costermongers, too, kept themselves to themselves in their leisure, the band at twopenny hops 'provided by the costermongers, to whom the assembly is confined' and the galleries at the popular theatres on the Surrey side of the Thames dominated by them. With their devotion to sparring and boxing, to dog-fighting and pigeon fancying, with their own language, and with their willingness to cheat at cards when playing with non-costers, the costermongers had developed a way of life in leisure that was inseparable from their work.[66]

The costermongers probably had a closer relationship between work and leisure than other occupations, but, in any community where one occupation dominated, work was likely to set the tune for leisure. Crewe, for example, depended on the employment offered by the London North Western Railway Company. Paternalistic employers provided some leisure facilities, commercial interests others, but much more important were activities organised by the workers themselves through trade unions, friendly societies and above all particular workshops and departments. Dinners, dances, smoking concerts, outings, bands, choirs, dancing troupes and sport, many of these activities linked with fund-raising for good causes such as the local hospital, stemmed directly from the world of work.[67]

Ferdynand Zweig, a former Professor of Political Economy at the University of Cracow who came to London in 1940, spent much time in the 1940s and 1950s looking at people's attitude to work and concluded that there was a fundamental ambivalence, a love/hate relationship, to work. 'The miners', he reported, 'who often hate their jobs, have at the same time a deeply-felt affection for them which is often expressed in the incessant talk about the pit.' The more skilled a man, the more likely he was to enjoy his work, but comradeship could often compensate for the dullness of work. 'I can safely say', Zweig reported in 1961, 'that most men in the works I visited liked their work or even enjoyed it – of course in different degrees; although some only tolerated it and a few merely endured it.'[68]

It's important to remember this mildly positive attitude to work because there is a tendency to think that work in the past was no more than something you had to do to make a living, a burden that you shed as soon as the hours of work were over. 'Pleasure in work', Eric Hobsbawm noted, 'is commoner than one thinks.'[69]

In terms of time, however, work was becoming less dominant. How was time liberated from work spent? It is common to think of the period from the later nineteenth century as one of commercially provided 'mass leisure', and there is much to support that case, yet it does not tell the full story. First, chapels and churches became major providers of leisure. Evangelicals in mid-century began cautiously to move away from their deep suspicion of modern leisure, to accept, in the words of Marianne Farningham, a prolific contributor to the popular nonconformist press, that 'we live too fast, we work too hard, there is too great a strain both on body and mind'. We needed relaxation. She ceased to 'believe that time absolutely given up to fun and nothing else is wasted. On the contrary, so it be free from sin, it is well spent.'[70] The Young Men's Christian Association (YMCA), formed under evangelical aegis in 1844, became a forum where the pros and cons of providing amusement were debated, its gymnasium building programme pointing to the future. Churches and chapels began to use the provision of amusements as a method of recruiting and evangelising.[71] In Reading, 'A major, or the major, thing churches and chapels were doing . . . was providing a varying but remarkably uniform range of ways of using or "improving" hours not worked'.[72] Certainly up to the First World War they remained key, and often the most important, providers of leisure. This was the case, for example, in Rochdale.[73]

Second, and often linked to church or chapel, the autodidact and self-improving culture of the eighteenth and first half of the nineteenth centuries was by no means spent or overshadowed in the period from 1850 onwards. Mutual improvement societies, many linked to chapel or church, proliferated. In Keighley in Yorkshire in 1881 they attracted about 6 per cent of the male population. Working men's clubs had libraries, held classes and staged musical and theatrical productions, as did many branches of co-operative societies.[74] Urban dwellers continued to campaign for access to land where they could walk. A potent combination of nonconformist seriousness, sometimes linked to temperance, love of the countryside and often an affiliation to radical or socialist political organisations provided a framework for sociability and enjoyment. The Clarion Cycle Clubs, with over eight thousand members in 1913, were one visible sign of it. Another was the formation in the 1890s of the Co-operative Holidays Association, closely linked to the National Home Reading Union, an organisation that strove to be 'a centre of life and light for thousands of earnest workers'. In 1913 the Co-operative Holidays Association had forty-two centres and welcomed twenty thousand guests. The outdoor movement flourished in the interwar years, ramblers, cyclists, youth hostellers and holiday-makers sustaining the spirit of the nineteenth-century pioneers.[75]

Leisure time was often spent at home. Martha Loane, a district nurse, writing before the First World War, described how

> My acquaintances among the poor, and they are numerous, . . . seldom enter theatre, dancing saloon, music hall, or concert room; they seem to have little or no connection with the vast crowds hanging around football and cricket matches, or on the outskirts of racecourses; they are not often to be found listening to improving lectures, nor attending political meetings, nor crowding into police-courts, and except very early or very late in life, they are not even regular attendants at church or chapel. Such enjoyments as they have seem to me to be of an entirely domestic nature.[76]

Long before sociologists in the 1950s and 1960s began to write of the privatisation of the family, its retreat into a self-contained world, there's ample evidence that many married men with young children were focused on family life. For Loane, 'The pleasures of a married man among the poor are chiefly connected with his children. When they are too old to interest him much – fortunately they are never too young – he falls back on papering, painting, gardening, carpentry, joinery, and wood-carving.'[77] If this was true of the first decade of the twentieth century, there is little doubt that home-based leisure was on the increase. By the late 1940s William Beveridge was reasonably confident that 'the greater part of the new leisure' was 'being used as it should be used, in developing better and more understanding relations in the family at home'.[78]

This privatised life of the family became a major focus of research in the 1950s and 1960s. Couples were described as spending their spare time together at home, often in gender-determined tasks, and not engaging with people outside the home, or indeed with the world of commercialised leisure except in the form of television. In Luton in the 1960s it was typical of wives to spend what they called their spare time doing housework, shopping (sometimes with husband) and watching television, often accompanied by knitting. Husbands also watched television (but without the accompanying knitting), did do-it-yourself jobs and slept.[79] Such time was rarely perceived as 'leisure' time. As an Ealing lorry driver put it in 1970, 'Leisure time – that's a laugh. When you come home you work', or as another respondent put it: 'Leisure? No, my wife keeps me too busy for that.'[80] But home they most frequently were, particularly at the weekend. In 1970 in the London region, husbands aged between thirty and forty-nine spent 66 per cent of time on Saturdays at home and 76 per cent of time on Sundays.[81]

One way of enlivening home-based leisure, or of getting men out of the house in leisure time, was to promote 'hobbies', a movement under way from the late nineteenth century onwards. In their hobbies men seem to have used their leisure time as a kind of antidote to the experience of work.[82] Hobbies were primarily for men. 'Without a hobby', working men told Ferdynand Zweig, 'you might as well be dead.' Zweig himself seemed to agree: 'A lack of hobbies is a very dangerous sign, and a man who loses all his hobbies should see a doctor about it'. Some men would say to Zweig, 'My work is my hobby', others 'My family life is my hobby', but these were probably a minority. For Zweig, and by implication his interviewees,

> Hobbies give a man something to love and something in which to find freedom. A working man has very little freedom, and like the rest of us he must often do what he dislikes. Work is often simply something which gives him a living, something he dislikes and would not do unless he is forced to it. But in his hobbies he regains his freedom; they are often the last thing left to modern man in which he can find freedom.

For Zweig, and he was not alone in this, the necessity of hobbies was specifically modern, a consequence of 'the dullness of our industrial civilization' and of 'an over-mechanical life'. The working man, Zweig said, looks for an 'equilibrium between work and play'. As to the hobbies that working men liked, manual were much more important than cultural, though within the manual people often looked for something 'as unlike their normal work as possible'. Another feature was that hobbies that brought in some monetary or material reward were often favoured, gardening or fishing for example, or breeding greyhounds or whippets for racing.[83]

A hobby that held out the hope of monetary gain was gambling, a matter not of luck but of serious study of form and odds, whether of horses, dogs or, from the interwar years with the development of the pools, of football teams. A concern about gambling came to the fore in the late nineteenth century, testimony to its importance evident in the large circulation of the sporting press. By the 1930s 'the majority of working-class men at least bet fairly regularly'. Expenditure on the pools rose from £10 million in 1934 to £40 million in 1938. Winning the pools was 'the great vision of ending worries and giving a man the chance to decide his own destiny, to be no longer at the mercy of all that his job represents'.[84]

The hobbies men pursued frequently extended from individual honing of a skill to a mix of sociability and competition. In communities across the country, individuals matched themselves against other individuals, pubs against pubs, clubs against clubs. Billiards, bowls, boxing, brass bands, choral societies, darts, fishing, horticulture, pigeon fancying and racing, rabbit coursing, rifle shooting and whippet racing all lent themselves to competition. The scale of this competitiveness was impressive. There were twenty thousand registered anglers in Sheffield at the end of the nineteenth century, most of them engaging in competition, half a million pigeon fanciers in the country.[85] The rewards for winners were sometimes material, beef or beer or a clock, sometimes a silver-plated cup or plate, chiefly perhaps the honour and self or group satisfaction of winning. Most competitions were local, within a community or with a neighbouring community but, in brass band playing for example, it could reach up to regional or national level. How do we explain it? The obvious answer seems the most persuasive one: that in leisure, more than in work, individuals and groups could gain some sense of achievement and control – for these competitions were for the most part organised by and for the working classes.

Sport was the most visible form of competitiveness, football the example that no one could ignore. In the early twentieth century half a million or more men were playing in leagues affiliated to the Football Association.[86] Football required a playing field, and for any semi-serious club one that was enclosed and where spectators paid gate money. It was in the last quarter of the nineteenth century, coinciding with the spread of the Saturday half-holiday, that clubs and leagues multiplied. In a mining community in east Northumberland between 1893 and 1898 the number of permanent enclosed football grounds escalated from three to thirty. The replacement of the old intermittent challenge matches by leagues was of fundamental importance. As Alan Metcalfe has put it, 'Increasingly time became structured and space became enclosed. The loose time and spatial boundaries of the traditional sports were eroded and replaced by regularly scheduled competitions played in specially created, enclosed grounds.'[87]

Football was not the only sport growing in importance. Some were distinctively local. In east Northumberland, for example, it is reckoned that before the First World War potshare bowling (throwing a handmade stone ball along a mile course with as few throws as possible) and quoits had more players and spectators among miners than did football.[88] Others had wider appeal, though still often a city or regional focus. In the Bolton area, for example, in the early 1930s there were 120 teams playing recreational cricket in a network of leagues, from the Sunday School Cricket League up to the Second Division of the Bolton and District Cricket Association.[89] More widely, professional or semi-professional league cricket in the Midlands and North, and rugby league, might have a large input of middle-class money and organisation, but they were played and watched by the working class.

Watching sport was another form of male comradeship and competitiveness, support for the local team on Saturday afternoons often the highpoint of the week. What was new from the late nineteenth century was not so much the size of crowds at sporting events, for there had been large crowds in the eighteenth century, as the regularity of opportunities to watch sport. Figures for spectatorship, nevertheless, both at matches and over a season grew inexorably. The average football cup tie attendance rose from six thousand in 1888–9 to twelve thousand in 1895–6 to over twenty thousand in the first round in 1903. In 1908–9 English First Division matches were watched by six million people with an average crowd size of sixteen thousand, rising to fourteen million watching in 1937–8 with an average crowd size of thirty thousand. Cricket rivalled football as a spectator sport with the average crowd size at eighty-one county cricket matches over fourteen thousand between 1891 and 1910 and continuing to rise in the interwar period. Greyhound racing in the London area alone attracted six and a half million spectators in 1928, about nine million in 1932.[90]

Hobbies, gambling and competitive sport did nothing to diminish the central role of the pub in male working-class life. Alcohol consumption peaked in the late 1870s and was thereafter in decline. But until the 1930s expenditure on alcohol made up over half of total expenditure on leisure goods and services, and the pub remained the main space for leisure time. Publicans continued to promote, sponsor and host leisure events. A prime example was the successful fostering of darts and darts competitions in the interwar period when the importance of the pub seemed under some threat from the competition of cinema and dance hall.[91]

Leisure and the structure of time

Leisure time increasingly structured people's lives, and thereby gave them their deepest meanings. Lives and leisure were moulded by four cycles, the life cycle, the annual cycle, the weekly cycle and the daily one.

After childhood, itself increasingly identified with play, a second phase of a leisure life cycle commenced with the first earnings. The time for pleasure, for enjoyment, for social life, came in the years that lay between starting work at the school leaving age and getting married – generally about eight to ten years. Living in the parental home, teenagers would hand most of their wages to their mothers, but as their earnings rose in their late teens and early twenties they could keep more for themselves, and feel that they had earned their leisure time and expenditure. Many teenagers were too poor or too isolated in the country to benefit from what was on offer. In the rural East Riding of Yorkshire, it was reported before the First World War, 'there is nothing in the way of amusement for the young people'. But in towns there was already by the end of the nineteenth century the beginning of a 'youth culture', with distinct styles of dress, of activities and of meeting places for young people. Attendance at football matches, music halls and cinemas, and purchase of reading matter aimed at the age range became hallmarks of teenagers and those in their early twenties. In the early twentieth century they might well take part in the weekly 'monkey parades' held in most towns when groups of boys and girls paraded past each other, eying each other up, and hoping for a click – it was the speed dating of its time.[92] In the interwar years, dancing escalated in popularity – and was of course an occasion for courting.

Marriage put men under pressure. To avoid sinking into poverty, Maud Pember Reeves reported, a married man with a family earning under thirty shillings a week must never smoke, he must never take a glass of ale; he must walk to and from his work in all weathers; he must have no recreations but the continual mending of his children's boots; he must neither read nor go to the picture palaces nor take holidays, if he is to do all that social reformers expect of him when they theoretically parcel out his tiny income.[93]

Of course the ideal of extremely restrained purchase of leisure goods and services was rarely strictly adhered to. Husbands kept back money from their wages, most of it spent on alcohol. 'Throughout the early decades of the twentieth century', concludes Andrew Davies, 'the need to balance the desire for leisure with the demands of the family housekeeping was acutely important for working-class families.'[94]

Many men tried to cope with the economic strains of married life with young children by working shifts and/or overtime so as to increase their wages. One manual worker in 1970 said of overtime, 'If you've got a growing family you need it'. In the London region in 1970 as many as 44 per cent of male full-time workers, especially those who were married, were either on shift work or doing weekend work.[95] The results were inevitably disruptive of family and social life. In a Banbury aluminium factory where a nightshift was common, 'Working life is out of time with home life, with wives' cooking and shopping and sleeping, and with the children's school life, out of time too with the social life of other people'.[96] Whatever the work schedule, fatigue outside work was common. A Dagenham assembly worker, asked what he had done the previous evening, responded, 'What did I do? I can't remember.' His wife could: 'You fell asleep, that's what you did. You went to sleep at half-past six after your tea, and at ten you got up off the settee and went to bed.'[97]

The pattern of the life cycle might suggest that as the children grew up and became wage-earners, leisure opportunities for the parents would have increased. Too often, however, habits had been formed, patterns of behaviour established, that were not easily broken. The leisure industries aimed mainly at the young. As for the old, their pleasures, as Loane put it, 'are scarce, although they need them more than the young and enjoy them quite as much'.[98]

The annual cycle of leisure gave a further time structure to men's lives. As holiday times became better recognised they exercised an increasing influence on the family sense of time and on the family economy – and men saw themselves as the providers. The year was broken into segments, the dividing points being Christmas or New Year, Easter and/or Whitsun, and holiday time, either the August Bank Holiday or the Wakes Week or equivalent break. Alfred Williams described these three periods of the year, and ascribed to each a different mood: hope and rising spirits between Christmas and Easter, a 'holiday in sight' in the middle period mitigating 'the hard punishment of the work in the shed', and 'almost despair' after the holiday, 'five whole months . . . to be borne without a break in the monotony of labour'.[99] Time was measured by these events and the family economy geared towards saving in anticipation of them ('bull' weeks, as they were called, sometimes preceded by 'cow' and 'calf' weeks when extra hours were put it) or, afterwards, work to make up for time lost and debts incurred. As a Mass Observation report noted in the 1940s, 'people tend to save because they haven't enough money to budget for a holiday without saving, not because they can spare enough money to save'.[100] The most important event was the summer holiday, the longest break from work and the most expensive, for it involved not simply time lost, expenditure on travel, and for the fortunate a guest house, but also new clothing.

The prospect or memory of the annual cycle of leisure gave shape to people's lives. Visits to the seaside were remembered through souvenirs and later photos. Celebration of Christmas became national in its scope, as it had not been in the eighteenth century. Children came to be at the centre of it, as they were of other celebrations; as Lyn Murfin has written of the Lake Counties, 'Cumbrians increasingly functioned as communities through their children'.[101] Beyond the personal level, public leisure events, most of them sporting, began to replace political and royal events as markers of the year. By the mid-twentieth century the year might be paced by the Boat Race, the Grand National, the Football Association Cup Final, Derby Day, the Lords test match, Wimbledon and the last night of the Proms instead of by Queen Elizabeth I's accession, the execution of Charles I, the Restoration and the Glorious Revolution.[102]

Immediately affecting annual time was the introduction of British summer time in 1916, aimed at reducing coal consumption. In 1925 British summer time was made permanent in law. In the Second World War clocks were moved forward by an hour to maximise productivity at munitions factories and to ensure people could get home before the blackout. This was then removed after the war, though British summer time was extended to winter in 1968, only to be ended in 1971 after panics about the safety of children going to school on dark mornings. Changing the clocks forwards and backwards was one way of marking the changing of seasons.

Besides the annual cycle there was also a weekly one. Monday, as we have seen, ceased, but not entirely, to be a holiday, and was noted for absenteeism and low productivity.[103] Pay day, Friday or Saturday, was the point around which the week and the family economy revolved, Saturday, as Thomas Wright noted in 1867, already by then seen as the best day of the week.[104] The weekly structure for those in regular paid employment was paralleled in the home by a cycle that started with washday on Monday and climaxed in cleaning on Friday. These two work cycles, paid and unpaid, might be consummated in the pub, music hall or cinema on Saturday evening, leaving Sunday as a day of some anticlimax, a long lie-in almost universal, men often drifting down to the barber in the morning, Sunday dinner the big occasion – its importance such that wives often absented themselves from church or chapel in order to cook it, saving religion for the afternoon or evening.[105] 'Sunday' thought Alfred Williams, 'is the day of complete inactivity with most of the workmen . . . If the weather is dull and wet a great number stay in bed till dinner-time, and sometimes they remain there all day and night, till Monday morning comes'.[106]

The daily cycle, from Monday to Friday, was marked by rigidity: time to get up, time to get to work, time to leave work, time for some leisure in the evening. But that routine could be subverted. Sport especially, just as it had in the eighteenth and early nineteenth centuries, could induce men to take time off. In Sheffield in 1893, when managers refused the men permission to go to a big game, they 'went all the same, and now the masters simply accept the inevitable and close the works'. In Bolton in 1908 local workshops stopped for the afternoon for an important game, and in Burnley in 1909 twenty thousand looms were stopped by a Burnley versus Tottenham match.[107]

Conclusion

The pessimistic view of both work and leisure came mainly from middle-class commentators. A more optimistic one stems from sources close to working-class experience. Certainly working-class men knew that they were better off, not only economically but also psychologically, than those without work. Unemployment attacked people on many fronts, not least the financial, but the sense of loss through not working is well-attested. Walter Greenwood in *Love on the Dole* described unemployed Salford men watching work take place on the new road between Manchester and Liverpool: 'A brand new thirty-odd-mile road, magnet for unemployed men of all trades who lined the cutting, lounging in the grass. Not in the expectation of work, it was merely an interesting way of killing time.'[108] In unemployment you had to find ways to 'kill time'. Retirement, too, confronted many people with a sense of the loss of any structure to their time – of having 'time on one's hands'. In the 1940s and 1950s when retirement at pensionable age became the norm for working-class men there was much concern that they found it difficult to adjust to – not least because their standard of living declined.[109] But it was not only money that was at stake. When sociologists asked people in the early 1970s whether they would continue to work if they didn't need the money, two-thirds said they would. Exactly the same two-thirds answered in the same way in the 1990s.[110]

Many men in the early and mid-twentieth century had achieved what we might call a work–leisure balance, both sides of the balance meaningful, the two together providing a sense of identity. Work by the mid-twentieth century occupied much less of the time of workers than it had in 1850. Their representatives had taken advantage of favourable bargaining positions in time of boom to negotiate shorter daily hours, more regular weekly hours and eventually holidays with pay. There is every sign that the additional leisure time was welcome. Men's work experience did not live up to the hopes of those who preached the gospel of work, nor did their leisure match the expectations of those who thought that in leisure the level of civilisation could be raised. But 'Eight hours a day and a holiday with pay' was a slogan to which all could respond. Moreover, in contrast to the late eighteenth and early nineteenth century, leisure time was recognised as necessary and legitimate. Class feeling was still often a regulator of access to space for leisure, rational recreationists and their successors still hoped to improve the quality and facilities for leisure, the state, both national and local, acted as a licensing body for leisure activities, but the balance of power was very different to what it had been. Workers had a right, and knew that they had a right, to leisure. There were many workers, especially those who were casual or part-time, who had benefited hardly at all from these changes, but an expected pattern and goal had nevertheless spread across the country. As Hubert Llewellyn Smith put it in the 1930s update of Charles Booth's survey of *London Life and Labour*, 'all the forces at work are combining to shift the main centre of interest of a worker's life more and more from his daily work to his daily leisure'.[111] The world of the work-leisure balance was, however, for the most part, a world inhabited by only one half of the human race – by men.

Notes

1 W. E. Houghton, *The Victorian Frame of Mind, 1830–1870* (New Haven and London: Yale University Press, 1957), p. 242.

2 T. Carlyle, *Past and Present* (1843; London: Chapman and Hall, n.d.), pp. 223–31.

3 Quoted in Houghton, *Victorian Frame of Mind*, pp. 243–4.

4 S. Smiles, *Self-Help* (1859; London: John Murray, 1911), pp. vii–viii, 33.

5 Carlyle, *Past and Present*, p. 231.

6 K. Marx, *Early Writings*, ed. T. B. Bottomore (London: C. A. Watts & Co., 1963), p. 125.

7 J. Ruskin, 'The nature of Gothic', in *Unto This Last and Other Writings by John Ruskin*, ed. C. Wilmer (Harmondsworth: Penguin, 1985), p. 86.

8 W. Morris, 'Useful work versus useless toil', in *William Morris Selected Writings and Designs*, ed. A. Briggs (Harmondsworth: Penguin, 1962), pp. 118–19.

9 W. Morris, 'How we live now and how we might live', in ibid., pp. 173–5.

10 J. Rose, *The Intellectual Life of the British Working Classes* (New Haven and London: Yale University Press, 2002), pp. 41–51.

11 R. H. Tawney, *The Acquisitive Society* (1921: London: Fontana, 1961), pp. 36, 39.

12 J. de Vries, *The Industrious Revolution: Consumer Behavior and the Household Economy, 1650 to the Present* (Cambridge: Cambridge University Press, 2008), pp. 186–237.

13 R. Samuel, 'The workshop of the world: steam power and hand technology in mid-Victorian Britain', *History Workshop*, 3 (1977), 13.

14 Nunquam [Robert Blatchford], *Merrie England: A Series of Letters on the Labour Problem* (London: Clarion Office, n.d.), p. 15.

15 P. Joyce, *Work, Society and Politics: The Culture of the Factory in Later Victorian England* (Brighton: Harvester Press, 1980).

16 C. Delheim, 'The creation of a company culture: Cadburys, 1861–1931', *American Historical Review*, 92 (1987), 13–44, quoting p. 27; H. Shpayer-Makov, 'Rethinking work and leisure in late Victorian and Edwardian England: the emergence of a police subculture', *International Review of Social History*, 47 (2002), 213–41.

17 B. Beaven, *Leisure, Citizenship and Working-Class Men in Britain, 1850–1945* (Manchester: Manchester University Press, 2005), pp. 141–8.

18 A. Smith, *The Wealth of Nations*, 2 vols (1776; London: J. M. Dent & Sons, 1910), vol. I, p. 73.

19 G. Stedman Jones, *Outcast London: A Study in the Relationship between Classes in Victorian Society* (1971; Harmondsworth: Peregrine, 1976), pp. 120–2.

20 A. J. McIvor, *A History of Work in Britain, 1850–1950* (Basingstoke: Palgrave, 2001), pp. 69–70.

21 A. Williams, *Life in a Railway Factory* (London: Duckworth, 1915), p. 48.

22 Samuel, 'Workshop of the world', pp. 50–2.

23 McIvor, *Work in Britain*, pp. 54, 56.

24 K. Marx, *Capital*, 2 vols (London: J. M. Dent & Sons, 1930), vol. I, pp. 435, 438, 443; see also E. J. Hobsbawm, *Labouring Men: Studies in the History of Labour* (London: Weidenfeld and Nicolson, 1964), pp. 344–70.

25 Marx, *Capital*, vol. I, p. 445.

26 Quoted in McIvor, *Work in Britain*, p. 67.

27 Williams, *Life in a Railway Factory*, p. 5.

28 McIvor, *Work in Britain*, pp. 68–73.

29 Ibid., pp. 131, 134; G. Cross, *A Quest for Time: The Reduction of Work in Britain and France, 1840–1940* (Berkeley, Los Angeles and London: University of California Press, 1989), p. 113.

30 McIvor, *Work in Britain*, pp. 93–8.

31 Ibid., p. 110.

32 Fred Williams to the author, 24 February 2010.

33 H. Cunningham, *The Children of the Poor: Representations of Childhood since the Seventeenth Century* (Oxford: Blackwell, 1991), pp. 186–7.

34 McIvor, *Work in Britain*, pp. 116–18, 132.

35 Ibid., pp. 120, 125.

36 Quoted in ibid., pp. 146–7.

37 Quoted in K. McClelland, 'Time to work, time to live: some aspects of work and the re-formation of class in Britain, 1850–1880', in P. Joyce (ed.), *The Historical Meanings of Work* (Cambridge: Cambridge University Press, 1987), p. 205.

38 R. Fraser (ed.), *Work: Twenty Personal Accounts*, 2 vols (Harmondsworth: Penguin, 1968), vol. I, pp. 11–12, 16, 23.

39 H. Beynon, *Working for Ford* (1973: 2nd ed., Harmondsworth: Penguin, 1984), pp. 124, 129.

40 Quoted in J. Rule, 'Time, affluence and private leisure: the British working class in the 1950s and 1960s', *Labour History Review*, 66 (2001), 239.

41 R. Whipp, '"A time to every purpose": an essay on time and work', in P. Joyce (ed.), *The Historical Meanings of Work* (Cambridge: Cambridge University Press, 1987), quoting p. 226.

42 J. Benson, *The Working Class in Britain, 1850–1939* (London: Longman, 1989), pp. 29–30.

43 R. Brown, P. Brannen, J. Cousins, M. Samphier, 'Leisure in work: the "occupational culture" of shipbuilding workers', in M. Smith, S. Parker and C. Smith (eds), *Leisure and Society in Britain* (London: Allen Lane, 1973), pp. 97–110.

44 Benson, *Working Class*, pp. 16, 19–26.

45 Quoted in H. Taylor, *A Claim on the Countryside: A History of the British Outdoor Movement* (Edinburgh: Keele University Press, 1997), p. 192.

46 Quoted in D. Erdozain, *The Problem of Pleasure: Sport, Recreation and the Crisis of Victorian Religion* (Woodbridge: The Boydell Press, 2010), p. 166.

47 Lady Bell, *At the Works: A Study of a Manufacturing Town* (London: Thomas Nelson, 1911), p. 192.

48 Quoted in McClelland, 'Time to work', p. 204.

49 W. Besant, *As We Are and As We May Be* (London: Chatto & Windus, 1903), p. 287; Beaven, *Leisure, Citizenship and Working-Class Men*, pp. 30–3.

50 C. Waters, *British Socialists and the Politics of Popular Culture, 1884–1914* (Manchester: Manchester University Press, 1990), quoting pp. 8, 41, 58.

51 C. Harris, *The Use of Leisure in Bethnal Green: A Survey of Social Conditions in the Borough 1925 to 1926* (London: The Lindsey Press, 1927), p. viii.

52 C. Langhamer, *Women's Leisure in England 1920–60* (Manchester: Manchester University Press, 2000), p. 19.

53 Quoted in K. Thomas (ed.), *The Oxford Book of Work* (Oxford: Oxford University Press, 1999), p. 581.

54 H. Durant, *The Problem of Leisure* (London: George Routledge & Sons, 1938), pp. 259, 2, 251–6.

55 R. James, *Popular Culture and Working-Class Taste in Britain, 1930–39: A Round of Cheap Diversions?* (Manchester: Manchester University Press, 2010), pp. 39–40, 49.

56 W. Beveridge, *Voluntary Action: A Report on the Methods of Social Advance* (London: George Allen & Unwin, 1948), p. 286.

57 Quoted in Langhamer, *Women's Leisure*, p. 19.

58 R. Hoggart, *The Uses of Literacy* (1957; Harmondsworth: Penguin, 1958), pp. 169–201.

59 F. Zweig, *The Worker in an Affluent Society: Family Life and Industry* (London: Heinemann, 1961), p. 79.

60 Quoted in Samuel, 'Workshop of the world', p. 6.

61 G. A. Williams, 'Introduction', in J. Gorman, *Banner Bright: An Illustrated History of the Banners of the British Trade Union Movement* (Harmondsworth: Penguin, 1976), pp. 10, 83.

62 Quoted in McClelland, 'Time to work', p. 205.

63 R. McKibbin, *The Ideologies of Class: Social Relations in Britain 1880–1950* (Oxford: Clarendon Press, 1990), p. 160.

64 Charles Clark to the author, 27 March 1982.

65 G. Porter, *The English Occupational Song* (Umeå: University of Umeå, 1992), pp. 11, 19–21, 91–101; miner's song quoted in H. Cunningham, *Leisure in the Industrial Revolution c. 1780–c. 1880* (London: Croom Helm, 1980), p. 68.

66 Cunningham, *Leisure in the Industrial Revolution*, pp. 69–71.

67 A. Redfern, 'Crewe: leisure in a railway town', in J. K. Walton and J. Walvin (eds), *Leisure in Britain 1780–1939* (Manchester: Manchester University Press, 1983), pp. 117–35.

68 F. Zweig, *The British Worker* (Harmondsworth: Penguin, 1952), pp. 104–5; Zweig, *Worker in an Affluent Society*, p. 67.

69 Hobsbawm, *Labouring Men*, p. 349.

70 L. Wilson, 'Marianne Farningham: work, leisure, and the use of time', in R. N. Swanson (ed.), *The Use and Abuse of Time in Christian History* (Woodbridge: The Boydell Press, 2002), pp. 347–55.

71 Erdozain, *Problem of Pleasure*, pp. 125–244.

72 S. Yeo, *Religion and Voluntary Organisations* (London: Croom Helm, 1976), p. 185.

73 P. Wild, 'Recreation in Rochdale, 1900–1940', in J. Clarke, C. Critcher and R. Johnson (eds), *Working-Class Culture* (London: Hutchinson, 1979), pp. 141–4; see also H. McLeod, '"Thews and sinews": nonconformity and sport', in D. W. Bebbington and T. Larsen (eds), *Modern Christianity and Cultural Aspirations* (London: Sheffield Academic Press, 2003), pp. 28–46.

74 Rose, *Intellectual Life of the British Working Classes*, pp. 78–9.

75 Taylor, *A Claim on the Countryside*, pp. 151–272, quoting p. 196.

76 M. Loane, *An Englishman's Castle* (London: Edward Arnold, 1909), p. 32.

77 M. Loane, *The Next Street But One* (London: Edward Arnold, 1907), pp. 38–41; see also Yeo, *Religion and Voluntary Organisations in Crisis*, p. 306.

78 Beveridge, *Voluntary Action*, p. 273.

79 J. E. Goldthorpe, D. Lockwood, F. Bechhofer and J. Platt, *The Affluent Worker in the Class Structure* (Cambridge: Cambridge University Press, 1969), pp. 97–103.

80 M. Young and P. Willmott, *The Symmetrical Family: A Study of Work and Leisure in the London Region* (1973: Harmondsworth: Penguin, 1975), pp. 209, 205.

81 Ibid., p. 99.

82 McKibbin, *Ideologies of Class*, pp. 138–66.

83 Zweig, *The British Worker*, pp. 7–8, 150–5.

84 McKibbin, *Ideologies of Class*, pp. 101–38, quoting p. 110; R. Holt, *Sport and the British: A Modern History* (Oxford: Clarendon Press, 1989), p. 183; N. Dennis, F. Henriques and C. Slaughter, *Coal Is Our Life: An Analysis of a Yorkshire Mining Community* (London: Eyre & Spottiswoode, 1956), pp. 36–7.

85 Holt, *Sport and the British*, pp. 189, 193.

86 Ibid., p. 135.

87 A. Metcalfe, *Leisure and Recreation in a Victorian Mining Community: The Social Economy of Leisure in North-East England, 1820–1914* (London: Routledge, 2006), pp. 33, 148–50, 156; on the importance of leagues, see T. Collins, *A Social History of English Rugby Union* (London: Routledge, 2009), pp. 42–4.

88 Metcalfe, *Leisure and Recreation*, p. 79.

89 J. Williams, 'Recreational cricket in the Bolton area between the wars', in R. Holt (ed.), *Sport and the Working Class in Modern Britain* (Manchester: Manchester University Press, 1990), pp. 101–20.

90 H. Cunningham, 'Leisure and culture', in F. M. L. Thompson (ed.), *The Cambridge Social History of Britain 1750–1950*, 3 vols (Cambridge: Cambridge University Press, 1990), vol. II, pp. 314–15.

91 P. Chaplin, *Darts in England, 1900–39: A Social History* (Manchester: Manchester University Press, 2009); Cunningham, 'Leisure and culture', p. 331.

92 H. Cunningham, 'Leisure', in J. Benson (ed.), *The Working Class in England 1875–1914* (London: Croom Helm, 1985), pp. 145–6.

93 M. Pember Reeves, *Round About a Pound a Week* (1913; London: Virago, 1979), p. 152.

94 A. Davies, *Leisure, Gender and Poverty: Working Class Culture in Salford and Manchester, 1900–1939* (Buckingham: Open University Press, 1992), p. 28.

95 Young and Willmott, *Symmetrical Family*, pp. 134, 183–4.

96 M. Stacey, *Tradition and Change: A Study of Banbury* (London: Oxford University Press, 1960), p. 9.

97 Young and Willmott, *Symmetrical Family*, p. 164.

98 Loane, *The Next Street But One*, p. 40.

99 Williams, *Life in a Railway Factory*, pp. 245–51.

100 S. Barton, *Working-Class Organisations and Popular Tourism, 1840–1970* (Manchester: Manchester University Press, 2005), pp. 87, 111, 217; W. Beveridge and A. F. Wells (eds), *The Evidence for Voluntary Action* (London: George Allen and Unwin, 1949), p. 64.

101 L. Murfin, *Popular Leisure in the Lake Counties* (Manchester: Manchester University Press, 1990), pp. 33–62, 225–6; N. Armstrong, *Christmas in Nineteenth-Century England* (Manchester: Manchester University Press, 2010), pp. 45–71.

102 P. Borsay, *A History of Leisure: The British Experience since 1500* (Basingstoke: Palgrave Macmillan, 2006), pp. 162, 200–5.

103 R. Samuel, 'Mid-Victorian Mondays' (cyclostyled notes), for figures on collieries and ironworks from Report on Intemperance, 1878, and for hours at work at John Bolton's, Warrington fustian-cutters, 1863 (Children's Employment Commission); McKibbin, *Ideologies of Class*, pp. 155–6; F. Zweig, *Men in the Pits* (London: Victor Gollancz, 1949), p. 9.

104 T. Wright, *Some Habits and Customs of the Working Classes* (1867; New York: A. M. Kelley, 1967), pp. 200–1.

105 Wright, *Habits and Customs*, pp. 206–7; C. G. Brown, *The Death of Christian Britain: Understanding Secularisation, 1800–2000* (London: Routledge, 2001), pp. 133, 144.

106 Williams, *Life in a Railway Factory*, p. 254.

107 Holt, *Sport and the British*, p. 61.

108 Quoted in Davies, *Leisure, Gender and Poverty*, p. 46.

109 P. Thane, *Old Age in English History: Past Experiences, Present Issues* (Oxford: Oxford University Press, 2000), pp. 385–406.

110 Young and Willmott, *Symmetrical Family*, p. 150; R. Crompton and C. Lyonette, 'Are we all working too hard? Women, men, and changing attitudes to employment', *British Social Attitudes*, 23rd Report (2006/7), 57.

111 H. Llewellyn Smith, *The New Survey of London Life and Labour*, 9 vols (London: King, 1930–5), vol. 8, p. 36.

7

The leisured class, 1840–1970

For the upper and upper-middle classes of Victorian Britain time was structured more by leisure than by work. As Thomas Malthus explained in 1820, 'The great laws of nature have provided for the leisure of a certain portion of society'.[1] Duties and obligations of various kinds were expected of the leisured, but they were unpaid. An annual calendar, marked by regular events, many of them sporting, gave shape to their lives.

A notch down the social scale, men did have to work for pay. Attracted by the lifestyle of the leisured class, they could at least ensure that their wives and daughters, in their freedom from paid work, testified to the high status of the family. In a society which in many ways appeared to place work at the apex of its value system, it was access to a life of leisure that accorded status. But leisure could be double-edged. By the late nineteenth century and with growing volume in the twentieth, it was being claimed that the leisured class, far from being useful and busy, were simply 'the idle rich'.

The leisured class, moreover, did not escape the sense running through the nineteenth and twentieth centuries that time was speeding up. Technological developments – the railway, the telegraph, the motor car, the radio – were both sign and symbol of the increased pace of life. Many people deplored the demise of 'old leisure', of more leisurely ways of living. They worried about the stress that it entailed, particularly for those they called 'brain-workers'.

The remedy lay in 'a gospel of leisure' to parallel 'the gospel of work'. Leisure must have a serious purpose, to make people fit for more work. Such thinking was the outcome of the deep-rooted Christian and particularly evangelical anxiety that leisure might be a misuse of God's time. Reconstituted as 'recreation', leisure became more legitimate. The middle classes embraced the new gospel and were at the forefront of an expansion of leisure, especially sport, each form of it carrying its own status label.

In the twentieth century the pressures of work for upper and upper-middle-class men mounted. By the 1970s a curious reversal seemed to be happening. While the better-off were devoting more time to work, the working classes had successfully reduced their working hours. They were, it was said, becoming the new leisured class. For everyone, however, time seemed to shrink. In response, those who were able to do so – an increasing proportion of the population – strove to make the most of their leisure, and they did so by spending money on it. In 1970 a Swedish economist coined the phrase 'the harried leisure class' to describe this modern phenomenon.

This chapter traces the shift from the 'leisured class' of mid-Victorian England to the 'harried leisure class' of 1970.

From 'leisured class' to 'idle rich'

Right at the end of the nineteenth century, in 1899, Thorstein Veblen, an American sociologist, published what was to become and remains a classic, *The Theory of the Leisure Class.* The fundamental reason for the development of a leisure class, Veblen argued, was that only in some combination of conspicuous leisure and conspicuous consumption could the wealthy achieve the status that they sought. In Veblen's analysis the origins of a leisure class lay far back in time, in any society where labour was devalued as a mark of inferiority, and where leisure – 'the non-productive consumption of time' – conferred prestige. It was not, Veblen argued, that time was simply idled away. It might be spent learning dead languages or manners, the value of these lying precisely in the fact that 'they are the voucher of a life of leisure'. Another voucher of such a life was for wives to become 'the ceremonial consumers of goods' which their husbands produced. In the leisure class, therefore, women's dress had to be not only expensive but by design impractical for productive labour. 'Waste', Veblen insisted, was at the heart of the repute that a leisure class gained by conspicuous leisure and conspicuous consumption, waste of time and effort, or waste of goods and money. Sport, an archaic survival for Veblen, however much it might be justified as fostering a manly spirit or improving physical culture, exemplified this wastefulness. It wasted time, effort and resources in a non-productive activity. The waste testified to the participant's high status.[2]

The leisure or leisured class, so-named, had been in existence for over half a century by the time Veblen wrote – he didn't coin the term. In Veblen's perspective it had in fact if not in name been in existence for very much longer than that. Peter Burke, from a historian's perspective, argued for 'the invention of leisure in early modern Europe'.[3] In England this new prominence of leisure can be seen in the social life of the aristocracy and bourgeoisie in the seventeenth and eighteenth centuries, in the emerging London Season, in the spa towns and in urban assemblies. Its lifestyle became one to be envied or emulated. As Thomas Malthus noted in 1820:

> It is not the most pleasant employment to spend eight hours a day in a count-ing house. Nor will it be submitted to after the common necessaries and con-veniences of life are obtained, unless adequate motives are presented to the mind of the man of business. Among these motives is undoubtedly the desire of advancing his rank, and contending with the landlords in the enjoyment of leisure, as well as of foreign and domestic luxuries.[4]

The pursuit of conspicuous leisure and conspicuous consumption ('foreign and domestic luxuries') was the spur which prodded men of business into emulation of the rich. Leisure, as Peter Borsay has argued, was a form of cultural capital, expenditure on it in the right forms the route to social accept-ability and advance.[5]

It required the spread of the language of class before the leisured class could be named, and that happened in the 1840s. In that critical decade, the spectre of revolution hanging over it, people began to think of those at the top of the society not only as the aristocracy or the ruling or landed class but also as the leisured class. It might be assumed that it was their enemies who branded them as a leisure class. Certainly they were not immune from criticism. The *Athenaeum* in 1845 was thankful that 'the leisure classes are not more misled and perverted than they are'. The fiercely independent MP J. A. Roebuck flattered his audience at the 1849 annual Festival of the Leeds Mechanics' Institution and Literary Society by declaring that 'All the great advances in knowledge, all the great works which have been done for mankind, have not been done by the leisure class (applause), but have been done by the labour-ing classes, those who have had to work for their livelihood'.[6]

It was more usual, however, to reflect on the positive role that the leisured class could play. John Stuart Mill, in 1848, felt that it needed to justify its existence, and to broaden out. He wanted there to be a limit on the amount that anyone could bequeath to an eldest child, leading to

> a great multiplication of persons in easy circumstances, with the advantages of leisure . . . ; a class by whom the services which a nation having leisured classes is entitled to expect from them, either by their direct exertions or by the tone

they give to the feelings and taste of the public, would be rendered in a much more beneficial manner than at present.[7]

The 'services' and the 'direct exertions' which Mill referred to were spelt out more clearly by W. E. Gladstone: 'The natural condition of a healthy society', he wrote, 'is that governing functions should be discharged in the main by a leisured class.' When 'the leisured class is depressed', he went on, 'that fact indicates that a rot has found its way into the structure of society'.[8] Gladstone pointed to evidence that the 'leisured class' was growing at a faster rate than the population as a whole, but emphasised that it needed 'to be constantly recruited from the fresh, lively, healthy energies of the bosom of the nation itself'. He feared the consequences of 'a growth of luxury and enjoyment'.[9] When his son inherited the Hawarden estate in 1875, Gladstone spelt out how he thought his time should be spent, the ideal for a member of the leisured class. With responsibilities as a Member of Parliament as well as for the estate, his son

> will have a well-charged, though not an over-charged life, and will, like professional and thoroughly employed men, have to regard the bulk of your time as forestalled on behalf of duty, while a liberal residue may be available for your special pursuits and tastes, and for recreations. This is really the sound basis of life, which can never be honourable or satisfactory without adequate guarantees against frittering away, even in part, the precious gift of time.[10]

In 1897 the Whig and Liberal Unionist Eighth Duke of Devonshire was as confident as Gladstone had been twenty years previously that the leisured class was growing, but he too worried that its members might spend 'lives of useless indolence' unless the education they received had instilled the duty of public service.[11] That worry grew, and was widely expressed. Twenty-seven bishops at the Lambeth Conference in 1908 declared that the Church must put 'plainly before the rich and leisured classes the sin of idleness, the responsibility of property, the paramount duty of public service, the incompatibility of selfish luxury with professing Christianity'. There was, it was reported in 1911, an increasing desire to sell land due to 'the increasing expenditure amongst the leisured classes in England' and their desire to free themselves from the shackles of local responsibilities. In 1913 the Ninth Duke of Devonshire headed a list of the great and good who called public meetings in London and ten other towns to press home the duty of service – they were aiming especially at 'men of the educated and leisured classes'.[12]

From a Conservative perspective the worry was that society might begin to ask too much of the leisured class. In 1894 the Marquis of Salisbury warned of the dangers of so increasing the machinery of government that the leisured class withdrew from it. His nephew and successor as Conservative party leader, A. J. Balfour, agreed, warning in 1910 that 'You must have a relatively leisured class to draw upon if you want your work to be done', but he saw no signs of its increase.[13]

The leisure class's functions stretched beyond politics. In 1868 the novelist Anthony Trollope, celebrating sport, was confident that Britain possessed 'the largest and wealthiest leisure class that any country, ancient or modern, ever boasted', the existence of a leisure class a necessary precondition for the health of sport.[14] More serious, perhaps, was the responsibility lying on the leisured class to provide social services. The Social Institutes' Union, founded in 1896, was 'an organized attempt by the leisured classes to provide for the recreation of the people'. By 1904 there were institutes in Liverpool, Bradford, Nottingham, Chester, Glasgow and nine in London.[15] In the 1920s Lord Eustace Percy, the Conservative President of the Board of Education, reflecting on the attempt to set up social centres in the new housing developments at Becontree and Dagenham, claimed that voluntary effort

> was nearly always supplied by what were usually called the leisured classes . . . At Becontree there was a large mass of people, in more or less the same economic circumstances, who had no leisure save during unemployment. It was the object of the present scheme to provide something which could only be supplied by people of leisure, and if people of leisure did not live in the place themselves there was no alternative but deliberately to organize a small centre of leisured people in the area.[16]

Critics would have disputed Percy's belief in the importance of the leisured class in bringing about social reforms, but perhaps it was initiatives of the kind Percy was associated with that led Clive Bell, the art critic and leading member of the Bloomsbury set, to claim in 1928 that 'the existence of a leisured class, absolutely independent and without obligations, is the prime condition, not of civilization only, but of any sort of decent society'.[17]

The leisured class justified its existence by reference to its social duties and obligations. But it became increasingly vulnerable to the idea that its members were more appropriately termed 'the idle rich'. The attack came first from the left. At a meeting of the unemployed in London in 1894, organised by the Social Democratic Federation, a leaflet condemned 'the insults with which the idle rich repeatedly assail those upon whose unpaid labour they live'. 'The idle rich' became an easy and constant target for socialists. Philip Snowden, for example, a future Labour Chancellor of the Exchequer, spoke on 'The Abolition of the Idle Rich' at a joint meeting of the Fabian Society and the Independent Labour Party in 1912.[18] But it was not only socialists who condemned 'the idle rich'. At the Church Congress in 1895 a speaker called on the clergy to take every opportunity to denounce the 'selfishness' of 'the idle rich'.[19] The term received even wider circulation when the author of *The Revolutionist's Handbook and Pocket Companion* in Bernard Shaw's *Man and Superman* (1903), is described as 'JohnTanner, M.I.R.C. (Member of the Idle Rich Class)'.[20] It was Lloyd George, however, who embedded the term in politics. In the run-up to the second general election in 1910 he spoke on 'Social Waste' to the Liberal Christian League, identifying 'the idle rich' as one of the symptoms and causes of that waste. The speech was virulently condemned by Conservatives, but Lloyd George had effectively transformed the leisured class into the idle rich.[21] As a correspondent for *The Times* noted in 1914, 'A decade or so ago the "leisured classes" was an accepted term for those members of society who are now stigmatized as the "idle rich"'.[22]

The 'idle rich' permeated the public discourse of the interwar years. As one critic put it in 1925, 'Their pathetic efforts at expensive time killing is portrayed by society journals and furnish telling texts for the revolutionary'.[23] Hit by surtax in Snowden's 1930 budget, many of the well-off deplored the description of themselves as the 'idle rich' – they were neither idle nor rich, they claimed.[24] But to the Labour candidate in the East Woolwich by-election in 1931 'The Tory Party is the party of the Idle Rich'.[25] That rhetoric put those who might be described as the 'idle rich' on the defensive. It was not true, it was claimed, 'that the car is a monopoly of the idle rich'. It was unfortunate, it was admitted, that so many musicians 'resent Glyndebourne as opera for the idle rich'.[26]

The 'leisured class' did not disappear without trace under this assault. Its members' response to the First World War – 'the leisured classes have come out magnificently' claimed Sir Frederick Milner in 1915 – gave them some respite.[27] Towards its end, however, their demise was claimed or foreseen, sometimes from unexpected quarters. In 1918 JB Side Spring Corsets promoted its products with the claim that 'There is no leisured class, and there are no leisured women'.[28] More predictably, the socialist and historian R. H. Tawney argued that 'Those to whom a leisure class is part of an immutable order without which civilization is inconceivable, dare not admit, even to themselves, that the world is poorer, not richer, because of its existence'.[29] Intellectual young men, it was said, turned to extremism 'because of the inanity which makes up a good deal of that which is put before the leisured classes as a fit life for men to lead'. The prewar fear that the leisured might avoid their responsibilities was even more acute. 'The supply of well-educated young men', wrote Henry Hobhouse, a man with long experience in local government, in 1929, 'is deficient, partly because the leisured class of public-spirited country gentlemen is rapidly disappearing owing to increased taxation, and partly because of the superior attractions of politics and sport'. The *Board of Trade Journal* in 1930 reiterated the economic difficulties: 'So far as the leisured classes are concerned, reduced dividends, combined with higher taxation, have left them with less spending power'.[30] Increasingly they were referred to as 'the so-called "leisured classes"'.[31] Or perhaps, as Lord Eustace Percy put it bluntly in 1931, less than three years after promoting his scheme for Becontree, 'The days of a leisured class are past, never to return'.[32]

Only in war could defence be turned into attack and the 'leisured class' reclaimed for the nation. 'The idle rich', wrote a correspondent of *The Times* in 1940, 'have never been either a graceful or an envied class in this country. On the contrary, the best of its leisured classes have always been eager to cast their possible leisure aside and to take on work which – in politics, literature, science, and many other fields – has been very largely responsible for the character and greatness of the national achievement.'[33] But war only delayed an imminent death. In 1954 a correspondent for *The Times* reflected that fifty or even thirty years ago there still survived 'the stratum of society which had once been known as the Leisured Classes'. It has, however, 'long been officially extinct'.[34]

Speeding up

The leisured class did not always have a leisurely way of life. Its members were as subject as the non-leisured to a sense that life was speeding up. People felt increasingly rushed, short of time. No one, it seemed, was free of the tyranny of the calendar and the clock.

Contemporaries and many historians have had a simple technological explanation for this feeling that things were speeding up. Travel was unquestionably speeding up. The telegraph and later radio, together with faster travel, meant that space was being conquered, and time was deeply implicated. Speeding up had been evident from 1700 if not before. In the eighteenth century stage coaches, competition and better roads slashed the time of travel between towns: London to Bristol took two days in 1754, only sixteen hours in 1784.[35]

Steam vessels from 1812 onwards were speeding up first estuary and then coastal travel. In 1827 there was the first crossing of the Atlantic by steam and by 1838 the first commercial steamship service across the Atlantic. The railway, the next phase in the speeding up process, allowed people to increase their speed of travel by over 400 per cent – from twelve to fifty miles per hour.[36] The telegraph, available to the public in 1843, enabled humans to communicate with one another in an instant. In 1851 a submarine cable was laid across the Channel, and in 1866 the first successful Atlantic cable.[37]

The spread of the railways prompted a change of both practical and symbolic importance. Different parts of the country operated their own times, making timetabling difficult, London time differing from that in Plymouth by sixteen minutes. In 1840 the Great Western Railway ordered London, or Greenwich, time to be kept for all stations, and other companies followed suit. In 1852 it became possible for true Greenwich Time to be automatically transmitted every hour from the Royal Observatory by electric telegraph. There was some, but muted, resistance to the imposition of Greenwich Time, particularly in the West Country, but by 1855 98 per cent of public clocks were set to Greenwich Time. This did not mean that all clocks showed the same time, far from it. In 1908 *The Times* carried a long correspondence about the variation in time shown on London clocks, causing, so it was claimed, great difficulty in transacting business. There followed a debate on the pros and cons of electrical timekeeping. Electrification won out, and public clocks began to display the same time.[38] The most important of these public clocks, Big Ben, from 1859 became the symbol of accurate time, first for Londoners, and then from 1924, with the BBC's broadcasting of its chimes, at national level. There was at first, however, no legal basis for Greenwich Time, and this caused problems in law cases where the exact time of an event could be important. In 1880 the Definition of Time Act made Greenwich Time the legal time.[39] In 1884 Greenwich Time also became the basis for world time.[40]

Contemporaries were fully alert to speeding up. Their metaphors incorporated the new world of steam. In *Coningsby* (1844) Disraeli wrote of life being lived at 'high-pressure'. 'We rush along at high pressure', reiterated Peter W. Clayden in 1867. In 1875 W. R. Greg published a much-quoted article on 'Life at High Pressure'. 'The most salient characteristic of life in this latter portion of the 19th century', he wrote, 'is its SPEED'. It was the speed of life more than of the railway that Greg had in mind, its causes as much cultural as technological. The Victorians, he thought, were living 'without leisure and without pause – a life of *haste* – above all a life of excitement, such as haste inevitably involves – a life filled so full . . . that we have no time to reflect where we have been and whither we intend to go'.[41]

George Eliot, in *Adam Bede* (1859), gave classic expression to the sense that a leisurely approach to life had passed away:

> Leisure is gone – gone where the spinning-wheels are gone, and the pack horses, and the slow wagons, and the pedlars, who brought bargains to the doors on sunny afternoons. Ingenious philosophers tell you, perhaps, that the great work of the steam-engine is to create leisure for mankind. Do not believe them: it only creates a vacuum for eager thought to rush in. Even idleness is eager now – eager for amusement: prone to excursion-trains, art-museums, periodical literature, and exciting novels: prone even to scientific theorising, and cursory peeps through microscopes.

'Old Leisure', by contrast, was easy-going, lived in the country, and 'was fond of sauntering by the fruit-tree wall, and scenting the apricots when they were warmed by the morning sunshine'. He 'was free from that periodicity of sensations which we call post-time'.[42]

Elizabeth Gaskell was similarly aware that an old world had passed. In *Sylvia's Lovers* in 1863 she described the drawn-out bargaining in the market in Whitby in the 1790s. In those days, she wrote, 'There was leisure for all this kind of work'.[43] Eliot and Gaskell were not writing about leisure as an activity but leisure as time, or perhaps even more leisure as a cast of mind. Their writing, like that of all those who wrote about the pace of modern life, was critical and nostalgic for a simpler time. And there was no escape from the pace. The Rev. H. H. Snell, reflecting in 1901 on Queen Victoria's reign, described life at the beginning of the twentieth century:

> Lines and wires and pipes, in entangling complexity cover the face and subcutaneous tissues of the land, throbbing and pulsating every moment of the day with the conveyance of living people and living speech . . . No one has time to read his paper through before the next edition treads upon its heels with other matter of importance. The physical powers of active and responsible men are strained to their utmost to keep their places in the van of life when it is being run at such a headlong pace.[44]

In 1911 the 'super-tramp', W. H. Davies, captured the felt need to escape from this 'headlong pace' when, in two lines much-quoted throughout the century, he asked:

> What is this life, if full of care
> We have no time to stop and stare.[45]

Brain-workers – and their wives

Speeding up at work (see Chapter 6) was experienced most directly by the working-class. It also affected the middle classes, though the evidence for it is hard to reconcile with that for the relaxed working hours outlined in Chapter 5. There is no denying, however, the extent of worry about speed up and overwork. In 1851 W. R. Greg wrote about the strain and stress of existence being 'by no means confined to the lower orders. Throughout the whole community we are all called to labour too early and compelled to labour too severely and too long. We live sadly too fast.'[46] By the time he wrote 'Life at High Pressure' in 1875 it was the professions alone he had in mind: 'The eminent lawyer, the physician in full practice, the minister, and the politician who aspires to be a minister – even the literary workman, or the eager man of science – are one and all condemned to an amount and continued severity of exertion of which our grandfathers knew little'.[47]

Greg was articulating a widespread worry, evident from the 1860s, about excessive 'brainwork'. Addressing the Royal Literary Fund in 1865 the archbishop of York thought that there were 'hundreds of writers in London overworking their brains without knowing it'.[48] *The Times*, in a review article on 'Longevity and Brainwork' in 1872, accepted 'that a belief in the perils of overwork is generally entertained', though it set out to argue the opposite case, highlighting anxiety, rather than brainwork itself, as the problem. 'It is anxiety chiefly which is the cause of premature corrosion of brain', a correspondent concluded.[49] The *Lancet* agreed, arguing that 'a constant and rather high degree of intellectual activity is a preserver rather than a destroyer of nervous health'. Problems ascribed to 'over-work', it thought, were more often due to excessive use of alcohol and tobacco and to 'severe and harassing anxiety'.[50] But anxiety itself, our modern-day 'stress', could be both cause and consequence of overwork. Hard work, too much work, seemed to be an unavoidable ingredient of the modern world. Disraeli, for example, in 1879 worried about the 'deleterious effects . . . if there were no cessation from that constant toil and brainwork which must characterize a country like this, so advanced in its pursuits and civilization'.[51]

Contemporaries constantly reflected on the harmful consequences of too much brainwork, death too often the result. John Leech, the *Punch* artist, died young in 1864, the 'incessant brainwork' which had induced in him 'a peculiar irritability' being thought to blame. When the Irish politician Isaac Butt was indisposed in 1878 (he died the following year), a colleague claimed that 'There was no man now living who had gone through more brainwork than the hon. gentleman'.[52] On one day in 1887 *The Times* carried obituaries of Adolphus Warburton Moore, private secretary to Lord Randolph Churchill, who had died in Monte Carlo where he had gone 'suffering from over-work', his death 'through a too rigid subservience to duty another valuable life . . . sacrificed'; and of the Rev. Dr Stevenson formerly of Brixton Independent Church until 'compelled by over work to take rest'.[53]

The widespread belief in the dangers of overwork is nowhere better exemplified than in the fact that one man who was propagating it by the 1880s was the prophet of work, Samuel Smiles. That work called the tune, Smiles was in no doubt: 'The life of man in this world is, for the most part, a life of work . . . Every man worth calling a man should be willing and able to work.' Time must be used productively, 'made the most of': 'It is astonishing how much can be done by using up the odds and ends of time in leisure hours. We must be prompt to catch the minutes as they fly, and make them yield the treasures they contain ere they escape for ever.'

But there was, wrote Smiles in 1887, a lurking danger, particularly in middle-class occupations. 'Overwork', he claimed, 'has unfortunately become one of the vices of our age, especially in cities. In business, in learning, in law, in politics, in literature, the pace is sometimes tremendous, and the tear and wear of life becomes excessive.' Smiles was particularly worried about 'brain-workers'. 'Brain excitement', he wrote, and he did so with the authority of a doctor, 'reacts upon the nerves, the stomach, the heart, the liver, and indeed upon the entire vital framework of the system. We have few buxom and rosy-faced thinkers.'[54] Alexander Wylie in the same decade, the 1880s, was equally worried. Bewailing 'the tide of over-labour which has swept over this country with desolating effects', he found the effects of 'intemperate labour' worse among mental than manual workers: 'Its baneful effects are found in the impaired digestion, general physical debility, relaxed will, and (in extreme cases) the softened brain, clouded reason, idiocy, or madness of its devotees . . . Cases are not rare in which men of letters wear down their brains to soft pulp in a few years.'[55]

The medical profession did nothing to reduce the anxiety. George M. Beard's *American Nervousness*, published in 1881, ascribed to the increased tempo of life the spread of neurasthenia, neuralgia, nervous dyspepsia, early tooth decay and premature baldness. In England Sir James Crichton-Browne in 1892 found deaths from heart diseases, cancer and kidney disease escalating, and explained it by the tension, excitement and mobility of modern life.[56]

What were the remedies for all this worry about brainwork? Entrepreneurs sensed a new market. Drink Gerolstein, a mineral water, urged an advertisement, it is 'Invaluable to brainworkers and persons of sedentary life'. In 1889 Phosphorate of Quinine was recommended for 'Depression of Spirits arising from over-work or over-study'. The more appetising-sounding Mariami Wine, with unsolicited testimonials from the Pope, President McKinley and no fewer than eight thousand physicians, could counter-balance 'the Effects of Mental or Physical Over-work'.[57] Others urged the necessity of an annual holiday. Whereas manual labourers, always envisioned, quite unrealistically, as working on the land, kept physically fit by work, brain-workers needed recreation and holidays. R. W. Dale, preaching to the well-off Congregationalists of Birmingham in the 1860s, suggested a month's holiday in the summer.[58] 'Over-tasked by excessive brainwork', men acted on his advice, heading for respite on the continent in what by the 1880s was termed 'the tourist season'.[59]

On a wider canvas the solution to overwork lay in recreation. What Smiles called 'The gospel of leisure and recreation' had to be set alongside 'the gospel of work; and the one', he wrote, 'is as necessary for the highest happiness and wellbeing of man as the other'.[60] Time, in this perspective, was going to be divided between work time on the one hand, and leisure and recreation time on the other, the latter a necessary condition for overall wellbeing.

Smiles wrote about men. What about 'the highest happiness and wellbeing' of woman? This was of much less concern to Smiles. He was fiercely opposed to women doing too much studying – the effects on them far more serious than the effects on men.[61] There was a clear line of demarcation between work and recreation for men while for women it was never clear when one began or the other finished. But they were, according to contemporaries, as stressed as the men. Home in the new suburbs became separated from city-centre workplace, and women found themselves marginalised if not excluded altogether from running the business. They had to structure a new way of life based on the home and on cultivating and maintaining a circle of appropriate acquaintances within calling card range. To fill their time, to overfill it some thought, were what *The Times* in 1876 called 'modern amusements':

> A mingled mass of perfectly legitimate pleasures ever thrusting themselves forward in a variety of shapes, some known, some unknown, to our more easily contented ancestors, and all together making continually increasing demands upon our time, upon our money, and not least, upon our strength and powers of endurance.[62]

Leisure, it seemed, was exacting a toll on time, money and health. The modern holiday, lamented *The Times* in 1861, 'is work, and it is tiring work . . . it entails a perpetual attention to time, and all the anxieties and irritations of that responsibility'.[63]

As Veblen had seen, wives and daughters testified to the status of their husbands or fathers in the way they conducted their lives, in the clothes and jewellery that they wore. This was a serious and expensive business. It demanded unremitting adherence to a remorseless code of conduct, and to a timetable – daily, weekly and by season – that was as strict in its way as the timetable of the factory. Bernard Shaw in the 1920s noted how those whom he called 'the idle rich' 'bind themselves to a laborious routine of what they call society and pleasure which you could not impose on a parlormaid without receiving notice instantly'.[64]

If women had problems of their own, they were also, for some people, the cause of problems for their husbands. 'The modern married woman', it was asserted in 1904, makes 'ever-growing demands on her husband's time, energy, and money'. The husband as a result suffered from 'overstrain at the office, . . . seriously overworked in order to find the wherewithal for his wife's superfluous fancies and furbelows'. Moreover she made 'still more serious inroads on her husband's time', demanding that he 'dance attendance' at social functions.[65]

Dilemmas for Christians

The debates on speeding up and overwork raised fundamental issues about how time should be spent. Christians in particular had to rethink their priorities. They had a long road to travel before they could happily embrace Smiles's 'gospel of leisure and recreation'. Preachers were on hand to offer advice. They were heirs to centuries of Protestant and Puritan sermons on the account everyone would have to make as to how they had spent their time – God's time – on earth. Wilberforce in the 1790s wrote about the life of the 'nominal Christian': 'Its recreations constitute its chief business. Watering places – the sports of the field – cards! Never failing cards! – the assembly – the theatre – all contribute their aid – amusements are multiplied, and combined, and varied, "to fill up the void of a languid and listless life".'[66] For the evangelicals, accounting for time was a constant preoccupation. Fowell Buxton, who loved shooting from his Norfolk home, was uneasily aware that 'the same energy, disposed of in a different way, might have spread Bible and Missionary Societies over the Hundred of North Erpingham'. Richard Cecil allowed himself fifteen minutes each day to play the violin, but found himself unable to keep to the time allocated, and abandoned the instrument altogether.[67] Two prominent cricketers in the 1820s gave up the game on conversion to evangelical Christianity – how could they justify to God playing such a time-consuming game?[68]

The difficulty for the evangelicals was all the greater because they had constituted 'the world' and its amusements as their chief enemy. George Eliot wrote how around 1830 'Evangelicalism had cast a certain suspicion as of plague-infection over the few amusements which survived in the provinces'. Lucy Aikin described to an American in 1828 how evangelicals 'make religion exceedingly repugnant to the young and cheerful, by setting themselves against all the sports and diversions of the people'. For Edmund Gosse as a child brought up in an admittedly extreme version of an evangelical home, the hostility to 'every species of recreation' was 'a burden that could scarcely be borne'. [69]

The mid-century years saw anguished debates about precisely what kind of amusement was legitimate for the convinced Christian. 'What amusements are lawful to persons who wish to live a religious life' was, according to R. W. Dale in 1867, 'the question by which many good people are sorely perplexed. The stricter habits of our fathers are being everywhere relaxed, and there are very many who wish to do right, who know not what to think of the change; they yield to the current of the times, but yield with hesitation, discomfort, and apprehension.' Much depended on the environment in which amusements took place. Billiards in the home was acceptable, but not in the pub. Card games might similarly pass muster in the home, and provided there were no stakes. Racing was too incorrigibly linked with gambling and drinking to be acceptable. Theatre, totally off-bounds in the late eighteenth and early nineteenth centuries, was still a site of moral danger. Novel-reading, particularly for the young, had to be carefully supervised, but was acceptable: 'Sir Walter Scott regenerated fiction'.[70]

Leaving aside the question of the legitimacy of this or that form of amusement, there was a general lesson which all could endorse, though its application was aimed more at men than at women. The purpose of recreation, a word middle-class Victorians infinitely preferred to leisure, was to re-create you for work. William Wilberforce had laid out the ground rule in the 1790s: 'There can be no dispute concerning the true end of recreations. They are intended to refresh our exhausted bodily or mental powers, and restore us with renewed vigour, to the more serious occupations of life.'[71] 'Unless recreation leaves us ready and willing to begin work again', proclaimed one clergyman, 'there has been something wrong in its use.' Pleasure, said another, was 'a legitimate incident of life, but not a legitimate end'.[72] 'The object of all recreation', preached Dale, 'is to increase our capacity for work, to keep the blood pure, and the brain bright, and the temper kindly, and sweet.'[73] Not without debate, not without opposition, in the second half of the nineteenth century Christians came to accept and in many cases to embrace the idea that recreation and leisure were a legitimate and necessary part of a religious life.

The sporting solution

Physical exercise was the recreation most recommended. In his *Lawful Amusements* (1805), the evangelical George Burder sanctioned 'bodily exercise' but not much else. Charles Simeon, a potent influence on many evangelicals, held that 'exercise, constant regular and ample, is absolutely essential to a reading man's success'. He recommended riding and tennis to his students, and a daily six-mile walk.[74] With such sanction physical exercise became legitimate and from the middle of the century there was a huge investment of the upper and middle classes in the invention of sports exclusive to themselves.

The new sports were often designed for the middle-aged rather than the young. The 'lawn' games, archery, bowls, croquet and tennis, were exemplary. Their great advantage was that they could be played in private, in people's gardens. Shooting, too, enjoyed privacy on private land, and was booming. Between 1870 and 1914 the number of guns licensed rose by 148 per cent, and the number of gamekeepers from nine thousand in 1851 to twenty-three thousand in 1911.[75] In fishing there was a division, by no means entirely adhered to, between 'game' fishing (salmon, trout, grayling) for the middle classes and 'coarse' fishing (all other freshwater fish) for the working classes. Many towns had distinctly exclusive angling clubs. Yachting, cruising and climbing, all growing strongly, also had access to space that kept non-participants at a distance.

The game that best exemplified this drive for exclusivity was golf. It enjoyed extraordinary growth with over a thousand courses in England by 1914.[76] Golf required both considerable space and a lot of time. Access to land was the key issue, many areas seeing 'the systematic encroachment upon and alienation of open, often "common", land from its customary uses'.[77]

There were innumerable disputes and long-running court cases, with the law normally on the side of the golfers. 'Artisans' were sometimes allowed to play, but only early in the morning. Comparing England and Scotland in 1909, 'in the one country', it was claimed, 'golf is the amusement of a comparatively well-to-do and leisured class, in the other it is that of all classes. The artisan golfer in England is still so rare as to be a negligible quantity, while among clerks and small tradesmen the game is practically non-existent.'[78]

Sport took up time, in some sports, golf or cricket, a lot of it. In first-class cricket, wrote one commentator in the first decade of the twentieth century, 'there is a waste of time that would never be tolerated in any other pursuit'.[79] In May 1914 *The Times*, in a leading article on golf, claimed that 'No sport has yet been invented that eats so insidiously into the day's routine or makes attention to business and affairs seem so much to resemble a churlish form of asceticism'. There were thousands, it claimed, who 'twenty years ago really worked and felt bound to apologize when caught in their chance hours of relaxation' who now expected a weekend of golf as a matter of routine. If golf was ever ended, 'multitudes of men and women would miss one of their main interests in life and be utterly at a loss how to turn their leisure hours to account'.[80] Players began to excuse time on the golf course as not really leisure time, but time for establishing business contacts. Even so, there was before the First World War a growing literature on 'golf widows', women whose husbands seemed to be perpetually on the golf course.

If sport received much early support as an antidote to the pressures of 'brain-work', by the end of the century there were strong voices saying that it was taking time and attention away from more serious concerns. The *Fortnightly Review*, inclined towards liberalism, in 1897 claimed that 'It is the introduction of easier pastimes which is wasting so much time that ought to be spent, if not at the desk, at least in taking stock of oneself, in associating with other minds, and bringing out one's latent powers'. From a right-wing perspective, the problem was more serious. For W. E. Henley,

> The nation, in a dream
> Of money and love and sport, hangs at the pap
> Of well-being, and so
> Goes fattening, mellowing, dozing, rotting down
> Into a rich deliquium of decay.

Sport, some argued, could be part of the solution. The London Playing Fields Committee in 1891 solicited support from 'all who detest the thought of national degeneracy, and abhor nervousness and effeminacy'. But it was the critics of sport who increasingly commanded attention. Robert Baden-Powell, always attuned to the drift of public opinion, wrote in 1906 how 'Our fore-fathers did not depend upon games in building up the British Empire; neither have games kept it together, and certainly they will not in the future'. German victory, it was said, might be 'won on the golf-links of Britain'. [81]

The sporting solution to the problem of middle-class overwork was never uncontested. It absorbed too much time. And by the twentieth century time seemed increasingly scarce.

The harried leisure class

By the late nineteenth and running into the twentieth century there was a tension at the heart of upper and middle-class society between a desire for and participation in leisure and a sense that time was in short supply. The old Christian barriers to spending time in recreation now dismantled, leisure and consumption became more openly flaunted, more expensive and more time-consuming. Arguably these trends could be found in all ranks of society. In 1909 Charles Masterman wrote of 'the "speeding up" of living which has taken place in all classes in so marked a fashion within a generation. The whole standard of life has been sensibly raised, not so much in comfort as in ostentation.'[82] Speeding up and conspicuous consumption and leisure were inextricably linked.

It was amongst the urban elite that the tension was greatest, resulting in significant social change. Back in the 1840s and thereafter city centres had been reconstructed on monumental lines, and in them 'a new world of bour-geois leisure had opened up, encompassing public exhibitions and concerts, gentlemen's clubs, restaurants and department stores'.[83] The boundaries of this world were contained within each city, the elements of it, however, remarkably similar in all of them. Leading men in the professions, business and commerce formed an elite at the apex of civic life, in control of the key cultural and political institutions. By 1900 these self-contained worlds had broken down, the elite's attachment to their cities weakened. They began to have town houses in London, estates in Scotland, villas by the sea. As Katherine Chorley wrote of Manchester, 'Their leisure interests and recreations were elsewhere and the time they gave to civic duties dwindled. The city was no longer the centre of their cultural lives.'[84]

No one could escape the signs and sight of the new plutocracy. 'Wealth in its motor cars is conspicuous everywhere', wrote one disenchanted observer in the West Country.[85] Much of the wealth came from the City of London, and London was certainly the place where it was most conspicuously displayed. At national level, the London Season set the parameters for an annual cycle of leisure. Wealth now rivalled birth as the passport to entry. You could buy your way into London Society. Outside the Season, members of the plutocracy retreated to their country estates, entertaining, patronising suitable events in their fields of influence, shooting and hunting. Many packs of fox hounds became dependent on City of London money. Leisure was expensive.[86] And it made demands on time. R. H. Tawney caustically described it: 'London in June, when London is pleasant, the moors in August, and pheasants in October, Cannes in December and hunting in February and March; a whole world of rising bourgeoisie eager to imitate them, sedulous to make their expensive watches keep time with this preposterous calendar'.[87]

But if this move towards a wider leisured society was one trend, there was another in tension with it, the sense that time 'is an article of which there seems a great scarcity nowadays'.[88] In 1970 a Swedish economist, Staffan Linder, in *The Harried Leisure Class*, linked together these two trends. If time as a resource was scarce, people would calculate how to get a decent yield from it – they would spend more and more of their money on it. Linder was not the first to make this argument. Over a century previously, *The Times* in a leading article in 1866 had reflected how 'We work so hard, and our craving for periodical diversion becomes so strong, that no price is too high to pay for the alternative required'. The new wealthy, it continued, 'want travel, field sports, some absolute contrast to intense civilization and brainwork at high pressure', and they were prepared to pay for it.[89]

From the dawn of the twentieth century observers were beginning to claim that an extraordinary transformation was happening: the middle classes were working harder, the workers were becoming the leisured class. In 1901 Lord Avebury, opening the new Central Free Library in Hull, declared that 'Working men . . . were the leisured classes. To-day merchants, lawyers, shop assistants, and others worked much longer hours than those we were accustomed to call working men.'[90] Chairing Bovril's AGM in 1921, Sir George Lawson Johnston agreed:

> We are all workers to-day – either brain-workers or sinew-workers. The manual labourer, with a legalized tendency towards a 40-hour week; the brain-worker up to, say, 60 hours, and often unable to keep his mind off his work during the rest of his hours awake. (Hear, hear) The days of being proud of belonging to what was called a 'leisured class' are gone, and the few in good health who permanently have no occupation are rather at pains to conceal the fact.[91]

William Beveridge wrote in 1948 of 'a redistribution of leisure, giving more to those who had least, taking leisure from those who had most'.[92] Ten years later, in 1958, Sir Robert Fraser, Director-General of the Independent Television Authority, foresaw 'a whole population becoming a leisured class'.[93]

Linder picked up this change in the social rank of those with leisure. He argued that by 1970 the pressure to spend on leisure time was felt not only by the rich but also by 'the average earner'. And, in the face of majority opinion at that time, he doubted whether hours of work would continue their long decline. The pressure to produce more, thereby raising incomes and increasing consumption, would be too great. In such circumstances the orthodox distinction between 'work time' and 'free time', between work and leisure, was out of place. 'Free time' was essentially 'consumption time', and there was no end to the amount that could be consumed in it, the pressure to be able to afford this leading to a trend towards longer hours of work.[94]

Conclusion

The leisured class of Victorian England, bolstered by the new plutocracy, survived into the twentieth century, but it came under increasing political and economic pressure. Its members were portrayed as 'the idle rich', they were subject to heavy taxation, and in a democracy their political, cultural and social role could be met in other ways. The public mood had no place for the idle. 'Spare time', it was noted in 1954, 'like unearned income, has become vaguely disreputable'; when we say that we have no spare time 'it generates a vague feeling of self-righteousness'.[95] By mid-century the old leisured class was no longer discernible.

But leisure itself had far from disappeared – on the contrary it had grown in amount, in its social range, and in the legitimacy attached to it. To some it seemed that the old working class had now become the new leisured class. Many working-class people, especially women, would have found that laughable. The articulation of the idea pointed, perhaps, to something different – that middle-class men were finding it difficult to cope with the demands of their work and their desire for leisure. Short of time themselves, they imagined that working-class people had an easier time of things. They became a harried leisure class. The harried leisure class encompassed a much larger proportion of the population than had the Victorian leisure class. Its existence foreshadowed the issue that emerged in clear focus in the late twentieth century and continues into the twenty-first, how to achieve a 'work–life balance': it was there in embryo by 1970.

Notes

1 T. R. Malthus, *Principles of Political Economy*, ed. J. Pullein, 2 vols (Cambridge: Cambridge University Press, 1989), vol. I, p. 463.
2 T. Veblen, *The Theory of the Leisure Class: An Economic Study of Institutions* (1899; London: Allen and Unwin, 1925).
3 P. Burke, 'The invention of leisure in early modern Europe', *Past & Present*, 146 (1995), 136–50.
4 Quoted in J. Hatcher, 'Labour, leisure and economic thought before the nineteenth century', *Past & Present*, 160 (1998), 115.
5 P. Borsay, *A History of Leisure: The British Experience since 1500* (Basingstoke: Palgrave Macmillan, 2006), pp. 79–85, 96.
6 *Athenaeum*, 1 Feb. 1845, p. 110; Roebuck reported in *The Times*, 5 Nov. 1849.
7 J. S. Mill, *Principles of Political Economy*, ed. D. Winch (Harmondsworth: Penguin, 1970), p. 379.
8 G. M. Young, *Today and Yesterday* (London: Rupert Hart-Davis, 1948), p. 37.
9 *The Times*, 17 Feb. 1876; 4 Nov. 1879.
10 J. Morley, *The Life of William Ewart Gladstone*, 3 vols (London: Macmillan, 1903), vol. 1, pp. 345–6.
11 *The Times*, 15 Jan. 1897.
12 Ibid., 7 Sept. 1908; 27 Feb. 1911; 14 Oct. 1913.
13 Ibid., 6 Feb. 1894; 9 Apr. 1910.
14 A. Trollope (ed.), *British Sports and Pastimes* (London: Reprinted from *St Paul's Magazine*, 1868), p. 18.
15 *The Times*, 5 Feb. 1904.
16 Ibid., 7 Nov. 1928.
17 Quoted in D. L. LeMahieu, *A Culture for Democracy: Mass Communication and the Cultivated Mind in Britain Between the Wars* (Oxford: Clarendon Press, 1988), pp. 128–9.
18 *The Times*, 5 Feb. 1894; 13 Jan. 1912.
19 H. W. Hill in ibid., 12 Oct. 1895.
20 B. Shaw, *Man and Superman* (1903; Harrnondsworth: Penguin, 2004), p. 211.
21 *The Times*, 18 Oct. 1910, and, e.g., 1 Dec. 1910.
22 Ibid., 2 June 1914.
23 Ibid., 25 May 1925.
24 Ibid., 23, 25, 26, 29 Apr. 1930.
25 Ibid., 8 Apr. 1931.
26 Ibid., 17 Apr. 1933; 22 May 1937.
27 Ibid., 8 Sept. 1915.

28 Ibid., 18 Sept. 1918.

29 R. H. Tawney, *The Acquisitive Society* (1921; London: Fontana, 1961), p. 136.

30 *The Times*, 15 Oct. 1919; 9 Jan. 1929; 25 Sept. 1930.

31 E.g. ibid., 19 Feb. 1927; 6 July 1928.

32 Ibid., 20 May 1931.

33 Ibid., 7 Oct. 1940.

34 Ibid., 26 Apr. 1954.

35 D. S. Landes, *Revolution in Time: Clocks and the Making of the Modern World* (Cambridge, Mass.:, Harvard University Press, 1983), p. 228.

36 W. E. Houghton, *The Victorian Frame of Mind, 1830–1870* (New Haven and London: Yale University Press, 1957), p. 7.

37 D. Howse, *Greenwich Time and the Discovery of Longitude* (Oxford: Oxford University Press, 1980), pp. 83–4, 117–18.

38 H. Gay, 'Clock synchrony, time distribution and electrical timekeeping in Britain 1880–1925', *Past & Present*, 181 (2003), 112–18.

39 Howse, *Greenwich Time*, pp. 87–94, 107–14, 169–70; A. C. Davies, 'Greenwich and standard time', *History Today*, 28, 3 March 1978, 194–9.

40 S. Kern, *The Culture of Time and Space 1880–1918* (Cambridge, Mass.: Harvard University Press, 1983), pp. 11–12.

41 Houghton, *Victorian Frame of Mind*, pp. 6–8; Clayden quoted in P. Bailey, *Popular Culture and Performance in the Victorian City* (Cambridge: Cambridge University Press, 1998), p. 24.

42 G. Eliot, *Adam Bede* (1859; Edinburgh and London: William Blackwood and Sons, n.d.), p. 443 (Chapter 52).

43 E. Gaskell, *Sylvia's Lovers* (1863; London: Smith Elder, 1906), p. 12.

44 Quoted in S. Yeo, *Religion and Voluntary Organisations in Crisis* (London: Croom Helm, 1976), p. 294.

45 W. H. Davies, 'Leisure', in *Songs of Joy and Others* (London: Fifield, 1911).

46 Quoted in Houghton, *Victorian Frame of Mind*, p. 60.

47 Quoted in ibid., p. 6.

48 *The Times*, 12 May 1865.

49 Ibid., 24 Sept. 1872; 28 Sept. 1872.

50 *Lancet* in *The Times*, 4 Jan. 1873.

51 *The Times*, 6 May 1879.

52 Ibid., 31 Oct. 1864; 18 Jan. 1878.

53 Ibid., 3 Feb. 1887.

54 S. Smiles, *Life and Labour; Or Characteristics of Men of Industry, Culture and Genius* (1887; 3rd ed., London: John Murray, 1912), pp. 1, 4, 308, 242.

55 A. Wylie, *Labour, Leisure and Luxury* (London: Longmans, Green & Co., 1884), pp. 18–20.

56 Kern, *Culture of Time and Space*, p. 125.

57 *The Times*, 13 March 1880; 19 June 1889; 27 Dec. 1899. In the early twentieth century Eno's fruit salts, Genasprin and Sanatogen were all advertised as relieving excessive brainwork, the latter apparently used by 'nearly all the famous writers of

these days', including H. G. Wells, Arnold Bennett, John Masefield and Compton Mackenzie. *The Times*, 3 Nov. 1917; 18 Mar. 1919; 27 Nov. 1924.

58 R. W. Dale, *Week-Day Sermons* (London: Alexander Strahan & Co., 1867), pp. 260–83.

59 *The Times*, 7 July 1881.

60 Smiles, *Life and Labour*, p. 310; Herbert Spencer, too, wrote about 'The gospel of recreation': see P. Bailey, *Popular Culture and Performance in the Victorian City* (Cambridge: Cambridge University Press, 1998), p. 216.

61 Smiles, *Life and Labour*, pp. 301–3.

62 Quoted in Bailey, *Popular Culture and Performance*, p. 13.

63 Ibid., p. 17.

64 B. Shaw, *The Intelligent Woman's Guide to Socialism, Capitalism, Sovietism and Fascism*, 2 vols (1928; Harmondsworth: Pelican, 1937), Vol. 1, p. 75.

65 Cloudesley Brereton in *The Times*, 17 Sept. 1904.

66 Quoted in D. Erdozain, *The Problem of Pleasure: Sport, Recreation and the Crisis of Victorian Religion* (Woodbridge: The Boydell Press, 2010), p. 71.

67 D. Rosman, *Evangelicals and Culture* (London: Croom Helm, 1984), pp. 121, 135.

68 P. Scott, 'Cricket and the religious world in the Victorian period', *Church Quarterly*, 3 (1970), 134–44.

69 Erdozain, *Problem of Pleasure*, pp. 77–8, 83, 66.

70 Dale, *Week-Day Sermons*, pp. 218–59; Rosman, *Evangelicals and Culture*, pp. 75–80.

71 Quoted in Rosman, *Evangelicals and Culture*, p. 121.

72 Bailey, *Popular Culture*, pp. 23–4.

73 Dale, *Week-Day Sermons*, p. 237.

74 Rosman, *Evangelicals and Culture*, p. 124.

75 J. Lowerson, *Sport and the English Middle Classes 1870–1914* (Manchester: Manchester University Press, 1993), pp. 38, 192.

76 Ibid., p. 125.

77 Ibid., p. 144.

78 *The Times*, 19 Oct. 1909.

79 Lowerson, *Sport and the English Middle Classes*, p. 81.

80 *The Times*, 23 May 1914.

81 Lowerson, *Sport and the English Middle Classes*, pp. 278, 281, 285.

82 C. F. G. Masterman, *The Condition of England* (1909; ed. J. T. Boulton, London: Methuen, 1960), p. 60.

83 S. Gunn, *The Public Culture of the Victorian Middle Class: Ritual and Authority in the English Industrial City 1840–1914* (Manchester: Manchester University Press, 2007), pp. 28–9.

84 K. Chorley, *Manchester Made Them* (London: Faber & Faber, 1950), pp. 138–9; Gunn, *Public Culture*, pp. 195–6.

85 'Labour and brain-work', *The Times*, 27 March 1911. The writer was almost certainly Stephen Reynolds.

86 L. Davidoff, *The Best Circles: Society, Etiquette and the Season* (London: Croom Helm, 1973); R. Carr, *English Fox Hunting: A History* (London: Weidenfeld and Nicolson, 1976), pp. 147–52.

87 Tawney, *Acquisitive Society*, p. 36.

88 *The Times*, 2 June 1914.

89 Ibid., 6 Oct. 1866.

90 Ibid., 7 Nov. 1901.

91 Ibid., 26 Feb. 1921.

92 W. Beveridge, *Voluntary Action: A Report on Methods of Social Advance* (London: George Allen & Unwin, 1948), pp. 221–2.

93 *The Times*, 10 June 1958.

94 S. B. Linder, *The Harried Leisure Class* (New York: Columbia University Press, 1970); *The Times,* 6 Oct. 1866.

95 *The Times*, 26 Apr. 1954.

8

Towards 'work–life balance'

From the mid-nineteenth century it became common to think of time as being divided between work and leisure. To do this, however, was to see the world through the eyes of men. Women, whether or not they were in paid employment, had very little sense of time being so neatly divided into work and leisure. Work provided the dominant motif of their lives, and there was no time on the clock when it began or ended. Life was task-oriented, and there were always tasks to be done.

In the twentieth century there were fundamental changes in how women spent their time, the most crucial of them being the increased participation in the employment market by married women. In response, in the 1990s the male discourse of work and leisure began to be replaced by a female one of work–life balance, and in the twenty-first century this has become the dominant way of thinking about time.

Coinciding with this vital change was another of equal import: the long, if intermittent, decline in the hours of work since 1830 sputtered to a halt in the 1970s, and at least in some sectors of the workforce began to go into reverse. Far from fulfilling the hope and expectation of the 1960s that work time would decrease and leisure time increase, for many people work began to occupy more of their time. This trend, together with a persistently high level of unemployment, was explicable in large part by the rise of neo-liberal economics and the push for a flexible workforce.

Women and time 1900–1950

Women's experience of time was structured by the life course. Although working-class girls had more family obligations to fulfil than boys, childhood and youth were the years when time seemed relatively plentiful. Like boys, when they started earning on leaving school they tipped up their wages to their mothers, and as they grew older and earned more they were able to keep more for themselves. The space between leaving school and marriage, some eight or ten years, was a time when they could expect to be able to pay for leisure. Young women outnumbered young men in the two boom popular amusements of the interwar years, dancing and cinema. Those aged sixteen to twenty-one formed the key clientele of the Mecca dance halls of the 1930s, girls often dancing with each other. As to cinema, Miss K, a participant in a mid-twentieth-century survey, was perhaps representative of attitudes. Aged nineteen, a counter clerk at the post office, living at home, 'She says she will not marry for a long time as she wants to have years and years of fun first. Miss K is a keen cinema fan. She goes two or three times a week, and never misses the crowd outside a film premiere to see the stars arrive.'[1]

Miss K was realistic in wanting to enjoy her fun while she could. In the more affluent classes married women with a servant might 'find time hang rather heavy on their hands'.[2] But for the working and lower middle classes marriage and the coming of children marked a new phase in the life course in which women's opportunities for leisure sharply contracted. 'Really my leisure ended when I started my family' said one woman.[3] Once ended, it was never regained. Marriage normally meant the end of paid work, and women felt that, not bringing any money into the household, they hadn't earned the right to leisure.[4] This of course didn't mean that they weren't working, but rather that their work was unpaid, and without any clear boundaries daily, weekly or annually. Home and the children became the focus of life, time without any clear structure. Women amongst the poor, wrote Martha Loane, 'generally abjured, from the very day of their marriage, all pleasures but those of a strictly domestic nature'.[5] As one woman in interwar Salford put it, 'Your entertainment was your children'.[6]

Wives, as Lady Bell noted of Middlesbrough, 'have no definite intervals of leisure'.[7] In the 1930s the Women's Health Enquiry Committee found that 65 per cent of their respondents had two hours of 'leisure' a day, but this 'leisure' turned out to be 'spent in shopping, taking the baby out, mending, sewing and doing household jobs of an irregular kind which cannot be fitted into "working hours"'. Although mothers who had few children or were 'efficient managers' might find time for leisure activities outside the home, the much more common story from their 1,250 respondents was that 'such leisure time as there is is spent in some sedentary occupation as a rest from the long hours of standing – and that it is spent entirely in mending'. Quite a number of respondents, for example, never went to the cinema.[8] Many felt a weight of expectation that they would always be at home. As one woman put it, 'I believe myself that one of the biggest difficulties our mothers have is our husbands do not realise we ever need any leisure time'.[9] The outcome was that, as Seebohm Rowntree reported of York, 'working-class women with young families have far fewer hours of leisure on which they can definitely depend than the men'.[10]

Married women who were in employment, a minority in the first half of the century, were in an even worse situation as far as leisure was concerned. In Preston in Lancashire, life for one employed woman 'was all bed and work'. In the words of Mrs Macleod, who brought up a family in Salford in the interwar years,

> A treat for me was a glass of beer and a cig, I used to go out for a couple of gills on a Friday night, that was during the war. Before that, it took you all your time to get out. The pictures was my treat. You couldn't afford it. You didn't bother. And more or less you didn't have time. I used to take the children to my mother's [and then] go to work . . . 8 o'clock you started, 6 o'clock you finished. Well by the time you collected your children, took them home, gave them their tea, washed them for bed, got your husband's tea, you had no time. I did my housework of a night.[11]

Sybil Horner, a factory inspector, noted in 1933 that 'women's work often begins where it nominally ends. The house and dependants make their claims upon the woman worker. Her work is never done.'[12] The end of one kind of work, paid work, led on to the beginning of another, housework.

The Second World War for its duration changed women's lives in fundamental ways, but in its aftermath things seemed much as they had always been. 'Spare time', a concept that women were more likely to use than 'leisure', was in short supply – one-quarter of women surveyed by Mass Observation in 1947 said that they had no spare time. In the words of a forty-five-year-old mother with three children from Dagenham, 'I have no spare time. When I am through with my work I am ready to sleep.' About half of the women interviewed by Mass Observation a year later cited 'sewing, knitting and mending' as their chief leisure activity.[13] William Beveridge in 1948 confirmed the gender divide: 'Nothing short of a revolution in housing would give to the working housewife the equivalent of the two hours' additional leisure a day on five days of each week that has come to the wage-earners in the past seventy years' – 'the wage-earners' by definition male.[14] A woman, reported Ferdynand Zweig in the early 1950s, 'has little time to spare. A working man is a man of leisure compared with his working wife. The whole conception of our leisured society, society gaining in leisure with the progress of mechanisation and productivity, applies primarily to men, much less to women in jobs.' The term 'hobby', thought Zweig, 'is a purely masculine conception'.[15] Ten years later, he found that the majority of employed women 'have no hobby or only a pastime such as is often part of their domestic duties, such as knitting and darning or dressmaking. Anyway, the impression one gains is that women do not need hobbies to the same extent as men; their energies are more fully spent in the two jobs they have to combine.'[16]

Women, work and leisure

From the middle years of the twentieth century women's use of time began to change in a fundamental way. They increasingly participated in paid employment after marriage. For men the twentieth century, with extended education and old age pensions, was marked by a substantial reduction in the number of years they spent in employment. For women the opposite was the case, each birth cohort working an increasing number of years.[17] Most women were employed at some point in the life cycle right at the beginning of the twentieth century, but they tended to stop employment when they got married: as late as 1931 only 16 per cent of the female labour force was married.[18] Young women between the school leaving age and twenty-four made up nearly half of the female workforce, and an increasing percentage of them were in employment, up from 47 per cent in 1911 to 72 per cent in 1951. Moreover they had widening expectations of the jobs they might do and the rewards they might get. True, it was only with the Second World War that domestic service began to decline – and it collapsed precipitously – but already back in 1918 the War Cabinet Committee on Women in Industry noted that young women were reluctant to return to 'living-in service, except as a last resort. They want more freedom and limited hours of work.' The new jobs were in clerical work, and the earnings and sense of independence gained made these young women 'at times more prominent consumers of leisure than young men, and pioneers in the development of working-class youth culture'.[19]

It was perhaps this relatively positive experience of working before marriage for those growing up in the 1930s and 1940s that played some part in the increase in the employment of married women after 1951. In 1951 just over one-quarter of all married women aged between fifteen and fifty-nine in Britain were in employment, in 1981 62 per cent.[20] Perhaps even more remarkable was the subsequent increase in the proportion of mothers with pre-school children who were employed, up from 28 per cent in 1980 to 53 per cent in 1999.[21] The entry of married women into the labour force was accompanied by a huge increase in the numbers working part-time. Women were increasingly working full-time up to marriage or the birth of the first child, then returning to the workforce part-time as the children grew up.

These changes, already by the mid-1950s seen as the second stage of a 'revolution' in women's social and economic position and in how they spent their time, were made possible by a matching of supply and demand. The decline in the age of marriage, the increased prevalence of marriage and the raising of the school leaving age to fifteen meant that there were fewer single women on the job market. Smaller family sizes meant that child-rearing and family care occupied less of women's lives. Further, as divorce rates rose, the instability of marriages gave women the incentive to gain the skills to maintain themselves. Coinciding with increased supply, there was a demand for labour in the postwar economy, together with an ongoing shift towards jobs in the service and clerical sectors and in light industry that were likely to recruit women. The demand for labour found its supply amongst married women – as well as from immigration.[22]

There were other facilitating factors that made married women's employment both easier and more attractive. The removal of the marriage bar on many forms of employment in the 1940s and 1950s, the waning of the strong domestic role preached to women in the 1950s and Barbara Castle's Equal Pay Act of 1970 all contributed to a view that paid employment was a legitimate and workable aspiration for married women.

The spread of labour-saving appliances in the home also facilitated employment. Using evidence from time diaries kept by women, and comparing 1937 with 1961, the time spent by women doing housework moved upwards from about 400 minutes per day to about 450 minutes. The increase was particularly sharp for middle-class women who no longer had easy access to servants, but even for working-class women there was an increase up to 1952 to over 500 minutes per day, though it was down to about 450 by 1961. Thereafter, for both classes, it was down to 350–75 minutes in 1974–5. These figures match quite closely the diffusion pattern of appliances. In the mid-1930s less than two-thirds of households were wired for electricity, a proportion still at only 83.5 per cent in 1950. Clothes washing machines, fridges and vacuum cleaners had to wait on the availability of electricity. Only

7.5 per cent of households had clothes washers in 1950, rising to 63 per cent in 1970. Fridges started from an even lower base of 3.2 per cent of households having one in 1950 rising to 57.6 per cent in 1970. Just over half of households had a vacuum cleaner in 1955, but nearly three-quarters by 1960. Potentially then from the 1960s the spread of appliances does seem to have released time from housekeeping, and made it available for paid employment, though it was often noted that appliances, and the way they were advertised, encouraged greater emphasis on cleanliness, and that attempting to achieve this ate into the time otherwise released.[23]

Given these facilitating factors making married women's employment easier, it might seem obvious that the reason married women sought employment was simply that it would increase family income. A change in the family economy seems to add weight to that possibility. Throughout the nineteenth and first half of the twentieth centuries, and probably before that too, families preferred to turn to the earnings of children rather than mothers. Children, when they started work, tipped up their earnings to their mothers. In the middle of the twentieth century this ceased to be the case. Children kept at least a significant proportion of their earnings. The 'teenage consumer' identified by Mark Abrams in the 1950s began to loom large in contemporary consciousness. Was it the case, then, that mothers entered the labour market in order to replace the income previously provided by children? The chronology seems to fit, and yet in all the research asking mothers why they went to work, none mentions this possible substitution. Indeed, a rise in men's real earnings by 40 per cent between 1950 and 1968 may have made it easier at that point in time to achieve an older ideal of the male breadwinner family economy where the husband and father provided what was needed.[24]

There is no doubt, however, that the money that could be earned in employment was a vital attraction. Paying for labour-saving appliances, often bought on hire purchase credit, was an incentive for women to enter paid employment. 'The diffusion of time-saving durables', write Bowden and Offer, 'has run considerably ahead of income.' Even more was this the case for what they call 'time-using goods', radio and television, whose diffusion was much more rapid than for time-saving durables. This reflected gendered consumption patterns, men having a much greater interest in the time-using than in the time-saving durables.[25] The decision to purchase a clothes washer may have been a dominantly female decision, the finance for it coming from her earnings. Saving towards a consumer durable, TV, a washing machine, a fridge, for a better house, for holidays, were amongst the reasons women gave for wanting to go to work.[26] As Pearl Jephcott concluded from a study of married women working in Bermondsey, they did it 'to provide more generous food, better footwear, and larger wardrobes, to buy durable consumer goods, to give the family a seaside holiday, and to acquire a cheap second-hand car'.[27]

There was, however, another factor entering into the decision to enter employment: boredom and loneliness at home. Married women in employment in the late 1950s, when asked whether they would prefer to stay at home or go out to work, by a large majority preferred work, responding, for example: 'I dread the four walls'; 'Fed up at home'; 'Nothing to do at home'; 'Would worry me more to be at home'.[28] A 1965 study showed that, after the financial benefits as a reason for working, respondents put most emphasis on 'a desire for company and the wish to escape boredom'.[29] Boredom could lead to depression, particularly high for working-class women with children at home in a flat. One woman in Bermondsey with three children, living in a block of flats without a lift with eighty-five steps to negotiate to the ground, took on a night job at least partly because her daily life was so isolated. Employment could in some circumstances halve the risk of suffering from depression.[30] Social contacts established at work, therefore, encouraged women to get out of the home – 'You can have a laugh here', they said about work.[31]

Psychological reasons meshed with economic ones to explain why so many married women entered the labour market. In Bermondsey the body language of working women with their 'purposeful walk . . . contrasted strongly with the bored looks of the mothers sitting about with a single child'. Women's self-esteem rose with work. 'You do feel nice', said one, 'when you get your bit of money on a Friday and know that you've earned it.'[32]

There was, however, a price to be paid for working – a curtailment of leisure time in a period when non-employed working-class women were enjoying something of a surge in it; from just under three hours a day in 1937 up to nearly five hours in 1961 and nearly six in 1975.[33] In Bermondsey in the 1950s, where 'the women have always expected to be over-occupied', married women equated leisure with physical rest, putting your feet up, having a lie down, doing nothing. Knitting was 'the recognized time-killer' for those not working, 'loss of leisure' the price that working women paid.[34] Not much seems to have changed by the 1980s. 'Unlike their husbands', it was reported, 'the women found it difficult to define their leisure. After some thought, they cited time spent with their children in the afternoon, when domestic work was temporarily complete, as their major source of leisure.' Since my son came along, said one mother, 'my leisure time is playing with him'.[35] Married women's entrance into the labour force did give them a sense of entitlement to leisure, and they began to mark off time for their own leisure: 'Saturday night's mine', as one woman put it. But even so fatigue and other commitments often took the edge off any pleasure. One woman worker described how 'With work I am standing all day and it is very tiring. When I come in I don't want to move. I feel exhausted. I'm entitled to a little relax. I sit down with a cup of tea and a fag. That time belongs to me.' A part-time home help described how 'I spend the afternoons cleaning, and preparing the dinner. I don't have much free time. I have half an hour before the children come in from school when I have a cigarette and relax.' Married working women craved above all for time for themselves. 'If I don't get time to myself', said one, 'I get very irritable and very resentful.'[36]

Hours of work

The entry of married women into the employment market coincided with another momentous change. The long decline in hours worked, stretching back to the 1830s, came to a halt in the 1970s, and since then has in some respects gone into reverse. Until the 1970s there was an almost unquestioned assumption that hours of work would continue to decline. In the 1950s Alva Myrdal and Viola Klein reckoned that if married women entered the labour market after a period of bringing up their children the hours for both men and women could be reduced to six a day, making possible 'a complete renaissance of home life'.[37] In the 1960s reputable forecasts were that by 2000 working hours in industrialised countries would be no more than thirty hours a week for forty weeks in the year, or might even be below one thousand hours per year.[38] Robots, it was said, would replace human beings on assembly lines, and hours of work could be radically shortened, perhaps down to four hours a day or four days a week. When Rhona and Robert Rapoport in 1971 reported on what was for the time a 'highly unusual' social formation, the dual-career family, they were confident that a thirty-hour week 'may become something like full time for many professions before long'.[39]

This prognosis of the future turned out to be false. What has happened since the 1970s is complicated, and different authorities arrive at different conclusions, some asserting a rise in hours worked, others seeing a fall, both camps drawing significant conclusions from the results they have reached.[40] The difficulty in assessing what has been happening arises from the changing nature of the labour market. First, there was a decline in the proportion of jobs that were manual, from nearly two-thirds of all jobs in 1951 to 38 per cent in 1991.[41] Manual working hours, the easiest to determine, were often, before the later twentieth century, taken as a proxy for all workers' hours. That then ceased to be viable. Since manual hours were higher than the hours of all those in employment, the shift in focus from manual workers to all those in employment had a built-in tendency to suggest a reduction in hours. Second, the gender composition of those in employment changed dramatically, with women constituting 31 per cent of all those in employment in 1951, rising to 46.4 per cent in 1998.[42] Since women's full-time hours have always been less than men's (we have seen this back in the eighteenth century), it follows that if women make up a higher proportion of all employees, there will be a tendency, irrespective of other factors, for hours to fall. A third complicating factor is that an increasing proportion of women who worked did so part-time. In 1951 only 11 per cent of women who worked did so part-time, a proportion that had risen to one-third by 1971 and was over 45 per cent by the end of the century.[43] If figures conflate full-time and part-time working (as they not infrequently do), there will again be a tendency for overall hours to be seen as in decline. Fourth, changes in the labour market began to render categories such as 'full-time' or 'part-time' a decreasingly helpful way of understanding people's working lives. In a 24/7 economy shift-working became increasingly common. In addition, many workers were on short-term contracts for weeks or months without any definition of hours to be worked. Finally, there was a growth in self-employment, from 7.3 per cent of the total labour force in 1979 to 12.1 per cent in 1998, and the self-employed, by quite a considerable margin, work longer hours than the employed, for males forty-six hours in 1992 compared to forty hours for those in employment.[44]

Given these complexities, figures that purport to give trends in average working hours across the whole economy are unlikely to be particularly helpful. The figures need to be disaggregated. For full-time employees, there was remarkable stability between 1979 and 1998, 38.5 hours in 1979, 38.2 hours in 1998, with men working more hours than women. In this twenty-year period 'there is no sign of a decrease in the working hours of full-time employees'.[45] Between 1998 and 2003 hours for men fell marginally, by less than one hour per week. Hours for women are difficult to disentangle, an apparent increase of three and a half hours per week explained by an increase in the number working full-time.[46] It is possible that in so far as there was decline it owed something to Britain's partial acceptance in 1998 of the EC Working Time Directive. This laid down a limit of an average of forty-eight hours a week over a seventeen-week period that a worker can be required to work. The Working Time Regulations, however, allowed for employees to opt-out, and one-fifth of the workforce, mostly under pressure from their employers, agreed to do so. Moreover, since the hours worked by those who were self-employed also declined in this period, and they were not subject to the Working Time Regulations, there may have been other reasons for it, though what they were has eluded commentators.[47] If the focus is narrowed to full-time manual workers in manufacturing, weekly hours rose from 42.2 in 1975 to 44.2 in 1997. Break this down by gender, and the hours for men rose from 43.6 to 45.1 and those for women from 37.0 to 40.2.[48]

Figures such as these conceal a critical change, the rise of a long hours culture in certain sectors of the economy. It could be assumed for most of the twentieth century that manual workers' hours would be longer than those of others. This changed in the late twentieth century. In stark contrast to the nineteenth century, by 1970 those in managerial and professional jobs often worked longer hours than manual workers. If for Veblen the highest-status group constituted a 'leisure class', by 1970 they appeared to have less leisure time than anyone else.[49] By the mid-1970s it had become 'a feature of contemporary society that the "leisure class" – in the sense of time at their disposal – is no longer the élite. The latter, now comprising the professional/ managerial superstructures of the occupational system, work longer hours'.[50]

Working over 48 hours a week is now normally taken as the indicator of long hours. The percentage of the UK workforce so doing stood at 11 per cent in 2003, having increased between 1988 and 1998, then dipped, only to rise to 13.1 per cent in 2007.[51] Men, particularly those with children, are significantly more likely than women to work long hours; over one-third of men with children in the household worked more than 50 hours per week in 1998, a six per cent rise over the previous decade. Managers, professionals and operative and assembly workers are those most likely to work long hours. Amongst women, those working in managerial and professional occupations constitute two-thirds of the total of long hours workers.[52] If hours of work are matched with income, those in the top 10 per cent income group work over thirteen hours more a week than those in the bottom 10 per cent.[53]

For those in manual work the compensation or attraction of working long hours in the form of overtime has always been the higher rate of pay for those hours. Countries like Britain with high income inequality tend to have long hours, overtime possibly helping to compensate for low hourly rates in normal time. Manual workers who boost their pay packets through working overtime are resistant to attempts to reduce their working hours, and between 1988 and 1998 there were sharp increases for both men and women in paid overtime. Non-manual workers have no such incentive towards long hours; over two-thirds of managerial and professional long hours workers were neither paid nor given time off in lieu.[54] Nevertheless, nearly all managers, 89 per cent of them in a 2008 survey, worked over their contracted hours, and effectively did the equivalent of forty days a year in unpaid overtime.[55]

Jonathan Gershuny has suggested that, in a marked shift away from the late nineteenth-century world described by Veblen, high social status has come to be marked, not by leisure, but by being busy, by working long hours. His research indicates that those with a high degree of human capital (in terms of time spent studying, qualifications gained and so on) work longer hours than those with low human capital (those leaving education at the earliest possible moment). The 'working class' in the early twenty-first century was amongst those at the top of the social scale: it was, however, not subordinate, but superordinate.[56] Being at work, however, was not always being busy. A significant contribution to long hours was often a culture where 'being present' was taken to indicate a commitment to work, and thus to enhance promotion prospects.[57]

Long hours of work co-existed, and not accidentally, with another new phenomenon of the period since the mid-1970s – the rise and persistence of unemployment and underemployment. Trade unions in the nineteenth century bargained for shorter hours in part to reduce the likelihood of unemployment. The 'full employment' that Beveridge pressed for in the 1940s was close to a reality in the 1950s and 1960s. The weakened trade unions since the 1980s, combined with government endorsement of a 'flexible labour market', have led to a situation where some work too much, others not enough. As one study of the 1980s put it, 'The labour process of the 1980s is one of rapidly growing flexibility in labour use patterns, chronically high unemployment and underemployment.'[58] In the recession since 2008 underemployment has matched unemployment – over three million workers in 2012 would like to work longer hours, mostly the young, women and the low-skilled, those whose incomes are insufficient to meet basic needs.[59]

International comparisons shed some light on Britain's experience of working hours. Men in the UK in 2002 worked about four and a half hours longer per week than those in France and Germany, five and a half hours longer than those in Sweden, and seven hours longer than those in Denmark and the Netherlands.[60] Just over one-fifth (22 per cent) of UK men employed full-time work long hours compared to an average of one-tenth in the other EU member states. Professional women in the UK are more likely to work long hours than their EU counterparts. In short, compared to other EU states, though not to the USA, Australia and Japan, long hours are prevalent in Britain.[61]

It might be thought that there was compensation for these long hours in the greatly extended holiday time to which everyone became entitled. Already in 1950 over 90 per cent of employees had some paid holiday entitlement, but often only a week. Half a century later, in 1998, British workers gained the right to four weeks' annual paid holiday.[62] However, entitlement is one thing, exercising that entitlement another: the demands of work are such that less than half of all workers take their full holidays. In 2012 more than one-third of senior civil servants took no annual leave. Of those working long hours 71 per cent are likely to go to work on some public holidays.[63]

Work–life balance

The phrase 'work–life balance' seems to have originated in the feminist movement in the late 1970s. It was used by the Working Mothers' Association, established in 1975, an organisation that became in time first Parents at Work and then Working Families.[64] The feminists who began to put the case for work–life balance in the 1970s were arguing for policies and facilities that would make it easier for mothers to engage in paid work.

By the early 1970s it was possible to predict that the pattern of work within families was altering radically. Married women were by then a permanent and growing element in the employed labour force. At the same time, as was widely noted, relationships within families were changing. The companionate marriage began to replace the patriarchal one. In 1973, in their book *The Symmetrical Family*, Michael Young and Peter Willmott with considerable foresight described the world we now inhabit: 'By the next century . . . society will have moved from (a) one demanding job for the wife and one for the husband, through (b) two demanding jobs for the wife and one for the husband, to (c) two demanding jobs for the wife and two for the husband . . . Instead of two jobs there will be four.' If, in consequence, they wrote, 'people by their own hyper-activity threatened their own inner stability, they would slowly turn the line of march in another direction. But which?'[65]

For some twenty years after its coinage the phrase 'work–life balance' had a muted life. Only in the mid-1990s did it spring into public awareness, and it was from the outset an issue primarily for women. In 1998 the Work–Life Balance Trust was founded 'to publicise the issue of Work–Life Balance' to everyone in Britain. When it closed in 2005, its Founder President, Shirley Conran, proclaimed that it had 'accomplished what it set out to do. Most people in Britain now know what "work–life-balance" means; everyone knows whether they've got it or not; everybody wants it'. But 'everyone' was female. As the Trust's '12 step girls' guide to personal work–life balance' put it:

> The key to personal work–life-balance is: time management and realistic expecta-tions, plus life coaching and mentoring, or self-improvement courses that include self-identity and assertiveness. Very few women – even high fliers – get 10/10 for self-identity. Have working mothers ever been made to feel guilty? Yes. Do *working fathers* feel guilty? No. Have you ever seen any articles on the problems of children with *working fathers*? Never . . . That's why these 12 steps are for women only.[66]

Here, and in innumerable articles addressed to a female readership, work–life balance was seen as not only exclusively a women's issue but also one to which the solution was primarily personal – self-improvement, the establishment of self-identity, assertiveness and so on.[67]

Alongside this strand of literature, however, was a parallel one that saw work–life balance as a policy issue, one taken up by the EU in a bid to bring about what it called 'the reconciliation of work and family life'.[68] True, the achievement of work–life balance was still seen as largely a personal respons-ibility: as the Department of Trade and Industry exhorted in 2001, 'Work–life balance isn't only about families and children. Nor is it about working less. It's about working "smart". About being fresh enough to give you all you need for both work and home, without jeopardising one for the other. And it's a necessity for everyone, at whatever stage you are in your life.'[69] But there were issues beyond the personal in work–life balance policies: governments were trying to square the circle both of encouraging women to have babies at a time when the birth rate was in decline and of persuading these same women to engage in paid labour, not least in order to increase tax revenue and decrease payment on benefits. This required putting pressure on employers to devise 'family-friendly' employment practices, such as flexible working hours.[70]

Few people noted in the flurry of activity that marked the first decade of the twenty-first century that 'life' had become confined to caring for your family. Work–life balance, for example, was defined in one report as 'having a level of flexibility in your working arrangements such that you can dovetail work with home responsibilities'.[71] Life as a whole was made up of 'working arrangements' and 'home responsibilities'. Leisure had disappeared. It is possible to see some continuity in this. As we have seen, women in history have often been hard put to see any of their time as leisure and in so far as the work–life balance discourse is focused on women it continues in this vein. It is nevertheless worth recalling that in the 1970s there was an assumption that leisure would be something for everyone. When Rhona and Robert Rapoport studied *Leisure and the Family Life Cycle* (1975), they specifically focused on the interactions between family life, work and leisure. In work–life balance discourse, leisure is simply absent, or at the very least subordinate.

This has not gone unchallenged. Clare Ungerson and Sue Yeandle have pointed out that 'work–life balance' might more properly be renamed as 'Paid/Unpaid work balance'.[72] Paul Ransome has suggested that we look at the 'total responsibility burden' of each household, dividing it into three parts: 'necessary labour', one part of it paid, the other 'unpaid', and what he calls 'recreational labour', the latter covering community activities, self-care, personal time, leisure, pleasure and enjoyment. Although the experience of 'recreational labour' is essentially personal and subjective, it can nevertheless 'contribute to the infrastructural security of the household because happy household members are bound to be more productive than unhappy ones'. This reads like a secular twenty-first-century version of nineteenth-century evangelicalism, with recreation justified because it made you fitter for your important responsibilities. Ransome seems to conceive of life being constituted of, and confined to, a 'total responsibility burden', with recreation reduced to 'labour'.[73] It is a telling instance of some of the absurdities of 'work–life balance' thinking, and of how narrowly some people have come to think of time in the twenty-first century – all the more so as this is an attempt to escape from the restrictions of the work and life dichotomy.

There is another largely unquestioned feature of work–life balance thinking. 'Life' is centred on families, and almost always families consisting of parents and dependent children, despite the fact that they constituted a mere 22 per cent of households in the UK in 2006.[74] In Ransome's terms, dependent children (presumably up to the age of eighteen) are part of the 'total responsibility burden' of parents. There is no suggestion that these children, certainly as they progressed beyond infancy, might contribute to the alleviation of that burden, might do some of the unpaid work of the household. Such an assumption at the very least misrepresents reality. Many children, 175,000 of them, have important caring roles, often of disabled family members. It also encapsulates a way of thinking about children unknown before the late twentieth century, that childhood, almost indefinitely prolonged, should be as far as possible a time of irresponsibility. Most parents through history have seen children as at least in part a resource that can contribute to the family economy.[75]

To assess how women have been affected by changing experience of time use, the hours for paid work need to be set alongside those for unpaid work. Unpaid work includes shopping and the travel associated with it, cleaning, cooking, laundry, odd jobs and child care. The amount, and type, of unpaid work has been calculated from a series of time diaries from 1961 onwards. Overall, there appears to have been a steady but not dramatic increase in the amount of unpaid work for men and women from 191 minutes per day in 1961 to 218 minutes in 1995. These figures conceal the fact that both part-time and full-time employed women with children under five increased the amount of time given to unpaid labour by a considerable amount in the twenty years after 1975, by an hour and a half a day for part-timers, by seventy minutes a day for full-timers. Women overall did far more unpaid work than men. Nevertheless the gap between the genders narrowed. In 1961 women did 130 minutes more unpaid work per day than men, in 1995 90 minutes. Non-employed women did about double the amount of unpaid work that full-time employed women did.[76]

Within the overall figures for unpaid work, there is a striking increase since 1975 in time spent on child care. In 1975 non-employed women with a co-resident child under five spent just over an hour a day (62 minutes) on child care, by 1985 103 minutes, and by 1995 148 minutes.[77] It is possible that this represents less a change in behaviour than in attitude: a woman in 1975, ironing while keeping an eye on her child, might describe her time as 'housework'; by 1995 she might have seen it as child care. But even the change in attitude is important: parents now spend more time with and worry more about their children.

If the amount of time spent on paid and unpaid work is aggregated, the figures suggest a decline between 1961 and 1975 from 487 minutes a day to 458, but from then up to 1995 rough stability. For some women, for example those with children working part-time, hours of paid and unpaid work were higher in 1995 than in 1961. Overall, too, 'women do substantially more work than men', though the difference between the sexes has declined from about eighty-five minutes to about fifty minutes.[78]

What did these changes mean for the way women divided up and thought about time? The mid-1970s represented a peak for leisure time (the residue left over after paid and unpaid work and sleep), succeeded by a plateau. Daily leisure for women who were employed full-time rose from just over four hours in 1961 to nearly five hours in 1974, but only by a further six minutes by 1984. For men there was a decline in leisure time of about seven minutes per day between 1974/5 and 1983/4.[79] Over the next two decades men's leisure time hardly changed, but women's fell by about forty minutes a day, a consequence almost certainly of women being more likely than previously to be in paid work.[80]

If people are asked what they feel about their work, the responses since the late twentieth century suggest a quite sharp deterioration. Women are particularly likely to be adversely affected by the long hours culture, reporting poor health much more frequently than those women who work shorter hours. Overall, 'Long hours working is associated with (but is not proved to cause) various negative effects, such as decreased productivity, poor performance, health problems, and lower employee motivation'.[81] It's hardly surprising that over the 1990s the proportion of men reporting that they were 'very happy' with their hours declined from 35 per cent to 20 per cent, and the proportion of women from 51 per cent to 29 per cent, not least because nearly 46 per cent of men and 32 per cent of women worked more hours than they were contracted for.[82] Half or more of full-time workers said they would like less time at work, three-quarters of such workers would like more time with their families. Three-fifths of those in employment said that the demands of their job interfered with their family lives.

Long hours at work were made worse by an increase in the intensity of work and a decline in control over work. Stress levels have risen. The 1980s and 1990s 'saw a steady decline in the levels of discretion experienced by British workers' and 'unambiguous' evidence 'of a widespread intensification of work effort and its detrimental impact on well-being'.[83] In 1970 in the London region only 4 per cent of married men working full-time cited 'stress, worry and overtiredness' at work as interfering with their home and family time.[84] Contrast this with the turn of the century: between 1990 and 2001–2 the prevalence of self-reported stress caused or made worse by work more than doubled, from 207,000 to 563,000. Nearly one-fifth of British workers (five million of them) categorised their work as very or extremely stressful. Asked whether they had experienced an increase in the speed of work and the effort they put into their jobs between 1992 and 1997, 64 per cent reported the former, 61 per cent the latter. An Institute of Management Survey in 1999 found that 69 per cent of its members reported an increased workload in the previous year.[85]

Men and women differ in how they perceive work and non-work time. For men, at least until the later twentieth century, the coupling of work and leisure seemed entirely appropriate and dominated all thinking about time. The entry into paid employment of married women challenged this, and in response the language shifted towards work–life balance. But in the burgeoning literature on the work–life balance the invocation of 'life' is a rhetorical flourish, an attempt at optimism in a world where 'life' all too often turns out to be a set of obligations to home and family. The most that can be hoped for are a few snatched moments of time for oneself. The work–life balance poses a problem, rather than describing reality. It is less a balance than a tension.

Conclusion

The entry of married women into the workforce, the increase in hours of work in key sectors of the economy, the evidence of greater intensity in that work, the removal since the 1970s of what were regarded as impediments to a flexible labour force, but were actually means of preventing exploitation, have combined to produce the crisis in time use that is wrapped up and concealed by talking about work–life balance. There is a further factor in the situation, the fear of unemployment or the experience of underemployment; it can drive people to submit to conditions at work that they know are harmful to their well-being.

Flexible working hours are the widely promulgated solution to the problems of time use in the early twenty-first century. From one perspective no one can doubt its sense. But however flexible work hours become they're unlikely to produce a situation where women (and many men) feel anything other than pressed for time. Three in five of all those in employment, we need to remember, say that the demands of their job interfere with their family lives. There are of course numerous individual exceptions to this – women who have so organised their lives that they do have time to do things on their own account and for fun. As children grow and become less of a tie, organising in that way becomes easier. The widespread experience, however, is that women with children are expected to be in the paid workforce without much diminution of the norm that they will also play the major role in keeping the home and family going.

From a historical perspective the experience of time in the late twentieth and early twenty-first century, particularly for women, is unprecedented. The challenge posed by Young and Willmott in 1970 remains: if people feel threatened by their 'hyper-activity', they will eventually change direction: but what will the direction be?

Notes

1 J. J. Nott, *Music for the People: Popular Music and Dance in Interwar Britain* (Oxford: Oxford University Press, 2002), pp. 168–90; B. S. Rowntree and G. R. Lavers, *English Life and Leisure: A Social Study* (London: Longmans, Green, 1951), pp. 114–15.

2 C. F. G. Masterman, *The Condition of England* (1909; London: Methuen, 1960), p. 58.

3 C. Langhamer, *Women's Leisure in England 1920–60* (Manchester: Manchester University Press, 2000), p. 22.

4 Ibid., p. 133.

5 M. Loane, *An Englishman's Castle* (London: Edward Arnold, 1909), p. 13.

6 A. Davies, *Leisure, Gender and Poverty: Working-Class Culture in Salford and Manchester, 1900–1939* (Buckingham: Open University Press, 1992), p. 60.

7 Lady Bell, *At the Works: A Study of a Manufacturing Town* (London: Thomas Nelson, 1911), p. 236.

8 M. Spring Rice, *Working-Class Wives: Their Health and Conditions* (Harmondsworth: Penguin, 1939), pp. 108–15.

9 Ibid., p. 94.

10 Quoted in Langhamer, *Women's Leisure*, p. 157.

11 E. Roberts, 'Working-class standards of living in three Lancashire towns, 1890–1914', *International Review of Social History*, 27 (1982), p. 52; Davies, *Leisure, Gender and Poverty*, p. 59.

12 Quoted in A. J. McIvor, *A History of Work in Britain, 1880–1950* (Basingstoke: Palgrave, 2001), p. 146.

13 Langhamer, *Women's Leisure*, pp. 25, 41.

14 W. Beveridge, *Voluntary Action: A Report on the Methods of Social Advance* (London: George Allen & Unwin, 1948), p. 275.

15 F. Zweig, *Women's Life and Labour* (London: Victor Gollancz, 1952), p. 141.

16 F. Zweig, *The Worker in an Affluent Society: Family Life and Industry* (London: Heinemann, 1961), p. 186.

17 P. Johnson, 'Work over the life course', in N. Crafts, I. Gazeley and A. Newell (eds), *Work and Pay in 20th Century Britain* (Oxford: Oxford University Press, 2007), pp. 98–116.

18 G. Holloway, *Women and Work in Britain since 1840* (London: Routledge, 2005), p. 150.

19 S. Todd, *Young Women, Work, and Family in England 1918–1950* (Oxford: Oxford University Press, 2005), pp. 1, 20–4, 35, 196.

20 Holloway, *Women and Work*, p. 197.

21 D. M. Houston (ed.), *Work–Life Balance in the 21st Century* (Basingstoke: Palgrave Macmillan 2005), p. 2.

22 A. Myrdal and V. Klein, *Women's Two Roles: Home and Work* (London: Routledge & Kegan Paul, 1956), pp. 1–12, 78–89; S. Horrell, 'The household and the labour market', in N. Crafts, I. Gazeley and A. Newell (eds), *Work and Pay in 20th Century Britain* (Oxford: Oxford University Press, 2007), pp. 117–42.

23 S. Bowden and A. Offer, 'Household appliances and the use of time: the United States and Britain since the 1920s', *Economic History Review*, 48 (1994), 725–48.

24 H. Cunningham, 'The decline of child labour: labour markets and family economies in Europe and North America since 1830', *Economic History Review*, 53 (2000), 420–6; I. Gazeley, 'Manual work and pay, 1900–70', in N. Crafts, I. Gazeley and A. Newell (eds), *Work and Pay in 20th Century Britain* (Oxford: Oxford University Press, 2007), p. 70.

25 Bowden and Offer, 'Household appliances'.

26 F. Zweig, *Women's Life and Labour* (London: Victor Gollancz, 1952), p. 74; Zweig, *Worker in an Affluent Society*, p. 175.

27 P. Jephcott, *Married Women Working* (London: George Allen and Unwin, 1962), p. 165.

28 Zweig, *Worker in an Affluent Society*, pp. 172–3; see also Jephcott, *Married Women Working*, p. 109.

29 M. Young and P. Willmott, *The Symmetrical Family: A Study of Work and Leisure in the London Region* (1973; Harmondsworth: Penguin, 1975), p. 103.

30 G. W. Brown and T. Harris, *Social Origins of Depression: A Study of Psychiatric Disorder in Women* (London: Tavistock Publications, 1978), pp. 278–9; Jephcott, *Married Women Working*, pp. 110–11.

31 Zweig, *Worker in an Affluent Society*, p. 173.

32 Jephcott, *Married Working Women*, p. 108.

33 J. Gershuny, 'Technical change and "social limits"', in A. Ellis and K. Kumar (eds), *Dilemmas for Liberal Democracies* (London: Tavistock Publications, 1983), p. 40.

34 Jephcott, *Married Women Working*, p. 134.

35 F. Devine, *Affluent Workers Revisited: Privatism and the Working Class* (Edinburgh: Edinburgh University Press, 1992), p. 146.

36 Ibid., pp. 148–9; R. Deem, *All Work and No Play? A Study of Women and Leisure* (Milton Keynes: Open University Press, 1986), p. 106.

37 Myrdal and Klein, *Women's Two Roles*, pp. 192–3.

38 P. Basso, *Modern Times, Ancient Hours: Working Lives in the Twenty-first Century* (London: Verso, 2003), p. 27.

39 R. and R. Rapoport, *Dual-Career Families* (Harmondsworth: Penguin, 1971), pp. 7, 298.

40 For the opposing views, both at international level, Basso, *Modern Times*, and J. Gershuny, *Changing Times: Work and Leisure in Postindustrial Society* (Oxford: Oxford University Press, 2000).

41 D. Gallie, 'The labour force', in A. H. Halsey and J. Webb (eds), *Twentieth-Century British Social Trends* (Basingstoke: Macmillan, 2000), pp. 287–8.

42 Ibid., p. 293.

43 Ibid., p. 297.

44 Ibid., pp. 299–300; Office of National Statistics, 'Labour Force Survey'.

45 Gallie, 'Labour force', p. 307.

46 Chartered Institute of Personnel and Development (CIPD), 'Living to work' (2003).

47 CIPD, 'Working Hours in the UK', 2006; M. Bunting, *Willing Slaves: How the Overwork Culture Is Ruling Our Lives* (London: HarperCollins, 2004), p. 5.

48 Gallie, 'Labour force', pp. 306–7.

49 Young and Willmott, *Symmetrical Family*, pp. 134–41.

50 R. and R. Rapoport, *Leisure and the Family Life Cycle* (London: Routledge and Kegan Paul, 1975), p. 3.

51 *Guardian*, 28 Nov. 2007, reporting Labour Force Survey; CIPD, 'Living to work' (2003) sees a rise in the long hours culture from 10 per cent of the workforce in 1998 to 25 per cent in 2003; see also TUC, *Hard Labour: Britain's Longer Working Week* (TUC, 1995) which documents an increasing long hours culture 1984–94.

52 J. Kodz et al., 'Working long hours: a review of the evidence', www.bis.gov.uk/files/file11543.pdf.

53 T. Burchardt, 'Time and income poverty', CASE report 57, 2008, p. 37.

54 Kodz, 'Working long hours'; S. Harkness, 'Working 9 to 5?', in P. Gregg and J. Wadsworth (eds), *The State of Working Britain* (Manchester: Manchester University Press, 1999), pp. 90–4.

55 *Guardian*, 19 Feb. 2008, reporting survey by Chartered Management Institute.

56 J. Gershuny, 'Busyness as the badge of honour for the new superordinate working class', *Social Research*, 72 (2005), 287–314.

57 Kodz, 'Working long hours'.

58 G. Standing, *Unemployment and Labour Market Flexibility: The United Kingdom* (Geneva: International Labour Office, 1986), p. 136.

59 *Guardian*, 4 Sept. 2012.

60 Gallie, 'Labour force', p. 308; Bunting, *Willing Slaves*, p. 9.

61 Kodz, 'Working long hours'.

62 Gershuny and Fisher, 'Leisure', pp. 632–3.

63 Bunting, *Willing Slaves*, p. 10; CIPD, 'Living to work'; *Guardian*, 29 Jan. 2013.

64 www.workingfamilies.org.uk.

65 Young and Willmott, *Symmetrical Family*, pp. 278, 282.

66 Work–Life Balance Trust, www.w-lb.org.uk.

67 See, for example, J. Hobsbawm, *The See-Saw: 100 Ideas for Work–Life Balance* (London: Atlantic Books, 2009) which makes no mention of leisure but does recommend five minutes a day of 'me-time' (pp. 123–4).

68 Quoted in C. Ungerson and S. Yeandle, 'Care workers and work–life balance: the example of domiciliary care-workers', in D. M. Houston (ed.), *Work–Life Balance in the 21st Century* (Basingstoke: Palgrave Macmillan, 2005), p. 247.

69 Quoted in Houston (ed.), *Work–Life Balance*, p. 1.

70 J. Conaghan, 'Time to dream? Flexibility, families, and the regulation of working time', in J. Fudge and R. J. Owens (eds), *Precarious Work, Women, and the New Economy: The Challenge to Legal Norms* (Oxford: Hart Publishing, 2006), pp. 120–7.

71 A. Bell and C. Bryson, 'Work–life balance – still a "women's issue"?', *British Social Attitudes*, 22nd report, 2005/6, p. 47.

72 Ungerson and Yeandle, 'Care workers', pp. 246–62.

73 P. Ransome, 'The boundary problem in work–life balance studies: theorising the total responsibility burden', in C. Warhurst, D. R. Eikhof and A. Haunschild (eds), *Work Less, Live More? Critical Analysis of the Work–Life Boundary* (Basingstoke: Palgrave Macmillan, 2008), pp. 62–79.

74 Ibid., p. 63.

75 H. Cunningham, *The Invention of Childhood* (London: BBC Books, 2006), pp. 211–45.

76 J. Gershuny and K. Fisher, 'Leisure', in A. H. Halsey with J. Webb (eds), *Twentieth-Century British Social Trends* (Basingstoke: Macmillan, 2000), pp. 632–5.

77 Ibid., p. 633.

78 Ibid., p. 635.

79 J. Gershuny, I. Miles, S. Jones, C. Mullings, G. Thomas and S. Wyatt, 'Time budgets: preliminary analysis of a national survey', *Quarterly Journal of Social Affairs*, 2 (1986), 26–9.

80 Gershuny and Fisher, 'Leisure', p. 635.

81 Kodz, 'Working long hours', p. 7.

82 Bunting, *Willing Slaves*, pp. 10, 147.

83 F. Green, *Demanding Work: The Paradox of Job Quality in the Affluent Economy* (Princeton and Oxford: Princeton University Press, 2006), pp. 50–8, 102–7, 173–4; R. Crompton and C. Lyonette, 'Are we all working too hard? Women, men, and changing attitudes to employment', *British Social Attitudes*, 23rd report, 2006/7, 55–70.

84 Young and Willmott, *Symmetrical Family*, p. 165.

85 Bunting, *Willing Slaves*, pp. 29–30, 180.

9

Conclusion

'Nuer are fortunate': so in 1940 the anthropologist E. E. Evans-Pritchard concluded his analysis of the Nuer's sense of time, so different to that in twentieth-century England.[1] In 1700 the English had a sense of time that bore only a faint resemblance to that of the Nuer. But were they for that reason, then and subsequently, unfortunate? Has a consciousness of time been a burden?

In two interlocking senses it is hard to deny that it has. Christianity and capitalism, singly and in combination, imposed on people an acute awareness of time, whether it was time that belonged to God or time sold to an employer. It was difficult in either case not to be anxious about time, for people became accountable for time misspent or time late for work. It's tempting to argue that, though people still have to worry about being late for work, in a largely post-Christian age worry about time misspent has at least diminished. Perhaps so, but that worry can easily take a secular turn. 'Punctuality' took on its modern sense only in the eighteenth century, and remains in the twenty-first century a prime virtue for many people, the failure to adhere to it causing stress in others. The 'time management' skills that are urged upon us are a modern version of Puritan worries about the use of time.[2]

Anxiety about time is most likely in societies where the sense of time is dominantly linear rather than cyclical. If time is ever marching onwards, then any time misspent or wasted is time gone for ever; we cannot recover it. In societies, like that of the Nuer, where thinking about time is dominantly cyclical, by month with the moon, by season, there is much less likely to be a sense that time has been lost; on the contrary, it will come round again. In England in the eighteenth century a cyclical experience of time, alongside practices such as fortune-telling that came to be labelled 'superstitious', was widespread. Attempts to reform such attitudes to time were less than wholly successful, and much evidence exists of their continuance into the present. Nevertheless in the years since 1700 time sense has become more linear. People still have a clear sense of the cycle of the week or the year, but it does not dominate lives in the way it used to. If people had to describe their lives they would on the whole not do it in the way that came naturally in the eighteenth and early nineteenth centuries by rehearsing what came to be called calendar customs, from New Year to Christmas. They would be more likely to talk of a 'career', a linear way of thinking.

The life course is very different now to what it was in 1700. Lives are longer. Instead of ten per cent or less of the population being sixty or over, there are now over twenty per cent. Combined with the lengthening of childhood and the twentieth-century invention of retirement funded by pensions, this has meant that a much smaller amount of people's lives is spent working, in the sense of working for pay. For the majority of the population in 1700 work started around the age of nine or ten and ended with death or incapacity. By and large Sunday in 1700 (in ways that it is not in the twenty-first century) was a day without work, but no other day in the year was sacrosanct. Local custom might sanction other days, normally religious festivals, or even a week to celebrate the wakes, but paid holidays were unknown. Perhaps it is not surprising that in the favourable economic conditions of the late seventeenth and first half of the eighteenth centuries many workers exercised what powers they had to take other days of leisure – that they had a leisure preference.

In the second half of the eighteenth century, and particularly towards its close and into the nineteenth century, economic conditions were much less favourable. Hours of work increased, not because people were caught up in a frenzy of consumerism, but as a matter of survival. Where machinery, water- or power-driven, could begin to dictate the pace and length of work, hours became exceptionally long, and it was only a combination of worker protest and legislation that brought them under some control. From the 1830s through to the 1970s, largely through trade union action, reflecting the demands of their members, hours of work declined, by day, by week, by year. And then, since the 1970s, against the prognoses of experts, the decline has stalled or gone into reverse. In the twenty-first century another gain is being eroded as the pressure grows for the pensionable age to rise.

The change since the 1970s coincided with an increase in the size of the workforce as married women, largely excluded from it in the later nineteenth and early twentieth century, began to enter it. Women, as Mary Collier was well aware in the eighteenth century, always worked longer hours than men, and had no clear division between work and non-work time. The work and leisure division of time was a male division. Why then did women take on more work in the second half of the twentieth century? There was no single over-riding reason, and the easing of the housework burden was a precondition, but having some money of your own was perhaps the most important incentive.

If that was the case it is easy to jump to the conclusion that consumption had a higher value in the allocation of time than leisure. This case has been argued for the whole period since 1700. It is based on a misunderstanding: leisure is a form of consumption. It nearly always costs money, not simply foregone earnings that might have come from more work, but in the commercialised leisure market that has been so evident since the eighteenth century.

In the later twentieth and early twenty-first centuries the better-off began to work some of the longest hours. Overwork, and the need for some release from it, had been the subject of much comment since the mid-nineteenth century, but the pressures on time mounted. The old leisure class transmuted into Staffan Linder's 'harried leisure class'; time-poor and money-rich, they spent heavily in the limited leisure time at their disposal. At the highest levels, sceptics might point out, they managed to incorporate quite a lot of what most of the population would regard as leisure into their working hours, in the hospitality suites at Wimbledon or Lords. But it was the challenge of Linder's analysis that the majority of the population, not just the elite, constituted a 'harried leisure class', work setting the pace of their lives.

In the twenty-first century work has been accorded a value that would have pleased Thomas Carlyle. Politicians of all parties appeal to 'hard-working families'. Against this, there is a long history of hope that time at work could be reduced. William Godwin in his radical *Political Justice* of 1793 thought that in an equal society 'half an hour a day employed in manual labour by every member of the community would sufficiently supply the whole with necessaries'. John Stuart Mill expressed a more realistic hope when he wrote in 1848 that 'The desirable medium is one which mankind have not often known how to hit: when they labour, to do it with all their might, and especially with all their mind; but to devote to labour for mere pecuniary gain, fewer hours in the day, fewer days in the year, and fewer years of life'. Mill's disdain for 'mere pecuniary gain' might not have been widely shared, but it would have been reasonable to conclude by the middle of the twentieth century that what he hoped for had been achieved: workers had shorter hours, paid holidays and a retirement that stretched ahead as life expectancy rose. Looking ahead in 1930, J. M. Keynes could foresee a time when work would be reduced to three-hour shifts or a fifteen-hour week. Bertrand Russell, 'In Praise of Idleness' in 1932, thought that 'If the ordinary wage-earner worked four hours a day, there would be enough for everybody, and no unemployment'.[3] More surprising perhaps, Winston Churchill as prime minister in 1953 was hoping that if he could negotiate global peace 'we might be able to give to the working man what he has never had – leisure. A four-day week and then three days' fun.'[4]

If these hopes for less work haven't been fulfilled, the reason lies in the removal of controls over the capitalist labour market. Looking over the twentieth century, Gary Cross has argued that workers, mistakenly, shifted their goals away from more time away from work – a movement reaching its high point in the 1920s – towards more financial rewards from work. They thus spurned the opportunities for what Cross calls 'democratic leisure', and were bought off with holiday time at the expense of a greater intensity and ultimately a greater amount of time at work. In sum, they opted for money over time.[5] A more plausible narrative of what has happened is that there was a sharp divide associated with the oil crisis of 1973. Broadly speaking, from the 1930s to the 1970s workers were in an increasingly strong position to demand higher wages which they used to improve dramatically their standard of living: housing above all, but the contents of houses also, the affordable consumer durables that made life both more comfortable and less tied up with endless housework, the purchase of a car and also, particularly noticeable in the 1960s and early 1970s, a sharp rise in 'out-of-home leisure service consumption'.[6] Overtime working, which might well imply the same number of hours but with some of those hours now attracting more pay, became a price worth paying for the benefits it brought. The same went for married women seeking employment. Levels of satisfaction with work were comparatively high.

The oil crisis of 1973 ushered in a new and much less optimistic period in the world economy. In its aftermath Keynesian growth-led economics were dethroned, and monetarism became the star by which governments guided their economies. Politicians turned their eyes on the large budgets of the welfare state and started to trim them. At the same time they began to attack the powers of trade unions, the organisations which had led and brought to fruition most of the campaigns for shorter hours. In Britain these processes were initiated, with a degree of reluctance, under the Labour governments in the mid- and late 1970s, and they were adopted with enthusiasm by Margaret Thatcher when she came to power in 1979. Her model was not continental Europe but the United States, and in the free labour market of the USA hours of work had never declined to the British level, and they now started an inexorable rise. The same was about to happen in Britain. Crucial to it was the smashing of the power of the trade unions, finally accomplished with the defeat of the miners' strike in 1984. Thereafter trade unions have been a much weaker force in British society, their membership in free fall and legislation reducing their power to call strikes.

Thatcher's commitment to a free market tilted the balance away from workers towards management – and management have rarely liked to concede shorter hours. As the emphasis of the economy shifted away from manufacturing towards services and finance, the latter embodied in the City of London as an international hub for financial services, so the ability of workers to control their hours diminished. The speed up of communications and the linkages between the US and British economies, the former of course in a very different time zone to the British, reinforced pressures to move towards an economy operating 24/7. In manufacturing the shift system had since the beginning of mechanisation tried to achieve the same 24/7 outcome, but no one had pretended that that pattern of work should extend beyond particular works. Now, a 'flexible labour market' became the touchstone of the whole economy.[7]

Industrial society for over a century, Guy Standing claims, organised life 'in time blocs'. That was certainly true for men, who kept a clear demarcation between work and leisure. But now there is no 'stable time structure'. 'Hours at work' are not the same as 'hours of work', especially for those, perhaps a quarter of the adult population, who belong to 'the precariat', those who lack security in their job or their employment. The members of the precariat have to spend long hours enhancing their attraction to potential employers, 'work-for-labour' as it has been called, and of course unpaid.[8] 'Time blocs' no longer exist. 'The current norm of a nine-to-five, five-day week in paid employment', observes the New Economics Foundation, 'does not reflect the way most people use their time.' Women are beginning to think of their lives in terms of 'work–life merge' rather than 'work–life balance', where work and free time are 'seamlessly jumbled up together'.[9]

The conclusion we can draw from over three centuries is that the amount of people's lives taken up by work depended on the organised strength or otherwise of workers themselves. Where that organisation was weak, as in many parts of the economy in the late eighteenth and early nineteenth centuries, and in the period since 1970, the employers' reluctance to concede shorter hours proved dominant. Significant gains in reduction of hours were achieved in the 1830s and 1840s and in the immediate aftermath of the First World War in times of considerable worker agitation. In short, there has been a politics of time acting against the pressures from free markets. One of the notable characteristics of more recent years has been the removal of time issues from the political to the personal.[10] A typical example is *Make the Most of Your Time* issued by the School of Life in 2012. 'Minute by minute', we are told, 'hour by hour, day by day, we struggle with time', yet the solution to that struggle lies entirely in individuals changing their habits and thoughts – mostly in an entirely banal and predictable way.

Leisure was part of the market economy. For most men, work was a powerful factor in their sense of their identity, and it might shape the kind of leisure activity they followed. Leisure was never wholly free and unconstrained time. The market, reinforced by class power relationships, by strong social norms, by moral injunctions, and often by legislation, to a large extent determined leisure activities. It marked out and controlled the space for leisure, it blessed or condemned particular activities (rational recreation as against bull-baiting), it limited the time for leisure. Nevertheless, within these limits, working-class men in the nineteenth and twentieth centuries created a leisure life that made them who they were. Their love of the pub, of professional sport, of gambling and of the football pools, of music hall and of cinema, met with the disapproval of middle-class moralists who could see only 'the problem of leisure'.

Women, for the most part, participated in this world only on the margin. Cinema was the exception, and it and dance appealed primarily to women, but, particularly if married, leisure was not for them. From one angle the shift in terminology from 'work and leisure' to 'work–life balance' looks like a retreat, a diminution of the significance of leisure, but for women the notion that there was anything besides work could be seen as liberating, even if 'life' turned out, to a disappointing degree, to be looking after a family and household.

Staffan Linder in 1970 argued that 'a constant hunt to secure the basic necessities of life is presently regarded as a degrading existence. Perhaps being constantly chased by a scarcity of time will some day be recognized as an equally undignified way of life'.[11] Norbert Elias in 1984 concluded *An Essay on Time* with a similar assertion that 'the pressure of time . . . in its present form creates problems which have yet to be resolved'.[12] No one could pretend that they have yet been resolved. We are still likely to think of the Nuer as 'fortunate'. This pervasive pessimism about the present – and the immediate future – arises from a sense that in a capitalist society there is no escape from the pressures exerted by time.

There are challenges to this pessimism. Richard Sennett, while alert to what he calls 'the corrosion of character' in the new flexible capitalism, also makes a powerful call for the revival of craftsmanship, extremely time-consuming but fundamental in any worthwhile society.[13] André Gorz argues that conditions are ripe from a move away from work as the primary preoccupation and marker of identity.[14] The New Economics Foundation proposes a shift to a norm of a twenty-one-hour working week, part of a programme to safeguard natural resources, enhance social justice and relieve people from a situation where 'we live to work, work to earn, earn to consume'. Robert and Edward Skidelsky, inspired by Keynes's belief in the possibility of a fifteen-hour working week, argue for a shift in emphasis away from growth and work and towards leisure.[15] Since 1993 Tom Hodgkinson in *The Idler* has promoted the virtues of laziness. All want to see a radical change in our use of and attitude to time. History is on their side: time can be changed.

Notes

1 E. E. Evans-Pritchard, *The Nuer* (Oxford: Clarendon Press, 1940), pp. 94–104, quoting p. 103.

2 J. Shaw, 'Punctuality and the everyday ethics of time: some evidence from the Mass Observation Archive', *Time and Society*, 3 (1994), 79–97.

3 K. Thomas (ed.), *The Oxford Book of Work* (Oxford: Oxford University Press, 1999), pp. 572, 580, 583, 567.

4 Lord Moran, *Winston Churchill: The Struggle for Survival 1940–1965* (London: Constable, 1965), p. 444.

5 G. Cross, *Time and Money: The Making of Consumer Culture* (London: Routledge, 1993).

6 J. Gershuny and K. Fisher, 'Leisure', in A. H. Halsey with J. Webb, *Twentieth-Century British Social Trends* (Basingstoke: Macmillan, 2000), p. 647.

7 J. Conaghan, 'Time to dream? Flexibility, families, and the regulation of working time', in J. Fudge and R. J. Owens (eds), *Precarious Work, Women, and the New Economy: The Challenge to Legal Norms* (Oxford: Hart Publishing, 2006), pp. 114–20.

8 G. Standing, *The Precariat: The New Dangerous Class* (London: Bloomsbury Academic, 2011), pp. 10, 24, 115–31.

9 New Economics Foundation, *21 Hours. Why a Shorter Working Week Can Help Us All to Flourish in the 21st Century* (New Economics Foundation, n.d.), p. 32; G. Hinsliff, 'The Merge', *Guardian*, 1 Jan. 2013.

10 For very different attempts to politicise time, see J. Gershuny, *Changing Times: Work and Leisure in Postindustrial Society* (Oxford: Oxford University Press, 2000), and V. Bryson, *Gender and the Politics of Time: Feminist Theory and Contemporary Debates* (Bristol: The Policy Press, 2007).

11 S. B. Linder, *The Harried Leisure Class* (New York: Columbia University Press, 1970), p. 145.

12 N. Elias, *An Essay on Time* (Dublin: University College Dublin Press, 2007), p. 162.

13 R. Sennett, *The Corrosion of Character: The Personal Consequences of Work in the New Capitalism* (New York: W. W. Norton, 1998); R. Sennett, *The Craftsman* (London: Allen Lane, 2008).

14 A. Gorz, *Reclaiming Work: Beyond the Wage-Based Society* (Cambridge: Polity Press, 1999).

15 New Economics Foundation, *21 Hours*; R. and E. Skidelsky, *How Much Is Enough? The Love of Money, and the Case for the Good Life* (London: Allen Lane, 2012).

Select bibliography

Adam, B., *Timewatch: The Social Analysis of Time* (Cambridge: Polity Press, 1995)

Allen, R. C. and Weisdorf, J. L., 'Was there an "industrious revolution" before the industrial revolution? An empirical exercise for England, c. 1300–1830', *Economic History Review*, 64 (2011), 715–29

Anderson, M., 'The emergence of the modern life cycle in Britain', *Social History*, 10 (1985), 69–87

Armstrong, N., *Christmas in Nineteenth-Century England* (Manchester: Manchester University Press, 2010)

Arrowsmith, J., 'The struggle over working time in nineteenth- and twentieth-century Britain', *Historical Studies in Industrial Relations*, 13 (2002), 83–117

Bailey, P., *Leisure and Class in Victorian England: Rational Recreation and the Contest for Control, 1830–1885* (London: Routledge and Kegan Paul, 1978)

Bailey, P., *Popular Culture and Performance in the Victorian City* (Cambridge: Cambridge University Press, 1998)

Barry, J. and Brooks, C. (eds), *The Middling Sort of People: Culture, Society and Politics in England, 1550–1800* (Basingstoke: Macmillan, 1994)

Barton, S., *Working-Class Organisations and Popular Tourism, 1840–1970* (Manchester: Manchester University Press, 2005)

Beaven, B., *Leisure, Citizenship and Working-Class Men in Britain 1850–1945* (Manchester: Manchester University Press, 2005)

Behagg, C., 'Controlling the product: work, time and the early industrial workforce in Britain, 1800–1850', in G. Cross (ed.), *Worktime and Industrialization: An International History* (Philadelphia: Temple University Press, 1988), 41–58

Bienefeld, M. A., *Working Hours in British Industry: An Economic History* (London: Weidenfeld and Nicolson, 1972)

Blanchard, I. (ed.), *Labour and Leisure in Historical Perspective* (Stuttgart: Vierteljahrschrift für Sozial- und Wirtschaftsgeschichte, 1994)

Borsay, P., *The English Urban Renaissance: Culture and Society in the Provincial Town 1660–1770* (Oxford, Oxford University Press, 1989)

Borsay, P., 'Health and leisure resorts 1700–1840', in P. Clark (ed.), *Cambridge History of Urban Britain, vol. 2, 1540–1840* (Cambridge: Cambridge University Press, 2000), 775–803

Borsay, P., *A History of Leisure: The British Experience since 1500* (Basingstoke: Palgrave Macmillan, 2006)

Boulton, J., 'Economy of time? Wedding days and the working week in the past', *Local Population Studies,* 43 (1989), 28–46

Bowden, S. and Offer, A., 'Household appliances and the use of time: the United States and Britain since the 1920s', *Economic History Review,* 47 (1994), 725–48

Brailsford, D., *Bareknuckles* (Cambridge: Lutterworth, 1988)

Brailsford, D., *Sport, Time, and Society: The British at Play* (London: Routledge, 1991)

Brewer, J. and Porter, R. (eds), *Consumption and the World of Goods* (London: Routledge, 1993)

Bryson, V., *Gender and the Politics of Time: Feminist Theory and Contemporary Debates* (Bristol: The Policy Press, 2007)

Bunting, M., *Willing Slaves: How the Overwork Culture Is Ruling Our Lives* (London: HarperCollins, 2004)

Burke, P., 'The invention of leisure in early modern Europe', *Past & Present,* 146 (1995), 136–50

Burnette, J., 'The wages and employment of female day-labourers in English agriculture, 1740–1850', *Economic History Review,* 57 (2004), 664–90

Bushaway, B., *By Rite: Custom, Ceremony and Community in England, 1700–1880* (London: Junction Books, 1982)

Capp, B., *Astrology and the Popular Press: English Almanacs 1500–1800* (London: Faber & Faber, 1979)

Carr, R., *English Fox Hunting: A History* (London: Weidenfeld and Nicolson, 1976)

Chaplin, P., *Darts in England, 1900–39: A Social History* (Manchester: Manchester University Press, 2009)

Chartered Institute of Personnel and Development (CIPD), 'Living to work' (2003)

Clapson, M., *A Bit of a Flutter: Popular Gambling and English Society 1823–1961* (Manchester: Manchester University Press, 1992)

Clark, G. and Van Der Werf, Y., 'Work in progress? The industrious revolution', *Journal of Economic History,* 58 (1998), 830–43

Clark, G., 'Farm wages and living standards in the industrial revolution: England, 1670–1869', *Economic History Review,* 54 (2001), 477–505

Clark, P., *The English Alehouse: A Social History 1200–1830* (London: Longman, 1983)

Clark, P., *British Clubs and Societies, 1580–1800: The Origins of an Associational World* (Oxford: Clarendon Press, 2000)

Clark, P. (ed.), *The Transformation of English Provincial Towns 1600–1800* (London: Hutchinson, 1984)

Clark, P. and Houston, R., 'Culture and leisure, 1750–1840', in P. Clark (ed.), *The Cambridge Urban History of Britain, vol. 2, 1540–1840* (Cambridge: Cambridge University Press, 2000), 575–613

Clarke, J. and Critcher, C., *The Devil Makes Work: Leisure in Capitalist Britain* (Basingstoke: Palgrave Macmillan, 1985)

Clayre, A., *Work and Play: Ideas and Experience of Work and Leisure* (New York: Harper & Row, 1974)

Coats, A. W., 'Changing attitudes to labour in the mid-eighteenth century', *Economic History Review*, 11 (1958), 35–51

Coats, A. W., 'The relief of poverty, attitudes to labour, and economic change in England, 1660–1782', *International Review of Social History*, 21 (1976), 98–115

Collins, T., *Rugby's Great Split: Class, Culture and the Origins of Rugby League Football* (London: Frank Cass, 1998)

Collins, T., *A Social History of English Rugby Union* (London: Routledge, 2009)

Conaghan, J., 'Time to dream? Flexibility, families, and the regulation of working time', in J. Fudge and R. J. Owens (eds), *Precarious Work, Women, and the New Economy: The Challenge to Legal Norms* (Oxford: Hart Publishing, 2006), 101–29

Crafts, N., Gazeley, I. and Newell, A. (eds), *Work and Pay in 20th Century Britain* (Oxford: Oxford University Press, 2007)

Cressy, D., *Bonfires and Bells: National Memory and the Protestant Calendar in Elizabethan and Stuart England* (London: Weidenfeld and Nicolson, 1989)

Cressy, D., 'The Fifth of November remembered', in R. Porter (ed.), *The Myths of the English* (Oxford: Polity Press, 1992), 68–90

Crompton, R., *Women and Work in Modern Britain* (Oxford: Oxford University Press, 1997)

Crompton, R. and Lyonette, C., 'Are we all working too hard? Women, men, and changing attitudes to employment', *British Social Attitudes*, 23rd report, 2006/7, 55–70

Cross, G., *A Quest for Time: The Reduction of Work in Britain and France, 1840–1940* (Berkeley, Los Angeles and London: University of California Press, 1989)

Cross, G. (ed.), *Worktowners at Blackpool: Mass Observation and Popular Leisure in the 1930s* (London: Routledge, 1990)

Cross, G., *Time and Money: The Making of Consumer Culture* (London: Routledge, 1993)

Cunningham, H., *Leisure in the Industrial Revolution c. 1780–c. 1880* (London: Croom Helm, 1980)

Cunningham, H., 'Leisure', in J. Benson (ed.), *The Working Class in England 1875–1914* (London: Croom Helm, 1985), 133–64

Cunningham, H., 'Leisure and culture', in F. M. L. Thompson (ed.), *The Cambridge Social History of Britain*, vol. 2 (Cambridge: Cambridge University Press, 1990), 279–339

Cunningham, H., *The Children of the Poor: Representations of Childhood since the Seventeenth Century* (Oxford: Blackwell, 1991)

Cunningham, H., *The Invention of Childhood* (London: BBC Books, 2006)

Curry, P., *Prophecy and Power: Astrology in Early Modern England* (Cambridge: Polity Press, 1989)

Davidoff, L., *The Best Circles: Society, Etiquette and the Season* (London: Croom Helm, 1973)

Davidoff, L. and Hall, C., *Family Fortunes: Men and Women of the English Middle Class 1780–1850* (London: Hutchinson, 1987)

Davidson, C., *A Woman's Work is Never Done: A History of Housework in the British Isles 1650–1850* (London: Chatto & Windus, 1982)

Davies, A., *Leisure, Gender and Poverty: Working Class Culture in Salford and Manchester, 1900–1939* (Buckingham: Open University Press, 1992)

Davies, A. C., 'Greenwich and standard time', *History Today*, 28, 3 (March 1978), 194–9

Davies, O., *Witchcraft, Magic and Culture 1736–1951* (Manchester: Manchester University Press, 1999)

Dawson, S. T., *Holiday Camps in Twentieth-Century Britain: Packaging Pleasure* (Manchester: Manchester University Press, 2011)

Deem, R., *All Work and No Play? A Study of Women and Leisure* (Milton Keynes: Open University Press, 1986)

Delheim, C., 'The creation of a company culture: Cadburys, 1861–1931', *American Historical Review*, 92 (1987), 13–44

Devine, F., *Affluent Workers Revisited: Privatism and the Working Class* (Edinburgh: Edinburgh University Press, 1992)

De Vries, J., 'The industrial revolution and the industrious revolution', *Journal of Economic History*, 54 (1994), 249–70

De Vries, J., *The Industrious Revolution: Consumer Behavior and the Household Economy, 1650 to the Present* (Cambridge: Cambridge University Press, 2008)

Durant, H., *The Problem of Leisure* (London: George Routledge & Sons, 1938)

Ehmer, J. and Lis, C. (eds), *The Idea of Work in Europe from Antiquity to Modern Times* (Aldershot: Ashgate, 2009)

Ekirch, A. R., *At Day's Close: A History of Nighttime* (London: Weidenfeld and Nicolson, 2005)

Elias, N., *An Essay on Time* (Dublin: University College Dublin Press, 2007)

Erdozain, D., *The Problem of Pleasure: Sport, Recreation and the Crisis of Victorian Religion* (Woodbridge: The Boydell Press, 2010)

Evans, C., 'Work and workloads during industrialization: the experience of forgemen in the British iron industry 1750–1850', *International Review of Social History*, 44 (1999), 197–215

Falkus, M., 'Lighting in the dark ages of English economic history', in D. C. Coleman and A. H. John (eds), *Trade, Government and Economy in Pre-Industrial England* (London: Weidenfeld and Nicolson, 1976), 248–73

Feinstein, C. H., 'Pessimism perpetuated: real wages and the standard of living in Britain during and after the industrial revolution', *Journal of Economic History*, 58 (1998), 625–58

Forman, F. J. (ed.), *Taking Our Time: Feminist Perspectives on Temporality* (Oxford: Pergamon, 1989)

Furniss, E. S., *The Position of the Laborer in a System of Nationalism* (Boston and New York: Houghton Mifflin Co., 1920)

Gay, H., 'Clock synchrony, time distribution and electrical timekeeping in Britain 1880–1925', *Past & Present*, 181 (2003), 107–40

Gershuny, J., *Changing Times: Work and Leisure in Postindustrial Society* (Oxford: Oxford University Press, 2000)

Gershuny, J., 'Busyness as the badge of honour for the new superordinate working class', *Social Research*, 72 (2005), 287–314

Glennie, P. and Thrift, N., *Shaping the Day: A History of Timekeeping in England and Wales 1300–1800* (Oxford: Oxford University Press, 2009)

Golby, J. M. and Purdue, A. W., *The Civilisation of the Crowd: Popular Culture in England, 1750–1900* (London: Batsford, 1984)

Gorz, A., *Reclaiming Work: Beyond the Wage-Based Society* (Cambridge: Polity Press, 1999)

Green, F., *Demanding Work: The Paradox of Job Quality in the Affluent Economy* (Princeton and Oxford: Princeton University Press, 2006)

Gregg, P. and Wadsworth, J. (eds), *The State of Working Britain* (Manchester: Manchester University Press, 1999)

Griffin, E., *England's Revelry: A History of Popular Sports and Pastimes 1660–1830* (Oxford: Oxford University Press, 2005)

Gunn, S., *The Public Culture of the Victorian Middle Class: Ritual and Authority in the English Industrial City 1840–1914* (Manchester: Manchester University Press, 2007)

Halladay, E., *Rowing in England: A Social History* (Manchester: Manchester University Press, 1990)

Halsey, A. H. with Webb, J. (eds), *Twentieth-Century British Social Trends* (Basingstoke: Macmillan, 2000)

Hannah, L., *Inventing Retirement: The Development of Occupational Pensions in Britain* (Cambridge: Cambridge University Press, 1986)

Harris, T. (ed.), *Popular Culture in England, c. 1500–1850* (London: Macmillan, 1995)

Harrison, B., *Drink and the Victorians: The Temperance Question in England, 1815–1872* (London: Faber & Faber, 1971)

Harrison, B., 'Religion and recreation in nineteenth-century England', *Past & Present*, 38 (1967), 98–125

Harrison, M., 'The ordering of the urban environment: time, work and the occurrence of crowds, 1790–1835', *Past & Present*, 110 (1986), 134–68

Harvey, A., *The Beginnings of a Commercial Sporting Culture in Britain, 1793–1850* (Aldershot: Ashgate, 2004)

Hatcher, J., 'Labour, leisure and economic thought before the nineteenth century', *Past & Present*, 160 (1998), 64–115

Heller, B., 'Leisure and the use of domestic space in Georgian London', *Historical Journal*, 53 (2010), 623–45

Herbert, T., *The British Brass Band* (Oxford: Oxford University Press, 2000)

Hill, B., *Women, Work and Sexual Politics in Eighteenth-Century England* (1989; London, UCL Press, 1994)

Hill, J., *Sport, Leisure and Culture in Twentieth-Century Britain* (Basingstoke: Palgrave, 2002)

Hobsbawm, E. J., *Labouring Men: Studies in the History of Labour* (London: Weidenfeld and Nicolson, 1964)

Hoggart, R., *The Uses of Literacy* (1957; Harmondsworth: Penguin, 1958)

Holloway, G., *Women and Work in Britain since 1840* (London: Routledge, 2005)

Holt, R., *Sport and the British: A Modern History* (Oxford: Clarendon Press, 1989)

Holt, R. (ed.), *Sport and the Working Class in Britain* (Manchester: Manchester University Press, 1990)

Holt, R. and Mason, T., *Sport in Britain, 1945–2000* (Oxford: Blackwell, 2000)

Hopkins, E., 'Working hours and conditions during the industrial revolution: a re-appraisal', *Economic History Review*, 35 (1982), 52–66

Houghton, W. E., *The Victorian Frame of Mind, 1830–1870* (New Haven and London: Yale University Press, 1957)

Houston, D. M. (ed.), *Work–Life Balance in the 21st Century* (Basingstoke: Palgrave Macmillan, 2005)

Howse, D., *Greenwich Time and the Discovery of Longitude* (Oxford: Oxford University Press, 1980)

Hutton, R., *The Rise and Fall of Merry England: The Ritual Year 1400–1700* (Oxford: Oxford University Press, 1994)

Hutton, R., *The Stations of the Sun: A History of the Ritual Year in Britain* (Oxford: Oxford University Press, 1996)

Ingold, T., 'Work, time and industry', *Time & Society*, 4 (1995), 5–28

James, R., *Popular Culture and Working-Class Taste in Britain, 1930–39: A Round of Cheap Diversions?* (Manchester: Manchester University Press, 2010)

Jephcott, P., *Married Women Working* (London: George Allen and Unwin, 1962)

Jones, G. S., *Outcast London: A Study in the Relationship between Classes in Victorian Society* (1971; Harmondsworth: Peregrine, 1976)

Jones, S. G., *Workers at Play: A Social and Economic History of Leisure, 1918–1939* (London: Routledge and Kegan Paul, 1986)

Joyce, P., *Work, Society and Politics: The Culture of the Factory in Later Victorian England* (1980; London: Methuen, 1982)

Joyce, P. (ed.), *The Historical Meanings of Work* (Cambridge: Cambridge University Press, 1987)

Kern, S., *The Culture of Time and Space 1880–1918* (Cambridge, Mass.: Harvard University Press, 1983)

King, S., *Poverty and Welfare in England, 1700–1850* (Manchester: Manchester University Press, 2000)

King, S. and Tomkins, A. (eds), *The Poor in England, 1700–1850: An Economy of Makeshifts* (Manchester: Manchester University Press, 2003)

Kirby, P., 'Attendance and work effort in the Great Northern coalfield, 1775–1864', *Economic History Review*, 65 (2012), 961–83

Kodz, J. et al., 'Working long hours: a review of the evidence', www.bis.gov.uk/files/file11543.pdf

Kussmaul, A., *Servants in Husbandry in Early Modern England* (Cambridge: Cambridge University Press, 1981)

Landes, D. S., *Revolution in Time: Clocks and the Making of the Modern World* (Cambridge, Mass.: Harvard University Press, 1983)

Lane, P., Raven, N. and Snell, K. D. M. (eds), *Women, Work and Wages in England, 1600–1850* (Woodbridge: The Boydell Press, 2004)

Langhamer, C., *Women's Leisure in England 1920–60* (Manchester: Manchester University Press, 2000)

Linder, S. B., *The Harried Leisure Class* (New York: Columbia University Press, 1970)

Lowerson, J., *Sport and the English Middle Classes 1870–1914* (Manchester: Manchester University Press, 1993)

Lowerson, J. and Myerscough, J., *Time to Spare in Victorian England* (Brighton: Harvester Press, 1977)

McCrone, K., *Sport and the Physical Emancipation of English Women, 1870–1914* (London: Routledge, 1988)

McIvor, A. J., *A History of Work in Britain, 1880–1950* (Basingstoke: Palgrave, 2001)

McKendrick, N., Brewer, J. and Plumb, J. H., *The Birth of a Consumer Society: The Commercialization of Eighteenth-Century England* (London: Hutchinson, 1983)

McKendrick, N., 'Josiah Wedgwood and factory discipline', *Historical Journal*, 4 (1961), 30–55

McKibbin, R., *The Ideologies of Class: Social Relations in Britain 1880–1950* (Oxford: Clarendon Press, 1990)

McLeod, H., ' "Thews and sinews": nonconformity and sport', in D. W. Bebbington and T. Larsen (eds), *Modern Christianity and Cultural Aspirations* (London: Sheffield Academic Press, 2003), 28–46

Malcolmson, R. W., *Popular Recreations in English Society 1700–1850* (Cambridge: Cambridge University Press, 1973)

Mangan, J. A., *Athleticism in the Victorian and Edwardian Public School* (Cambridge: Cambridge University Press, 1981)

Mason, T., *Association Football and English Society, 1863–1915* (Brighton: Harvester, 1980)

Mason, T. (ed.), *Sport in Britain: A Social History* (Cambridge: Cambridge University Press, 1989)

Mason, T., 'Sport and Recreation', in P. Johnson (ed.), *Twentieth-Century Britain: Economic, Social and Cultural Change* (Harlow: Longman, 1994), 111–26

Mathias, P., 'Leisure and wages: theory and practice', in *The Transformation of England: Essays in the Economic and Social History of England in the Eighteenth Century* (London: Methuen, 1979), 148–167

Mathias, P., 'Time for work, time for play: relations between work and leisure in the early modern period', *Vierteljahrschrift für Sozial- und Wirtschaftsgeschichte*, 81 (1994), 305–23

Matthews, R. C. O., Feinstein, C. H. and Odling-Smee, J. C., *British Economic Growth 1856–1973* (Oxford: Clarendon Press, 1982)

Meller, H., *Leisure and the Changing City, 1870–1914* (London: Routledge and Kegan Paul, 1976)

Metcalfe, A., *Leisure and Recreation in a Victorian Mining Community: The Social Economy of Leisure in North-East England, 1820–1914* (London: Routledge, 2006)

Muldrew, C., *Food, Energy and the Creation of Industriousness: Work and Material Culture in Agrarian England 1550–1780* (Cambridge: Cambridge University Press, 2011)

Murfin, L., *Popular Leisure in the Lake Counties* (Manchester: Manchester University Press, 1990)

Myrdal, A. and Klein, V., *Women's Two Roles: Home and Work* (London: Routledge & Kegan Paul, 1956)

New Economics Foundation, *21 Hours. Why a Shorter Working Week Can Help Us All to Flourish in the 21st Century* (New Economics Foundation, n.d.)

Nott, J., *Music for the People: Popular Music and Dance in Interwar Britain* (Oxford: Oxford University Press, 2002)

Offer, A., *The Challenge of Affluence: Self-Control and Well-Being in the United States and Britain since 1950* (Oxford: Oxford University Press, 2006)

Ottaway, S. R., *The Decline of Life: Old Age in Eighteenth-Century England* (Cambridge: Cambridge University Press, 2004)

Perkins, M., *Visions of the Future: Almanacs, Time, and Cultural Change 1775–1870* (Oxford: Clarendon Press, 1996)

Perkins, M., *The Reform of Time: Magic and Modernity* (London: Pluto Press, 2001)

Pimlott, J. A. R., *The Englishman's Holiday: A Social History* (London: Faber & Faber, 1947)

Plumb, J. H., *The Commercialisation of Leisure in Eighteenth-Century England* (Reading: Reading University, 1973)

Pollard, S., 'Factory discipline in the industrial revolution', *Economic History Review*, 16 (1963–4), 254–71

Poole, R., *Time's Alteration: Calendar Reform in Early Modern England* (London: UCL Press, 1998)

Porter, G., *The English Occupational Song* (Umeå: University of Umeå, 1992)

Quadagno, J. S., *Aging in Early Industrial Society: Work, Family and Social Policy in Nineteenth-Century England* (New York: Academic Press, 1982)

Quinault, R., 'The cult of the centenary, c. 1784–1914', *Historical Research*, 71 (1998), 307–23

Rapoport, R. and R., *Dual-Career Families* (Harmondsworth: Penguin, 1971)

Rapoport, R. and R. N., *Leisure and the Family Life Cycle* (London: Routledge and Kegan Paul, 1975)

Reay, B., *Rural Englands: Labouring Lives in the Nineteenth Century* (Basingstoke: Palgrave Macmillan, 2004)

Reid, D. A., 'The decline of Saint Monday, 1766–1876', *Past & Present*, 71 (1976), 76–101

Reid, D. A., 'Weddings, weekdays, work and leisure in urban England 1791–1911: the decline of Saint Monday revisited', *Past & Present*, 153 (1996), 135–63

Reid, D. A., 'Playing and praying', in M. Daunton (ed.), *Cambridge Urban History of Britain, vol. 3, 1840–1950* (Cambridge: Cambridge University Press, 2000), 745–807

Richards, J., *The Age of the Dream Palace: Cinema and Society in Britain, 1930–1939* (London: Routledge and Kegan Paul, 1989)

Rowntree, B. S. and Lavers, G. R., *English Life and Leisure: A Social Study* (London: Longmans Green, 1951)

Rule, J., *The Experience of Labour in Eighteenth-Century Industry* (London: Croom Helm, 1981)

Rule, J., 'Time, affluence and private leisure: the British working class in the 1950s and 1960s', *Labour History Review*, 66 (2001), 223–42

Russell, D., *Popular Music in England, 1840–1914: A Social History* (Manchester: Manchester University Press, 1987)

Russell, D., *Football and the English: A Social History of Association Football in England, 1863–1995* (Preston: Carnegie, 1997)

Samuel, R. 'The workshop of the world: steam power and hand technology in mid-Victorian Britain', *History Workshop*, 3 (1977), 6–72

Samuel, R. (ed.), *Miners, Quarrymen and Saltworkers* (London: Routledge & Kegan Paul, 1977)

Schofield, R., '"Monday's child is fair of face": favoured days for baptism, marriage and burial in pre-industrial England', *Continuity and Change*, 20 (2005), 93–109

Schwarz, L. D., 'English servants and their employers during the eighteenth and nineteenth centuries', *Economic History Review*, 52 (1999), 236–56

Schwarz, L., 'Custom, wages and workload in England during industrialization', *Past & Present*, 197 (2007), 143–75

Sennett, R., *The Corrosion of Character: The Personal Consequences of Work in the New Capitalism* (New York: W. W. Norton, 1998)

Sennett, R., *The Craftsman* (London: Allen Lane, 2008)

Sharpe, P., *Adapting to Capitalism: Working Women in the English Economy 1700–1850* (1996; Basingstoke: Macmillan, 2000)

Sharpe, P., 'The female labour market in English agriculture during the industrial revolution: expansion or contraction?', *Agricultural History Review*, 47 (1999), 161–81

Shaw, J., 'Punctuality and the everyday ethics of time: some evidence from the Mass Observation Archive', *Time and Society*, 3 (1994), 79–97

Shpayer-Makov, H., 'Rethinking work and leisure in late Victorian and Edwardian England: the emergence of a police subculture', *International Review of Social History*, 47 (2002), 213–41

Skidelsky, R. and E., *How Much Is Enough? The Love of Money, and the Case for the Good Life* (London: Allen Lane, 2012)

Smith, H. L. (ed.), *The New Survey of London Life and Labour*, 9 vols (London: King, 1930–5)

Spring Rice, M., *Working-Class Wives: Their Health and Conditions* (Harmondsworth: Penguin, 1939)

Steedman, C., 'The servant's labour: the business of life, England, 1760–1820', *Social History*, 29 (2004), 1–29

Storch, R. (ed.), *Popular Culture and Custom in Nineteenth-Century Britain* (London: Croom Helm, 1982)

Swanson, R. N. (ed.), *The Use and Abuse of Time in Christian History* (Woodbridge: The Boydell Press, 2002)

Taylor, H., *A Claim on the Countryside: A History of the British Outdoor Movement* (Edinburgh: Keele University Press, 1997)

Thane, P., *Old Age in English History: Past Experiences, Present Issues* (Oxford: Oxford University Press, 2000)

Thomas, K. (ed.), *The Oxford Book of Work* (Oxford: Oxford University Press, 1999)

Thomas, K., *The Ends of Life: Roads to Fulfilment in Early Modern England* (Oxford: Oxford University Press, 2009)

Thompson, E. P., *The Making of the English Working Class* (London: Gollancz, 1963)

Thompson, E. P., 'Time, work-discipline and industrial capitalism', in M. W. Flinn and T. C. Smout (eds), *Essays in Social History* (Oxford: Clarendon Press, 1974), 39–77

Todd, S., *Young Women, Work and Family in England 1918–1950* (Oxford: Oxford University Press, 2005)

Tranter, N., *Sport, Economy and Society in Britain, 1750–1914* (Cambridge: Cambridge University Press, 1997)

Underdown, D., *Start of Play: Cricket and Culture in Eighteenth-Century England* (London: Allen Lane, 2000)

Urry, J., 'Time, leisure and social identity', *Time & Society*, 3 (1994), 131–50

Veblen, T., *The Theory of the Leisure Class: An Economic Study of Institutions* (1899; London: Allen & Unwin, 1925)

Vincent, D., *Literacy and Popular Culture in England 1750–1914* (Cambridge: Cambridge University Press, 1989)

Voth, H.-J., 'Time and work in eighteenth-century London', *Journal of Economic History*, 58 (1998), 29–58

Voth, H.-J., *Time and Work in England 1750–1830* (Oxford: Clarendon Press, 2000)

Voth, H.-J., 'The longest years: new estimates of labor input in England, 1760–1830', *Journal of Economic History*, 61 (2001), 1065–82

Walton, J. K., *The English Seaside Resort: A Social History, 1750–1914* (Leicester: Leicester University Press, 1983)

Walton, J. K., *The British Seaside: Holidays and Resorts in the Twentieth Century* (Manchester: Manchester University Press, 2000)

Walton, J. K. and Walvin, J. (eds), *Leisure in Britain 1780–1939* (Manchester: Manchester University Press, 1983)

Walvin, J., *Leisure and Society, 1830–1950* (London: Longman, 1978)

Warhurst, C., Eiklof, D. R. and Haunschild, A. (eds), *Work Less, Live More? Critical Analysis of the Work–Life Boundary* (Basingstoke: Palgrave Macmillan, 2008)

Waters, C., *British Socialists and the Politics of Popular Culture, 1884–1914* (Manchester: Manchester University Press, 1992)

Webb, S. and Cox, H., *The Eight Hours Day* (London: Walter Scott, 1891)

Weber, M., *The Protestant Ethic and the Spirit of Capitalism* (London: Allen & Unwin, 1930)

Whitaker, W. B., *The Eighteenth-Century English Sunday: A Study of Sunday Observance from 1677 to 1837* (London: Epworth Press, 1940)

Wigglesworth, N., *The Social History of English Rowing* (London: Frank Cass, 1992)

Wigley, J., *The Rise and Fall of the English Sunday* (Manchester: Manchester University Press, 1980)

Winstanley, M., *The Shopkeepers' World, 1830–1914* (Manchester: Manchester University Press, 1983)

Wood, S. (ed.), *The Degradation of Work? Skill, Deskilling and the Labour Process* (London, 1983)

Woodward, D., *Men at Work: Labourers and Building Craftsmen in the Towns of Northern England, 1450–1750* (Cambridge: Cambridge University Press, 1995)

Woodward, D., 'Early modern servants in husbandry revisited', *Agricultural History Review*, 48 (2000), 141–50

Wrightson, K., *Earthly Necessities: Economic Lives in Early Modern Britain* (New Haven and London: Yale University Press, 2000)

Yeo, E. and S. (eds), *Popular Culture and Class Conflict, 1590–1914: Explorations in the History of Labour and Leisure* (Brighton: Harvester Press, 1981)

Yeo, S., *Religion and Voluntary Organisations in Crisis* (London: Croom Helm, 1976)

Young, M. and Willmott, P., *The Symmetrical Family: A Study of Work and Leisure in the London Region* (1973; Harmondsworth: Penguin, 1975)

Index

Lightning Source UK Ltd.
Milton Keynes UK
UKOW06f1900180616

276556UK00006B/81/P